What the World's Experts Are Already Saying About *Accountable Marketing*

Peter Rosenwald has elevated the term "accountable marketing" from an oxymoron to an exciting reality. His book may make old-time marketers cringe at the prospect of now having to justify heretofore unquestioned and unquestionable marketing budgets. Long overdue; it should occupy a permanent place on every marketer's desktop.

Jock Bickert
Database Psychologist
Member, Direct Marketing Hall of Fame

He's been there, done that and got the T-shirt. Now he's written the book and all you have to do is read it.

Peter's life is the story of *Accountable Marketing*. For him to share the wealth of the wisdom he's acquired along a lively and varied journey is fascinating and invaluable. If you're in business—and agree with Peter that "Average" is the most dangerous word in contemporary marketing—and seeking to maximise your share of your customer's wallet, then this book is priceless.

Buy this book and become accountable.

Andrew Fraser CMG
Global Marketing Consultant

From his global vantage point, Peter Rosenwald has made accountability interesting and accessible. Written in appealing prose, Peter reduces the barriers for success, providing templates that can be used in real world applications to help any organization grow in a systematic fashion. He reveals what every marketer needs to know . . . How to determine what they can invest to acquire a customer—the allowable cost per order (ACPO.) This is math for even the "quantitatively challenged." The formulas alone are worth buying the book for.

Ron Jacobs
President
Jacobs & Clevenger, Inc.
Co-Author, *Successful Direct Marketing Methods*

Peter has taken a complex science and turned it into an easy discipline for anyone and everyone to benefit from. This book ranks with the best ever written on the subject of Direct Marketing but it also allows you to apply it to other media. It provides an excellent foundation for anyone looking for a reliable, practical method of ensuring their marketing dollars are well spent. Every marketer wants a guaranteed return on investment. You won't find a better return than on this excellent book.

Accountable Marketing is a common sense guide to a complex subject. This is a very practical book, easy to read and full of helpful examples. A must have for everyone's marketing library.

Peter Jupp
CEO, Infocore

Peter Rosenwald's book is a must-read for today's marketer. Anyone associated with advertising and marketing today will now have the tools to truly measure the effectiveness of their advertising in our highly cluttered media world.

This is truly a breakthrough tool that any serious marketer will find of enormous value."

Jerry I. Reitman
Executive Vice President (retired)
The Leo Burnett Company
Author of *Beyond 2000: The Future of Direct Marketing*

Understanding the economics of Customer Management is crucial. This book teaches you everything you need to know to find, grow and keep profitable customers. There is no better book when you want to learn the economics of reaching the people who count, as opposed to counting the people you reach.

Reimer Thedens
Chairman/CEO Worldwide
OgilvyOne worldwide Ltd., London

This is a really good book that fills an important need in the market. Rosenwald presents a how-to approach to bring accountability to marketing where it wasn't before. His examples are clear and concise and easy to apply to new situations. Rosenwald shows how and why to look at what new customers are really worth. For many marketers, just this lesson will make it more than worth reading. Rosenwald shows how to compute profit—not just break-even or Lifetime Value—but profit. That's the kind of thing Marketers need on a day-to-day basis.

Alan Weber
President of Marketing Analytics Group
Co-author, *Desktop Database Marketing*

Once upon a time not so long ago, mass marketing ruled. No longer. In the 21st century, successful marketing is based on razor-sharp accountability, measurability, targetability, flexibility, and customer focus. In *Accountable Marketing*, respected industry leader and author Peter Rosenwald presents a veritable crash course in the dynamics of this new marketing world. This book is an outstanding and comprehensive resource for today's—and tomorrow's—marketing professionals.

H. Robert Wientzen
President & CEO
Direct Marketing Association

Peter Rosenwald has capped a long and successful career with his book, *Accountable Marketing*. This book should be required reading for any one engaged the business of marketing, advertising or any other form of commercial persuasion. It is a hands-on guide to the essential business of advertising accountability, whether it is image advertising, sales promotion, data-driven marketing, or the current favorite and least understood topic of customer relationship marketing. *Accountable Marketing* is a necessary primer and source of wisdom for every marketer. I found that even as a marketing veteran, I learned something valuable from every chapter. The book is readable, informative, and constantly interesting. It should take its place on the required reading list of anyone involved in marketing and advertising.

Lester Wunderman
Founder and Chairman Emeritus
Wunderman

▶ ▶ ▶ **Accountable
Marketing** ◀ ◀ ◀

Accountable ◄◄◄ ►►► Marketing: The Economics of Data-Driven Marketing

by Peter J. Rosenwald

RĀCꝊM
COMMUNICATIONS

AMERICAN
MARKETING
ASSOCIATION

THOMSON
—✳—™

Australia • Canada • Mexico • Singapore • Spain • United Kingdom • United States

Accountable Marketing: The Economics of Data-Driven Marketing
By Peter J. Rosenwald

Copyright © 2004 by TEXERE, an imprint of Thomson Business and Professional Publishing, a part of the Thomson Corporation. Thomson, the Star logo, Thomson Business and Professional Publishing, and TEXERE are trademarks used herein under license.

Text ISBN: 0-324-30468-4
Data CD ISBN: 0-324-30469-2
Package ISBN: 0-324-20359-4

Printed and bound in the United States by Phoenix Color
1 2 3 4 5 6 7 8 9 07 06 05 04

For more information, contact Texere, 622 Third Ave., 10th Floor, New York, NY 10017, or find us on the Web at *www.etexere.com.*

This publication is designed to provide accurate and authoritative information in regard to the subject matter covered. It is sold with the understanding that the publisher is not engaged in rendering legal, accounting, or other professional services. If legal advice or other expert assistance is required, the services of a competent professional person should be sought.

Consulting Editor in Marketing: Richard Hagle
Composed by: Sans Serif, Inc.

A CIP catalogue record for this book is available from the Library of Congress.

The names of all companies or products mentioned herein are used for identification purposes only and may be trademarks or registered trademarks of their respective owners. Texere disclaims any affiliation, association, connection with, sponsorship, or endorsement by such owners.

This book is printed on acid-free paper.

▶ ▶ ▶ Dedication

Accountable Marketing is dedicated to all the men and women in the international marketing industry who are constantly searching for ways to improve marketing performance and who embrace the idea that in making their efforts "accountable," they are adding a critical missing dimension to an industry all too often self-indulgent and mesmerized by its own *hype*.

It is also dedicated to the many industry professionals who have generously shared their knowledge and experience with the next generation through writing, teaching and allowing others to build on the foundations they have poured.

▶ ▶ ▶ Contents

▶ ▶ ▶ Exhibits

▶ ▶ ▶ Acknowledgments

I n the autumn of 1957 with my university diploma neatly tucked into a desk draw, no job and the little money I had fast running out, I prepared for a book club job interview the following day by going to the library to learn what I could about the "mail order" business, the forerunner of direct marketing. The only book I could find that had anything on the subject was Otto Kleppner's *Advertising & Promotional Methods*, which covered the subject in 17 concise pages. It was those 17 pages that helped me get started in a career that has spanned almost half a century and seen the industry grow and prosper. Today there are literally hundreds of titles in many languages on every aspect of direct marketing as well as undergraduate and graduate courses throughout the world.

While it would be ego satisfying to believe that the creation of *Accountable Marketing* and its accompanying Template software has been my work alone, it would be a fantasy. Works of this kind are the result of many different contributors and sources, of shared experiences and knowledge. Many colleagues have been extremely generous in their contributions and for that I am most grateful.

The Template programming of my original concepts has been done by the brilliant Brazilian software firm Assesso, by its owner Flavio Pires and principally by his wife Anna Chien. I can only marvel at their skill, endless good humor and friendship and their belief in this project. Without them it could not have been done.

Although it would be impossible to list all the people who have, knowingly or not, made valuable contributions, special thanks are due to Ron Jacobs, President of the innovative direct marketing advertising agency, Jacobs & Clevenger, Inc. in Chicago and co-author with Bob Stone of the classic reference, *Successful Direct Marketing Methods*, Jerry Shereshewsky of Yahoo; David Milne, senior consultant, Results Business Consulting; Peter Jupp, President of Infocore Inc.; James Johnson, Director of Stay in Touch; John G. Sanchez, President of Zunch Communications, Inc.; Eugene Raitt of AIG in Hong Kong; Solange Mata Machado and Humberto da Costa Guimarães of the American Chamber of Commerce of Brazil; Roberto Miranda, CEO of RBS Direct (Brazil), Efraim Kapulski, President of ABEMD, the Brazilian Direct Marketing Association and Paulo Vasconcelos, Director of CRMachine® in São Paulo.

The evolution of the Accountable Marketing concept and my own interest in the subject goes back a long way and has been influenced to varying degrees by many international industry leaders (some sadly no longer with us).

The first understanding of the ACPO concept and its role in all accountability in marketing came from the late Richard Benson, certainly one of the direct marketing industry's great circulation geniuses when we worked together at American Heritage Publishing Company in the late 1950s and early '60s. The company's founder and president, James Parton was another important influence.

My dear friend, mentor and "guru" Lester Wunderman has been a guiding influence to the entire industry. No one has done more to extend its frontiers and it was his initial articulation of the concept of "accountability" that was the inspiration for this book.

Walter Schmid, the visionary founder of the Montreux Direct Marketing Symposium invited me to be Chairman of the Symposium's Executive Committee and in that capacity to interact with almost all of the international DM "greats" for almost a decade. It was in the cauldron of the Symposium that many of the concepts found here were first explored and for the opportunity to be in that place at that time I personally owe Walter Schmid an enormous debt of gratitude.

Dr. Roberto Civita, Chairman of Grupo Abril, my close friend for more than a quarter of a century and employer during three and one-half wonderful years of working and living in Brazil, has always understood the importance of direct and data driven marketing and has supported my efforts to expand and improve the discipline. His encouragement and generosity are deeply appreciated.

Special thanks also go to my editor, Rich Hagle of Racom Communications who believed in this book from the start, suffered through its gestation and contributed unnumbered suggestions and resources. His patience and wisdom have been profound and without them, this book would never have been completed.

My wife and partner in life and work, Renée Comte Rosenwald has spent endless days wondering when I was going to have time for something other than "the book". She has read chapters, made constructive suggestions and provided unending tender loving care. To her I owe a debt of gratitude beyond measure.

▶ ▶ ▶ Introduction

Why a book on Accountable Marketing?

The answer is a reflection of the increasingly competitive economic environment, a commercial world in which businesses are intensifying the search for efficiencies in all their activities, and marketing, formerly largely immune from the demanding discipline of accountability, is being judged by new rules.

Recognizing that waste in marketing, as in all activities, is the enemy of profit, marketers are searching for every possible way to reduce or eliminate it. They are addressing new metrics to measure what they do and demanding accountability in their marketing to serve as a baseline to improve performance.

Marketers for all products and services want to get the maximum bang for their buck, and with information technology as their handmaiden, they are making large investments with the objective of knowing more about their customers and using that knowledge effectively.

The understanding that the value of a loyal customer has a much larger impact on brand values and profit than even market share, has fueled the explosive growth of a culture of "customer-focus" and created a new buzz phrase, Customer Relationship Management (CRM).

The thrust of this book and its accompanying templates is to contribute to the need of marketers to gain a better understanding of the economics that condition all marketing whether they are selling fast moving consumer goods (FMCG) at retail or highly complex financial products through institutions or direct and to provide some tools to facilitate marketing accountability. It is also intended to dispel some marketing myths and help the reader make the economic decisions so crucial to today's marketing success.

It grows out of almost fifty years of trying to understand this many-faceted business and helping colleagues around the world to do better strategic planning and economic management.

Accountable Marketing is for all marketers, and its templates provide tools for the often-complex calculations that are a requisite part of planning for accountability. Illustrations taken from sample template calculations throughout the book are intended both to illuminate the text and to provide an understanding of how the templates can best be used as aids to solve marketing economic problems.

While largely conditioned by the increasingly data-dominated disciplines of direct marketing (DM), a once relatively small part of the marketing scene that has grown in tandem with the desire of all marketers to get closer to their customers, its applications are important to every branch of the entire marketing continuum–image advertising, sales promotion, data-driven marketing and customer relationship management. If one thing is certain, it is that the right data, imaginatively used, becomes a critical element in all marketing efforts.

As many marketing programs migrate from a paradigm of "one-to-everyone" to "one-to-one" marketing, the way we approach the marketplace and measure our performance has radically changed. Even when dealing with millions of customers, new technologies and understandings allow us to return to the days when merchants operated at a micro rather than a macro level–one customer at a time. If "average" is the most dangerous word in marketing, we need new perceptions and tools to see and deal with each customer as a unique individual.

More than ever before, today, all the parts of the continuum have many things in common and the "learnings" from one can often illuminate opportunities for others.

The FMCG company that focuses on the lifetime value of its individual customers and invests promotional money to maximize that value, the financial institution that aggregates its customer's accounts, investments and insurance and provides an integrated basket of services to obtain the maximum share of wallet, the cable TV or satellite supplier that "tiers" its entertainment offering to the different interests of its viewers all have common problems. So, too, do retailers seeking to understand whether to focus on their traditional metric, the value of every square foot of store space or on the value of their customers.

They all need to be able to assess how much they can afford to spend on promotional activity for different customer segments of the market and how they can focus their spending better on individuals with different wants and needs. They need sophisticated tools to help develop their marketing strategies.

The eleven chapters of this book and the interactive templates that accompany it are intended to help marketers better understand and practice accountable marketing.

Beginning with an overview of the economics of the marketing continuum (Chapter 1), the book addresses such topics as:

▶ Understanding the economics of the Marketing Continuum and how accountability is critical to all four legs of the continuum (Chapter 1).

▶ How to determine the "allowable" marketing spend to achieve different objectives (Chapter 2).

▶ The importance of the customer and migrating to and maintaining customer focus (Chapter 3).

▶ Making CRM a reality and determining how much to spend on CRM initiatives (Chapter 4).

▶ How to plan the economics of simple and complex products and services (Chapters 5 and 6).

▶ The use of incentives to stimulate sales and their economics (Chapter 7).

▶ Building and executing tests as the foundation for accountability (Chapter 8).

▶ The challenges and economics of promotional planning in all media (Chapter 9).

▶ Strategic planning for accountability and selling that plan to management (Chapter 10).

▶ The future of marketing accountability (Chapter 11).

The templates have been designed to allow the user to easily address such issues as customer lifetime value, pricing, attrition, promotional planning in all media, upselling and cross-selling, CRM, projecting results, and many other tasks. Any Excel" user will find them easy to navigate: simply inputting data into the indicated blank cells will deliver the results and allow easy "what-if" calculations. While throughout the text, references to monetary numbers have been generalized, excluding currency identification except in specific circumstances, the templates will automatically produce results in whatever currency you normally use.

If "God is in the details" today's marketing throughout the continuum demands a new attention to metrics and detailed planning. It's the details that often confuse things and the purpose of this book is to make it easier for the marketer to harness these details and use them to assure marketing accountability and profits.

▶ ▶ ▶ A Note About Using the
Accountable Marketing Templates

The accompanying CD-Rom contains thirty-four templates to help you with every aspect of your accountable marketing calculations. Each template on the disk is titled and references the appropriate Exhibit in the text. *It is recommended that the user go to the Exhibit in the text for a practical example of the use of the template.*

The templates have been created using Microsoft® Excel™ and run in Excel 97 or higher. They will run on both the Windows™ and MAC platforms.

To use the templates for Windows, simply insert the disk and use Windows Explorer ™ to find the template that suits your need. If you are using MAC, simply insert the disk and an icon will appear on the desktop. In both cases, the template cells will all be blank. *You may input data in only the boxed white cells: the shaded cells have the formulae running behind them and will give you the results of the calculations.*

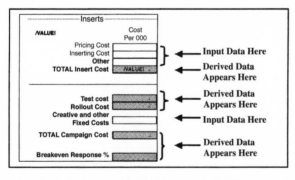

While it is not recommended, you may unblock any of the templates by using the code AMT. Be sure to keep a copy of the original for future use.

1

Understanding the Economics
of the Marketing Continuum

Advertising and marketing have come a long way since Eve seductively offered Adam that first apple. And it has become much more complicated in the process. Yet, while today's offers are far more complex than the single apple, the basic principles and philosophies haven't changed: Marketing should produce concrete and measurable results in terms of sales and financial results. In the last analysis, it's the numbers that matter.

Today's consumer is deluged with an enormous variety of products and services and marketers spend billions to capture the consumer's attention and interest, to get him to make an initial purchase and then to encourage his unending loyalty. These billions spent for marketing are the sum of multiple expenditures, and in our highly competitive marketplace those marketers most skillful at marshaling their resources and directing them with the most focus are richly rewarded, adorn the cover of *Forbes,* and are toasted at Harvard Business School.

This book is about *Accountable Marketing*—the process by which we can plan and measure our marketing initiatives for greater marketing success. Together with its accompanying Templates, it is about the essential economics that apply to all marketing actions in the continuum and how marketers can use them to have more successful businesses.

Where Accountable Marketing Started and How

In the beginning there was personal selling, a face-to-face presentation of a product by a seller to a buyer. This was followed by "mail-order"—the first form of distance personal selling—which used direct mail as its medium. As it matured, it took on the much more elegant title of direct marketing. Eventually, as computers allowed marketers to capture and use increasingly good data and the industry emerged into a main-line marketing form many professionals added the word "data" and the term Data Driven Marketing (DDM) came into currency. The latest and most fashionable form is Customer Relationship Management (CRM).

Direct marketing (DM) and CRM are the most "accountable" of the marketing disciplines and use the maximum amount of sophisticated data. However, the economics of DM and CRM have substantial relevance and applications not just to DM and CRM but to every aspect of the marketing continuum. Today DM and CRM account for more than 50% of the total marketing spend in the United States[1] and a growing share throughout the world.

In the mid-1970s, having merged his direct marketing agency Wunderman, Ricotta & Kline with Young & Rubicam, direct marketing guru Lester Wunderman gave a keynote speech in New York in which he defined direct marketing as "Accountable Advertising." His argument was straightforward: Every aspect of the direct marketing process could be economically measured, and the direct marketer could determine with great precision the return on each promotional investment. If one advertising medium returned orders for less cost than another did, the marketer knew it and could make subsequent media decisions accordingly.

The speech received a lot of comment, not least on the executive floor of Young & Rubicam's Madison Avenue headquarters. The then Chairman of Y&R, Edward Ney invited Wunderman to a breakfast where he patiently explained that while Wunderman's perception had unquestionable merit, it could be interpreted to suggest that if direct marketing was "accountable," general advertising was not. "That's not a positioning that Y&R can feel comfortable with," he concluded.

So in the interests of "corporate correctness," the term "accountable advertising" was submerged for a while. But it never really went away, and as more and more companies have discovered that the majority of their marketing efforts can be precisely measured, the trend towards accountable marketing has gained ever-increasing momentum.

In its early days the "mail order" business was a "fly-by-the-seat-of-your-pants" affair that relied more on instinct than process. Direct mail was its principal medium. Arriving at work in the morning, marketers stopped first in the mailroom to count the orders and projected profits were often calculated on the back of the nearest envelope. Few sophisticated systems existed and the word "model" was used exclusively to describe the handsome men and women pictured in the brochures and advertisements. Nevertheless, marketers did carefully track the numbers, and they did it without the benefit of computers that can handle thousands of variables on a single desktop.

"Brand" marketers were somewhat more sophisticated, but like their poor cousins in mail order, their efforts were largely "hit" and "miss," and planning for profitability was at best an imprecise science.

The ideas that "brands" have definable value and that the "customer" is a complex individual who passes through a number of different life stages had not been articulated. It was taken as a matter of faith that advertising drove sales and that the more advertising, the more sales. There was hardly a well-defined marketing continuum as there is today, flowing from image advertising through sales promotion and on to direct marketing and CRM and when properly managed, creating individual customer data for future use.

The arrival and ubiquity of the computer changed all that. Two powerful economic forces came into play. One was the ever-decreasing cost of data storage: the other was the soaring increase in the cost of reaching prospects through all media. At every point in the continuum, marketers began to recognize the power of data and increasingly to use it to shape their marketing strategies and actions. When it became more economical to hold data and use it for marketing purposes rather than spend increasing amounts to reach mass audiences, modern direct marketing was born and all marketers took notice.

As the industry matured during the late 1960s, marketers increasingly realized the power of data, not only to focus their marketing efforts but also to productively plan and manage their businesses. Process largely took over from instinct, and management became increasingly interested in the fundamental economics underlying their business.

The Marketing Continuum

All marketing efforts become part of a "continuum" that allows the marketing strategist considerable flexibility. He can enter the continuum where he likes and use all or only part of it. Commentators on the marketing process define the continuum in many different and equally legitimate ways. But the simplicity and clarity of the four-part process described in Exhibit 1-1 provides a framework for examining the accountability issues that are the subject of this book.

As can be seen, the Marketing Continuum has significant overlaps. As one moves from the left to the right of the diagram—from Image Advertising to CRM—the activities become increasingly measurable and "accountable."

Today, most marketing efforts begin with the creation of an "image" for a product or service and the building of a brand. It was not always the case. Before the "mass" production and distribution of goods, the burden of establishing confidence in the quality of a product lay almost exclusively with the seller, who was usually a local retailer who had established a reputation in his community and to whom the purchaser could go if he had a problem. Those were days when a good merchant knew his customers by name, knew their likes and dislikes and catered to each; what we now call the *integrated marketing database* was held in the totally integrated real-time head of the merchant. Things were much simpler then.

Because the customer has so much more choice than he had just a few decades ago and because he is exposed to so many different selling messages, the cozy loyal relationship that existed between merchant and customer has become highly promiscuous. No longer do parents take their offspring along to the family bank to open savings accounts solely on the basis of the family's historic banking relationship. Now they search together for the highest interest rates being offered and change their accounts from one bank to another in the quest for a half point more interest on their savings or a slightly lower borrowing rate. Commercial promiscuity based upon short-term benefits has largely replaced consumer

Exhibit 1-1 The Marketing Continuum

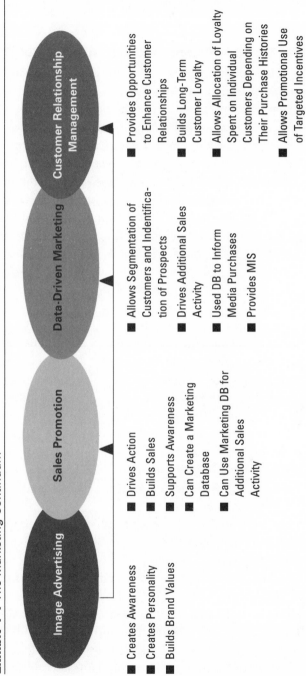

Image Advertising
- Creates Awareness
- Creates Personality
- Builds Brand Values

Sales Promotion
- Drives Action
- Builds Sales
- Supports Awareness
- Can Create a Marketing Database
- Can Use Marketing DB for Additional Sales Activity

Data-Driven Marketing
- Allows Segmentation of Customers and Indentification of Prospects
- Drives Additional Sales Activity
- Used DB to Inform Media Purchases
- Provides MIS

Customer Relationship Management
- Provides Opportunities to Enhance Customer Relationships
- Builds Long-Term Customer Loyalty
- Allows Allocation of Loyalty Spent on Individual Customers Depending on Their Purchase Histories
- Allows Promotional Use of Targeted Incentives

fidelity: The growing emphasis on CRM is a direct consequence of this trend.

Building the Brand Is Paramount; But at What Cost?

This change in the seller-buyer relationship caused a paradigm shift in the way mass manufacturers and service providers approached the marketplace. They reasoned that if they could establish a brand that the public would know and respect—a better mousetrap, so to speak—then the public should beat a path to the door of any merchant selling it without too much worry about *which* merchant. As the penetration of television in the home rose to its current level of almost 100% in most developed and developing countries, mass advertising using TV as the medium of choice has been used to create awareness of the brand and build its value in the mind of the consumer. Alongside TV, radio, mass magazines, and many other media were used to repeat and reinforce the brand story. Creating the brand and giving it value are clearly the first steps in the continuum.

As the marketplace has become increasingly competitive, mass marketers and their advertising agencies have continually increased their spending to capture the public's attention with the objective of making each brand "top-of-mind" when the consumer is interesting in making a purchase in the product or service category. How much to spend—while the subject of massive research and investigation—has often been dictated more by competitive pressure than by any tested rationale. Even the use of sophisticated models to try and determine the "right" level of spend to accomplish defined objectives falls short because of the difficulty in precisely measuring something as amorphous as brand loyalty.

When world economies were growing and profits were pouring in, *accountability* often took a back seat to arguments that brands had discernable values and that the greater the spend on building these brand values, the greater the stock market value of the company owning the brand.

Perhaps this lack of accountability is part of the reason a recent article in *The Wall Street Journal* said: "The faith of big-spending marketers in the power of traditional advertising is waning. . . . The most worrisome findings indicate that companies are increasingly skeptical of the power of advertising to boost sales." Mass advertising supports mass marketing at the beginning of the continuum, but the irony is that consumers increasingly do not wish themselves to be part of the "mass."

For years the leading analysts of the marketing scene have been calling attention to the increasing need to focus on individual customers. In the early 1990s, Tom Peters predicted correctly that Manic specialization meant that the 1990s would be the decade of one-to-one, not niche, marketing.

Every child's experience of looking first through one end of a telescope and then the other demonstrates how different things look close-up and from a distance. Marketers have tended to assess the economics of their businesses with the "big," macro, view, the profit and loss account, the cash flow statement, and the balance sheet. This is an obvious and important discipline. However, the problem with using only this perspective is that it often sees only the forest and overlooks the trees, individual details that could make the businesses much more profitable.

It is fair to say that the closer you are to the individual consumer, the greater the possibility of accountability in marketing. As you move from left to right in the continuum, your ability to measure and influence individual action grows accordingly.

The Real Cost of a Free Lunch

In an effort to keep current customers and acquire new ones, the number and type of sales incentives seem endless and our loyalty often goes to the highest bidder. Even the wealthiest individuals collect and use the "bonus" points proffered by marketers ignoring the famous observation that there is no such thing as a free lunch. Aggressive retailers use a wide variety of methods to stimulate purchases as illustrated by the "pile them high, sell them cheap" philosophy of a famous retail merchant. The economics of sales promotion can be measured with much greater accuracy than brand advertising.

Take for example the case of a small West of England bank that had a problem that needed a quick sales promotion solution. To fund their second mortgage lending operation, they determined that they needed to substantially increase the level of individual deposits. And they needed to do it quickly if they were to capture the desired share of a fast-expanding market.

Their experience with using direct response advertisements in the press to raise money had been variable, sometimes better and sometimes worse than the £70.00 they knew they could afford to secure a £1,000.00 deposit paying 5% annual interest. Experience had shown that this deposit would stay with the bank for at least one year and that many depositors would renew the deposits if the interest rates offered remained competitive.

When we recommended an aggressive advertising campaign that offered as an incentive "the highest bank interest rates in Britain," the bank's finance director went ballistic and thundered that there was no way the bank could afford this. The bank, he argued, was paying interest at near the top of the market, and there was no way to increase it.

Our recommendation was made not on the basis of thinking up a "best" headline and then trying to support it, but on a solid strategic and economic foundation.

It was well known that the British (like most other investors) chase the highest interest rates available for their spare savings. So we reasoned that offering the highest rate in the land ought to capture more than their attention: It should produce a substantial amount of money in deposits, more deposits for the same advertising expense. The economic question we asked ourselves was the same as any merchant planning a sales promotion campaign might ask: How much additional business would we need to generate to justify the cost of the incentive? Or, put in the specific terms of this offer:What reduction in the cost of attracting a £1,000.00 deposit would be necessary to justify how much of an interest increase?

The answer (as shown in Exhibit 1-2) was simple to calculate. There was an historic marketing cost of £70.00 to attract a one thousand pound deposit. This was also the "allowable"—the amount we could afford to spend. The cost of the additional interest would add £10.00 to the costs. However, an increase in the number and/or quality of the responses (deposits generated) of only 14.29% would totally fund the additional 1.00% or £10.00 of interest that would substantiate the claim. This same logic would apply to any sales promotion incentive.

Exhibit 1-2 Competitive Incentive Calculation

	Initial Incentive		Enhanced Incentive	
	%	Value	%	Value
Product Value		1,000.00		1,000.00
Allowable Marketing Expenditure	7.00%	70.00	7.00%	70.00
Incentive Cost (Percent of Value)	5.00%	50.00	6.00%	60.00
TOTAL Promotion & Incentive Cost	12.00%	120.00	13.00%	130.00
Additional Incentive Cost				10.00
Historic Marketing Cost Per Product		70.00		
Increase in Response & Relative Decrease in Marketing - Cost Per Product Value Needed to Justify Added Incentive			14.29%	

Even the Finance Director had to accept the logic of the argument. He was even prepared to go along with a test campaign so long as "you gentlemen remember that this extra cost of interest will be charged to the marketing budget, *not the financial one.*"

The question was then only whether or not the new advertising would be able to bring in the needed deposits at a marketing cost (the actual cost of raising £1,000) 14.29% lower than the historic allowable historic figure.

Some simple tests proved that the campaign would do much better. Actual results nearly doubled the best past campaign experience with an almost 50% *decrease* in the marketing cost of raising the needed funds. This difference between the actual and the allowable, less the additional interest cost, flowed directly to profit. Not surprisingly, the Finance Director never offered to share some of the excess profit with marketing.

There were incremental benefits as well at every step in the continuum, benefits that were not considered in the economic equation but were extremely valuable if less quantifiable.

The "highest bank interest rates in Britain" claim—not without a little help from the bank's PR agency-generated considerable positive financial page press comment that supported the bank's image as well as the specific sales promotion objective. The new depositors, having now dealt with the bank and having been satisfied with the service, produced excellent cross-sell results for other products. Having the expectation that the bank would always be at the top or near the top of the interest rate table, they were inclined to keep their deposits at the bank rather than switch. For those who did, the initial investment in acquiring them could be amortized over a longer period.

This is an almost classic case of what started out as a simple sales promotion exercise positively influencing every step of the continuum, first by accomplishing the primary marketing objective of economically raising new funds but also enhancing the bank's image and building its customer file.

When we see advertising that offers "interest free" credit or similar promotional financing (especially from automotive, white goods and furniture companies), we see applications of this concept. The promotional offer is a "cost" of the sales process and to be successful must create a sufficient number of incremental sales to reduce the normal cost of sales by a sufficient amount to justify this special expense. The success or failure of the sales promotion effort is clearly "accountable."

Recent developments in "scanner" technologies have begun to bridge the distinctions between sales promotion and direct marketing insofar as customers in retail outlets are individually tracked, their purchases are scanned and they are offered specific sales promotions relevant to their purchases. When this data is combined with historic purchasing data, it makes a powerful combination, but the essential economics do not change except with respect to the cost of the technology. Whatever is promoted to them has a "cost" in terms of discounts, etc., and this cost must be measured against increased sales—just as the increased interest rate for the British bank was measured—to determine how much sales have increased for how much expense.

When we plan sales promotions we must not forget that there are no free lunches and that the marketing budgets will almost certainly be charged for the costs of anything that is "free."

Strict Accountability: The Special Strength of Direct Marketing and CRM

Direct Marketing and CRM are the most accountable disciplines on the Marketing Continuum, and the lessons learned from them have been applied throughout this book and inform all branches of marketing. As noted above, counting the coupons and measuring the marketing cost of each order and the value of each customer were fundamental disciplines that spelled the difference between success and failure for mail order traders.

Today we have many different types of increasingly complex products and services sold to individuals or businesses using direct marketing in many different ways. The economics of single sales and continuities, subscriptions, and clubs have very different drivers. The many media options available to the marketer from personal selling to the Internet are dazzling. Each has different economic parameters. Choosing the right one or the right combination is a critical strategic marketing task.

When truly data-driven, Direct Marketing is a process—not as many of its practitioners have argued, a series of techniques—whose principles can apply profitably to each of these individual parameters. It begins with a process of thought about the relationship of the individual purchaser–"one-to-one" as Tom Peters predicted—to the product or service being offered. From that point of departure, to be successful, it demands attention to a wide spectrum of economic variables. These range from product or service prices and costs, fulfillment and distribution costs, attrition calculations, promotion and incentive options, overhead costs and intended profit expectations to assumptions about future purchases from the same customer. It demands rapt attention to the many details of the economic interaction between seller and buyer. If there were ever businesses that proved the adage that "God is in the details," they are direct marketing and CRM.

While nothing is more important than the right product being offered in the right way to the right customer, without a focus on the economics at every stage of the process, the likelihood of success is seriously diminished. The methodologies of the discipline have increasing resonance throughout the marketing continuum and appeal to the desire for accountability that management and shareholders are demanding. Marketing based on carefully calculated risk to reward ratios has growing appeal.

No matter how "brilliant" a promotional initiative, no matter how many industry prizes it wins, the ultimate judgment of its success will be found on the bottom line. The obsession with measurement that characterizes Direct Marketing and CRM is, more than anything else, what is attracting the attention of all the branches of Marketing.

But it isn't only the *measurement* of results that is important. The economic methodologies and database disciplines for planning that have come to characterize modern direct marketing are influencing all marketing no matter where it falls on the continuum.

There is general agreement among marketers that if direct marketing is the beginning of the process—the acquisition of a sale or a customer—then CRM is keeping that customer and enhancing the relationship for the purpose of maximizing the profitability of the relationship. Each sale has its own marketing cost, but it must also carry a portion of the cost of acquiring the customer in the first place. All things being equal, the more sales to the customer, the lower the share of the acquisition cost amortization. The economics of both are closely interrelated and should be considered together.

Investing in the Future

Image Advertising is Advertising. Direct Marketing is making an investment in a customer's future value.

One striking difference between image advertising and direct marketing is the different way the accounting profession treats marketing expenditures.

Because the effect of image advertising is difficult to measure with any degree of precision, auditors normally require advertising expenditures to be "written off" when they are made. They are seen as "costs" not as "investments."

Not so with marketing expenditures used to acquire a customer. Measurable advertising to acquire a magazine subscriber, an insurance purchaser, a credit card user or a host of other product and service customers with an up-front acquisition cost and a forward revenue flow can be capitalized over a predictable and conservative future time period. This has the effect of doing what accountants like to do: relating revenue and expense in a logical way. And it has a very positive effect on the ability of companies to make direct marketing investments, especially those companies that make their figures public.

Imagine a major successful subscription acquisition campaign run in the last three months of a fiscal year. Unless it was very unusual, there would be no way that the acquisition cost of the new subscribers could be recouped in that fiscal year. Thus, even if the campaign was highly successful and brought in far more subscribers at lower than forecast acquisition cost, the campaign expenditure would put a big hole in the company's annual profit.

Instead of forcing the marketer to write off all the expenditure in that fiscal year (as would be required of an image campaign), accounting rules allow the direct marketer to capitalize the acquisition cost and write it off over the term of the subscription. For example, if history shows that a subscriber is likely to stay for two years, a normal accepted procedure would be to write off the acquisition cost 50% over the first six months of the subscription, 25% over the second and the remaining 25% over the third six months, clearing the debt, so to speak, with six months of revenue still to be received.

This allows direct marketers to be less concerned with end-of-the-year acquisition marketing investments than they would be otherwise and reflects a much fairer picture of the business. Why not: The investment in marketing is just like any investment that is predictably revenue producing over time.

Average: The Most Dangerous Word in Contemporary Marketing

Despite readily available tools and technologies, marketers have tended to concentrate their attention on "macro" financial data instead of the far more helpful and meaningful "micro" data on each individual customer. Ask any room full of people if the "average" consumer will raise his or her hand. No hands will be raised. Yet traditional marketers (and many direct marketers) still think about the *average* customer as their target. Averages can badly distort reality. It is well known that if a dozen people are drinking beer in a bar and Bill Gates comes in, the "average" net worth of the people in the bar rockets up dramatically. But that doesn't all of a sudden make them all millionaires.

Imagine a portfolio of 66,000 clients of a small business. Knowing those 66,000 customers generated total revenue of $769,560 and that each had an *average* value of $11.66 is interesting, but it does little to help us manage the promotional planning for the enterprise. If our initiatives are driven by that average sales figure, we will almost certainly miss many exciting promotional opportunities.

Much more important than the average value is the knowledge

that only 1% of the customers accounted for 15% of total sales, with each having an average annual purchase value of $174.90. Five percent accounted for 50%, each with an average annual purchase value of $116.60 compared to the average value for the entire customer base of $11.66.

If marketing investment is based on the $11.66 expenditure it will *per force* be very limited. If it is allocated in relation to the relative spend of specific customer segments, it can be much more effective.

Without customers there is no business: The enterprise is dead. A business with customers is alive, and to the extent it focuses on the profitable relationship with these customers, it can flourish. Knowing which customer is which, the focus sharpens and we can see each tree, not just the forest.

With the appropriate data, marketing managers can now decide whether the same promotional and CRM resources should be directed *equally towards all the customers or whether the customer base should be segmented by their values and appropriate promotional resources deployed according to their relative values.*

Retailers are also coming to realize that their traditional paradigm of single-minded concentration on the value of every square foot of selling space may need adjustment. All retail space units, like all customers, are not equal. Thus, smart retailers are increasingly trying to understand the relative value of the retail space *and of each customer,* changing their focus to how best to use their available space to receive a greater share of the spend of their best customers.

These simple and real-life examples illustrate a significant (albeit obvious) truth: The most dangerous word in marketing today is the word *average.* And that's why marketing executives in all the disciplines of the continuum almost always answer "No!" when asked, "Would you spend your marketing monies the way you do today if you could differentiate between your highest, your middle and your low value customers?

The reason for this is that most image advertisers and sales promotion specialists continue to focus on that elusive *average* customer and do not understand or use the tools that exist to make this essential differentiation. Is it because using these tools would acknowledge that direct marketing is not a second-class citizen in the marketing hierarchy? Or is it perhaps that understanding the characteristics of specific customers instead of the "average" customer is too much like hard work?

Whatever the reasons, this differentiation is fundamental to practitioners of Direct Marketing and CRM, activities that by their nature depend more upon the purchasing performance of individual customers than of the customer base as a whole.

Professional direct marketing today is not about advertising. It is about a series of measurable and accountable promotional efforts to sell within a carefully structured economic framework. The economic edifice of the new Accountable Marketing is built on these four pillars of Direct Marketing and CRM:

▶ The *value of a specific sale.*

▶ The *value of a customer or prospect over time.*

▶ The *allowable marketing cost of acquiring a customer* or *making a specific sale.*

▶ The *allowable cost of the CRM activities that enhance customer performance.*

If we know the net value of a specific sale (the revenue that's left after all the product and distribution costs connected with that sale but before promotional expenses) and can reasonably project how many more sales we can make to that customer and in what period of time, we are more than half way towards a viable program. With this information, we can determine how much marketing money we can afford to invest to acquire that customer and how much to make that sale—the allowable cost per order (ACPO)—the most important economic equation in our business and one that is the subject of Chapter 2. And we can also know how much we should spend to make certain that we keep that customer. Because as we have seen, different customers have different values and the amount of resource we put against each one must be consistent with his individual value.

While the edifice described above is most strongly identified with Direct Marketing and CRM, it drives all marketing on the Marketing

Continuum comprising Accountable Marketing. It sounds simple and in many ways it is. It's the details that often confuse things.

To understand how much "margin" we will have on a specific sale we need to look closely at all the costs connected with that sale. These are often difficult to assemble and many judgment calls need to be made. Of the people who use the telephone to "order," what percentage will actually complete the transaction; how many will return the merchandise for one reason or another; how many will keep it but fail to pay? If we are offering an incentive to purchase, we need to be able to determine the true cost of this incentive against each actual sale. To calculate the number and value of additional sales likely to be made to this customer, we must either have data on his previous purchase performance or be able to make educated guesses.

Collecting and using data to inform our decision making and to help us make highly educated guesses is a very potent combination, the driving force behind an increasing number of highly successful businesses that use data to drive their marketing efforts. An understanding of the ways to use the economics underlying these "guesses" is a recipe for direct marketing success with significant application to all branches of marketing.

Whatever branch of marketing we practice, with today's knowledge and marketing database tools we can *know* a great deal about our customers and their purchasing performance. With that knowledge, the classic problem of knowing that you are wasting half of your advertising money but not knowing which half should be an historic footnote better used for after-dinner speeches than for the management of a successful business.

Notes

[1] Figures published by the Direct Marketing Association of the US showed direct marketing as representing 56 percent (US $193 billion) of the total US $344.8 billion spent in US advertising media in 2002.

▶▶▶ 2

Understanding Allowable
Cost Per Order (ACPO)

N
o matter what the branch of marketing a marketer is in or where that branch fits on the continuum, every successful marketer knows that there is a finite amount that an organization can afford to spend on each customer to promote its product or service. We call this the "Allowable Cost Per Order" or ACPO. (See www.acpomodel.com)

This amount can be determined through a calculation based on a mix of the revenue the marketer expects to receive for each product unit sold multiplied by the number of units the marketer expects to sell, less all the costs of the manufacturing or production of the product and its distribution. Stated as a formula, this can be expressed as

ACPO =
Total Revenue – all expenses including profit and/or contribution.

This formula can be applied to a single or multiple sale, a subscription, a club or any sales sequence to consumers or businesses.

If the marketer's promotional efforts are very successful and sell more than originally contemplated, the organization benefits on the bottom line by being able to amortize promotional spend over a greater number of sales, thus reducing the amount of promotional money that must be allocated to each sale. Conversely, if sales do not achieve the desired level, each unit of merchandise is burdened with a greater marketing cost than had been anticipated and is reflected in lower profits or unexpected losses. A recent article in *The Economist*[1] drew attention to this: "Last year . . . GM's [General

Motors] profit per vehicle was a scant $350—providing a wafer-thin profit margin of 1–2%. With manufacturing costs these days cut to the bone, *the only way for carmakers to raise their margins is to lower their marketing and warranty costs"* [Emphasis added].

Even with the benefit of highly sophisticated models, "image" advertisers are subject to a high degree of risk. This risk reduces the closer we get to individual or one-to-one relationships with our customers. We can see them much more clearly, and they are many times more accountable than when we are marketing to the average consumer or even selected consumer segments. All marketers share a common objective, to obtain an *actual cost per order* lower than our *allowable cost per order*.

The ACPO Informs All Marketing Actions

As Exhibit 2-1 shows, the concept of ACPO works at every stage of the marketing continuum.

Although the ACPO concept is least applicable to image advertising, it still plays a positive and profitable role, but it becomes an increasingly powerful tool when applied to sales promotion, direct marketing, and CRM.

Most "sales promotion" efforts are by their nature short term: Marketers make an exciting offer that will generate additional sales volume or clear existing inventory and then return to normal until the next promotion. The exciting offer is usually characterized by a discount or other incentive, and this has a measurable cost that must be recouped through increased sales and a lower cost-per-sale than would have been possible without the sales promotion. Sales promotion initiatives are increasingly used to move casual purchasers into regular customers.[2]

The existence of the marketing database and a growing understanding of the importance of differentiating customers in terms of their purchasing histories, demographics, and psychograpics has blurred the lines between sales promotion, direct marketing and CRM. No wonder that stores like Harrods in London invite their best charge-card customers to exclusive advance viewing of the sales merchandise. Who better to "reward" with the opportunity to purchase yet more merchandise, albeit at preferential prices, than the customers who have bought the most from you in the past?

Targeting Sales Promotions

Sales promotion efforts are even more targeted by practitioners of direct marketing than by general (or image) marketers. If you know, for example, that someone has recently purchased a digital camera or a computer, the opportunity to sell accessories is both obvious and highly cost effective. We know that any satisfied previous customer is a much better prospect than someone who has never purchased from you before and the costs of selling to such a customer will be lower than acquiring him or her in the first place. With data on the recency, frequency, and value (RFV) of the individual's purchases, the cost of selling relevant merchandise or services and increasing your share of the individual's total spend—often called "share of wallet"—will be far less than it would be selling to a stranger. Upselling (offering the customer a deluxe version or additional benefits for a higher price) and cross-selling (selling other related or unrelated products) therefore become important contributors to the total economic activity.

As indicated in the earlier exhibit, the two key economic determinants in assessing the allowable investment for a sales promotion activity are:

1. Having previously "acquired" the customer, *the amount that can be afforded to make the specific sale or drive each specific action (e.g., induce a retail visit).*

2. Promoting to prospects who are not part of your customer database, *determining how valuable the name and accompanying data will be for future marketing efforts and either factoring this into the "allowable" or not.*

While following the normal procedures for determining the allowable marketing spend for a single sale, we will almost certainly find that we can anticipate a substantially higher response rate from former customers than new prospects. Thus, we are likely to succeed with a substantially lower ACPO than were we to have to recruit the customers in the first place.

The "Micro" View: Better Than the Big Picture

What is important—even essential—in the economic planning of all marketing is determining the revenue and cost perimeters and

Exhibit 2-1 ACPO

CONTINUUM STAGE	APPLICATIONS OF ALLOWABLE COST PER ORDER CONCEPT	ECONOMIC DETERMINANTS	COMMENTS
Image Advertising	• Unless existence of marketing database, can only be applied in "macro" terms, thus low applicability • Getting potential consumers to identify themselves through "raising their hands" as first step in two or multi-step process, high applicability	• Total sales expectation in given time frame • Cost of media and wastage to reach target • Amount that can be afforded for each step of the process including cost of non-conversion	While having the lowest level of application specificity within the continuum, the use of image advertising to also generate a customer-specific show of interest is important. The amount you can afford to spend to get these expressions of interest can be calculated in the total ACPO and the costs of the image advertising are often shared between holders of each objective.
Sales Promotion	• When promoting to a customer database high applicability • When promoting to a prospect universe with the intention of building a marketing database high applicability	• Having previously "acquired" the customer, amount that can be afforded for each customer to make the specific sale or drive the specific action (i.e., get a retail visit) • How valuable the name and accompanying data will be for future marketing efforts	The line between sales promotion and direct marketing activities is a highly flexible one with considerable overlap. Often a cross-sell effort could just as well be called sales promotion or vice versa. The key issues in each effort are: • The amount you can afford to spend to make the specific sale • The value of the data obtained

Exhibit 2-1 ACPO (Continued)

CONTINUUM STAGE	APPLICATIONS OF ALLOWABLE COST PER ORDER CONCEPT	ECONOMIC DETERMINANTS	COMMENTS
Data-Driven Marketing	• *High applicability* in all measurable selling modes, one-shots, continuities, clubs & subscriptions for all products & services	• Lifetime value of the customer considering all revenue and cost parameters of the single or continuing transactions	All areas of the DDM process are impacted by the ACPO.
Customer Relationship Management High	• *High applicability* in all CRM resource applications as part of overall CRM program	• Amount of increased margin obtainable from customer as a result of CRM initiative • Comparable cost of acquiring a new customer to replace the existing one	Each CRM action has an allowable cost that must be factored into the total economics of the customer relationship. Often part of the acquisition allowable in the form of "points" or "miles" is allocated to CRM.

knowing, in advance, of the expenditure of large sums of promotional money, whether or not you can expect each customer's purchases to justify the expenditure in attracting that customer in the first place. This is the primary reason why image advertisers and sales promoters often seem to be looking at the marketplace through a different end of the telescope than direct marketers and CRM experts. The image marketers want to see the whole universe, the "macro" view. Direct marketers usually start from a "micro" view of the performance of each individual customer. This close-up view is consistent with the need to deal with each customer as a specific entity rather than an undifferentiated "average." It is a significant difference in the traditional starting point for the way image advertisers and direct marketers traditionally do their economics.

As we know, there is no such thing as an "average" customer. Each is different, and economic planning that depends upon averages even among defined groups of prospects and customers still misses the essential point of overcoming Pareto's Principle, better known as the 80/20 rule.

Where Accountability Begins

What we can afford to spend in promotional money to obtain an order of any kind, acquire a subscription, or enroll a club member, conditions all marketing activity no matter what the product or service or to whom it is being marketed. It doesn't matter whether the product is a tangible one, such as an article of wearing apparel or a cell phone, or something as ephemeral as a package holiday, a financial service or a charitable opportunity to support a worthy cause. And it is not important whether the product or service is delivered "direct" or through some other distribution channel.

A *prospect* is someone you hope to be able to attract to become a customer, but he is not a customer until he has made a purchase. The objective is to transform as many prospects into customers as possible and at costs below the allowable. The best prospects are people who meet the profile of your current customers, and the more demographic and psychographic data you have on each, the more likely you are to succeed in moving him or her from "prospect" to "customer" status. Determining the ACPO is the first step in making marketing more accountable.

There are two kinds of customers. One is a person who buys from you once and disappears–you don't know who he is or how to contact him again. The other is someone with whom you have established a one-to-one relationship; someone who has purchased from you and given you his name, address, and other relevant data, someone who has given you, explicitly or implicitly, the permission to contact him again.

There are also two kinds of orders. The first is for a single sale, the second for a sale that is part of a sequence. The only thing that differentiates them in ACPO terms is whether the marketing investment has to be recouped on the single sale or whether it can be "spread" over the sequence of sales. It should be obvious that if the marketing investment can legitimately be spread, the likelihood is that the marketer can afford significantly more to acquire the customer than if he is making a single sale.

The critical economic factor is always *how much we can afford in marketing spend to make the sale, transform the prospect into a customer and retain the customer's loyalty.*

How much we can afford to do each of these things depends upon a number of factors. Some are more obvious than others. There is the revenue we expect to receive. From this must be deducted the cost of the product we intend to sell, the cost of any sales incentives, the cost of handling and delivering the order, of collecting the money and much more. There is also the attrition rate of customers when the product is delivered and paid for over time and there is the cost of maintaining the customer relationship.

Finally, and importantly, there is the profit or contribution we plan to make. *What we can afford to spend for promotion is what's left after all these costs are deducted from the revenue.*

This is the *Allowable Cost per Order or per Customer (ACPO)*. It is arguably *the most important economic factor in marketing and the one that most profoundly affects the profits on the bottom line. It informs every aspect of the marketing economics and media strategy.* If you can't calculate the ACPO you are, so to speak, flying blind, an activity not known to contribute to getting you where you wish to go or even surviving the journey.

Moving from "Case Rate" to Customer Rate

Large packaged goods companies such as Procter & Gamble and Nestle calculate the percentage of the wholesale value of a case of goods that they can afford to spend for marketing—often called the "case rate." They stick rigorously to this percentage in calculating how much to spend for their advertising and marketing activities. Only relatively recently have they changed the focus somewhat and begun to examine what might be called "customer rate." This is the amount they can afford to spend to attract a specific customer to purchase a given amount of the product over a specific time period, a calculation that direct marketers call "Lifetime Value" (LTV).

The principle of LTV applies to all marketing. As marketers (whether selling fast-moving consumer goods (FMCG) through image advertising and sales promotion or vendors of highly specialized products and services selling to a limited market), our goal is to establish a franchise with a customer and have that customer regularly purchase our products or services.

Because it costs more to attract a new buyer than to sell to a satisfied former buyer, the economics favor promoting repeat purchases and gaining from each customer the maximum value over the lifetime of the relationship, a relationship discussed in detail later in this chapter.

Many years ago a colleague and I were sent to Hong Kong from London by our advertising agency employer to help P&G solve a local marketing problem it was encountering for its infant disposable product, Pampers. On the very long flight we consumed a fair amount of the airline's very fine offering of wines and spirits and arrived ready to go directly to the hotel and catch up on much-needed sleep.

But the client had other ideas. He picked us up at the airport and insisted on taking us to dinner. Over that delicious meal we got talking about the "problem," and, loosened by the effects of the flight, I asked provocatively: "How much would you pay me if I could guarantee you the two year spend of a new mother on 'disposables' for her baby?"

The client said he had never been asked that question before and thought for a moment—you could see him doing calculations in his head. When he finally answered, he apologized that he couldn't give us an exact figure without some homework, but it was sure to be "one hell of a lot." "What," I asked undiplomatically, "had the figure to do with the Pampers 'case rate'"? "Nothing whatever," he answered graciously.

Had the journey not been so long nor had my colleague and I not enjoyed the airline's hospitality so abundantly; had we had a good night's sleep before meeting the client and getting down to work, I would probably never have thought to ask the question so directly. But then we might also never have begun an analytic process, which looked at the real value of each Pampers customer instead of the case rate. It was a process that has had a profound effect on the marketing not only of Pampers but other fast moving consumer goods for which there is a clearly definable target market and an accountable and predictable "lifetime value." (See Exhibit 2-2.)

While a detailed Lifetime Value Calculation template exists (see Exhibit 2-10, Lifetime Valuation) and can be used to determine the allowable cost of acquiring a customer, a simplified look at the numbers for a disposal product such as Pamper shows the dynamic of the LTV.

The assumption in the model in Exhibit 2-2 indicates that the total value of a customer who buys the maximum number of individual or pack purchases[3] only of the single brand for all the disposals needs for a single baby is $832.00. However, prudence dictates that an allowance should be made for attrition for whatever reason, including switching to another brand or generic product. Obviously, the lower the percentage of attrition, the closer the LTV comes to 100 percent. In this example, assuming that CRM or other activities can mitigate any attrition, the lost 208.00 can be recovered to fund these activities or be used for customer acquisition and/or additional profit.

Against this revenue, we have product and distribution costs. For the purpose of this example we have assumed that the Percentage Distribution Discount is 30 percent, and therefore, the wholesale value after attrition is 436.80. In comparing the "Case Rate" to the "Customer Rate," the wholesale value (the basis for "Case Rate") is critical.

Exhibit 2-2 FMCG Allowable Cost Calculation

	Customer Rate	Case Rate
Product [Describe Product Below]: *Disposables*		
Maximum Number of Individual or Pack Purchases	104	
Value Per Individual or Pack Purchase	8.00	
TOTAL Value of Purchases if 100%	832.00	
Discounted by Attrition or Switch %	25.00%	208.00	
Adjusted Total Lifetime Value after Attrition or Switch		
Wholesale Value after Attrition or Switch	624.00	436.80
Less:		
Unit (Pack) Cost of Product	4.00	
Number of Packs Discounted for Attrition or Switch	78	
TOTAL Cost of Product	312.00	312.00
% Distribution Discount	30.00%	187.20	
% for Marketing	12.00%	52.42	52.42
TOTAL Costs	551.62	364.42
PROFIT	8.70%	72.38	72.38
If Precise Data on Target Customers **Exists**,		
Allowable Spend Per Customer	52.42	
If Precise Data on Target Customers **Does Not Exist**,		
Likely % of Marketing Wastage	40.00%	
Allowable Spend Per Customer After Wastage	31.45	

We have also assumed that 12 percent of the wholesale value can be used for marketing.

Our challenge as marketers is to use this data to find the best marketing mix. This raises the following questions:

▶ How much of this amount should be spent on general advertising?

▶ How much should be spent on sales promotion?

▶ How much should be spent on direct marketing and CRM?

The model tells us that we have $52.42 to spend per customer. If precise name and address data of new mothers is available then we would do well to use the majority of this money to target these prospects with specific promotions and incentives (which must be funded out of this amount). If this data does not exist, then we need to use this marketing money to try and reach the target market as best we can, mindful of the likely high degree of waste inherent in promoting to an audience, part of which may have no interest in the product. With a relatively low 40 percent level of waste, the amount that will be available for our actual prospects will drop to $31.45.

Without calculating the customer rate and LTV, the marketer would simply spend the 12 percent of wholesale value case rate in general advertising and sales promotion activities and be dependent for profit on the cumulative success of this effort. He could do little to capture and use the data on his customers. Using the LTV changes the focus and allows the marketer to concentrate his expenditure on customers rather than prospects.

Unfortunately, lists of women in their last trimester of pregnancy, and new mothers are hard to come by and exist only in a few markets. Thus, the majority of sales of Pampers and other FMCG products must rely on the combination of mass media advertising and sales promotion combined in Pampers case with in-hospital sample distribution and other name-gathering methods to build new mother lists allowing direct contact. The majority of sales are likely to continue to remain at the retail outlets, but if we can identify the new mothers, we can offer them special incentives to first try the brand and then to continue purchasing it.

Pet food is another FMCG category that invites the same direct marketing approach as Pampers. Just as babies at different ages need different sizes and types of disposables, pets have a wide spectrum of food needs. A young country dog has very different nutritional needs than a mature city dog. And no matter how much you love your pet, the purchase of weighty packs of pet food is a burden. Thus, the marketer who can provide a customized service providing the right food for specific pets and a delivery service to make sure that the pet owner is well served, has a major opportunity to use direct marketing methods to attract customers and keep them.

Customer Identification Potential at Retail

New technologies such as scanners built into shopping baskets and radio frequency identification (RFID) are likely to add strength to FMCG companies desirous of knowing more about their customers and giving them the ability to target those customers both at the retail outlet and with promotion designed to assure the brand sale when they visit the outlet. While scanners have been around since the 1980s and there have been numerous experiments, retailers have tended to use these technologies more for stock control than for customer purchase identification.

This may be changing. Said a press release from Symbol Technologies, Inc., "Symbol's Portable Shopper has changed the way people shop by allowing them to scan their own purchases as they go through the aisles, reducing checkout time and providing item and price checks, as well as a running total of purchases. . . . Supermarkets can use the collected data to better stock their stores [and] Special offers can be made to shoppers as a link to the store's loyalty program."

RFID technology relies on tiny microchips that are added to product labeling and "each chip broadcasts a unique ID code that can yield a wealth of information. . . ."[4]

Marketing executives have come to realize that there are many products, whether delivered "direct" or not, that can benefit from the same economic point of departure as P&G discovered for Pampers. They tend to be products that at any given time have a fairly narrow and definable potential customer base, products from disposable contact lenses to specialty coffees that have sufficiently high "lifetime" value and can benefit from the establishment of a direct relationship with the end user.

The Challenge: Minimizing Waste

If the users can be identified and included in a marketing database, promotional spend can be concentrated on acquiring them in the first place and sustaining their purchase cycle through carefully planned CRM activities. Much of the waste inherent in talking to everybody—even a carefully defined group of *everybodys*—can be eliminated. Just think how few members of even the most carefully targeted TV audience are prospects for disposable diapers, new mothers or women in the last trimester of pregnancy, or how many wear disposable contact lenses.

We tend to think of TV as a low-cost-per-thousand medium. And it is often the best means of efficiently reaching large numbers of prospects. But it is almost impossible to estimate with any accuracy the level of waste using the medium when promoting a product that has a narrow target market.

If the cost per thousand of a 30-second TV spot has a cost index of 100 and only 5 percent are *really prospects*, the real cost of reaching each of them jumps 20 times from a theoretical .10 to a cost per prospect of 2.00.

As David Milne, formerly Deputy Chairman of Saatchi & Saatchi and now Senior Consultant for Results Business Consulting in the UK, says; "TV shouts at all and has no heed to response. It speaks, indifferent to interest and incapable of dialogue. For these reasons alone media advertising can be very inefficient. If it's a sale you want, talk to the horse's mouth and heed what it tells you."

Calculating the ACPO

Calculating the ACPO for different types of products and promotions depends upon the marketer having sufficient data and tools to develop appropriate models. Subsequent chapters look in detail at ways to make these calculations from a single sale product to more complex forms such as continuities, clubs and subscriptions. To better understand the drivers that condition the ACPO calculation, it would be useful to look at a sale of a single product.

The simplest sale is a single sale to a single person. Its

economic requirements are rudimentary and every merchant who stays in business uses them in one form or another as second nature whether or not he includes direct marketing in his marketing armory. While the example below assumes this sale is made at a distance—what is usually called a "mail-order" or direct marketing sale—most of the criteria are the same if the product is delivered at the retail level.

Before direct marketers discovered the many advantages of acquiring a "customer" instead of simply making a "sale," this was the most common form of responsive offer. It is still used frequently and the template that follows, (Exhibit 2-3) has been designed to facilitate calculations. It allows the user to input the important data and delivers the results including sensitivities (defined by the user) to aid planning.

As can be seen in reviewing the template, the marketer needs the following information:

▶ The revenue value of an individual unit.

▶ How many units the person will buy.

▶ The total product cost per unit.

▶ The revenue from postage and shipping chargebacks if any.

▶ The cost of sales or other taxes.

▶ The total costs of fulfillment including distribution, handling, credit card charges, etc., if the product is to be delivered rather than sold at the retail.

▶ An assumption for bad pay.

▶ An assumption for product returns.

▶ The costs of any premiums or incentives to be given including shipping them if separate from the product shipment.

▶ Any miscellaneous expenses.

▶ The desired profit or contribution.

From these inputs we can compute the "Net Margin before Promotion." Using an estimated total promotion cost per thousand, both the

Exhibit 2-3 Valuing a Single-Unit Sale

Item Selling Price	60.00	
No. of Items	2	
TOTAL Product Revenue	**120.00**	
Less:		
Unit Product Cost	15.00	
No. of Items	2.00	
TOTAL Product Cost	**30.00**	
Gross Margin before other Costs	**90.00**	
Postage Charge Back for Package	3.50	
TOTAL Gross Revenue	**93.50**	
Less:		
Taxes included in price	9.00%	11.12
Fulfillment (inc. Credit Card charges)		15.00
Bad Pay at	3.00%	3.71
Returns at	4.00%	4.94
Premium		6.00
Misc.		5.00
TOTAL Non-Product Costs		**45.78**
Profit or Contribution	15.00%	**18.53**
Net Margin Before Promotion		**29.23**
Promotion Cost Per '000 (including media and lists, etc.)	500.00	
% Response needed to Breakeven and make desired Profit Margin is		**1.41%**
No.of Orders Per '000 Promotions needed to Breakeven and make desired Profit Margin is		**14**

Sensitivities (+ or -) To Target Response Percentage

Degree of Sensitivity	20.00%			Target		
% Response	1.10%	1.37%	1.71%	2.05%	2.46%	
Cost Per Response	45.65	36.52	29.22	24.35	20.29	
Profit (Loss) after Add-back of Profit or Contribution	2.09	11.22	18.53	23.39	27.45	
% Profit to Gross Margin	4.03%	9.04%	13.83%	18.54%	22.25%	

Chart: % Response (bars) — 1.10%, 1.37%, 1.71%, 2.05%, 2.46%; Profit (Loss) after Add-back (line) — 2.09, 11.22, 18.53, 23.39, 27.45

number of orders necessary to recoup the promotion expense and the percentage response needed to get them are simple to derive.

The example in the template looks at a single product with a unit price of 60.00 and a unit product cost of 15.00. There is also a "Postage Charge Back for Package," which is additional revenue to help cover the costs of postage or other distribution. The model contemplates the sale of two units of the same product to a single buyer. What we see when all the operational costs have been deducted is 29.22 (Net Margin before Promotion). The question is: How much marketing can we buy for 29.22 or put another way, what level of response do we need to attain the 15 percent profit or contribution margin that is our objective?

Using this model, we see that we would need a 2.74 percent response to meet the target. If experience teaches that this is unrealistically high, then the additional cost of making the sale will eat into the profit or contribution margin and may negate the project, sending its proponents "back to the drawing board."

To evaluate the effect of different response percentages, the template also calculates sensitivities. The user can input the degree of sensitivity by putting a percentage in the box provided (20 percent in Exhibit 2-4) and the template calculates the range of sensitivities on both sides of the "target"— the Net Margin Before Promotion developed in Exhibit 2-3. This assumes that this entire margin would be used to make a sale.

As seen in Exhibit 2-4, the target percentage response is 1.71 percent and reducing it by 20 percent gives us a percentage response of 1.37 percent. This allows us to do easy "what ifs": what if, for example, the response percentage was only 1.10 percent? How would this effect the profit? As can be seen, it would fall from the desired 15 percent or 18.53 to only 1.69 percent or 2.09.

Exhibit 2-4 Sensitivities (+/-) to Target Response Percentage

Sensitivities (+ or -) To Target Response Percentage					
Degree of Sensitivity	20.00%		Target		
% Response	1.10%	1.37%	1.71%	2.05%	2.46%
Cost Per Response	45.85	36.52	29.22	24.35	20.29
Profit (Loss) after Add-back of Profit or Contribution	2.09	11.22	18.53	23.39	27.46
% Profit to Gross Margin	1.69%	9.09%	15.00%	18.94%	22.24%

Exhibit 2-5 Sensitivities (+/-) to Target Response Percentage

Degree of Sensitivity	20.00%	Target			
% Response	1.75%	2.19%	2.74%	3.29%	3.94%
Cost Per Response	45.65	36.52	29.22	24.35	20.29
Profit (Loss) after Add-back of Profit or Contribution	2.09	11.22	18.53	23.39	27.45
% Profit to Gross Margin	1.69%	9.09%	15.00%	18.94%	22.23%

Obviously, changing the promotion cost per thousand people promoted from the 500.00 shown in the example to say 800.00 would also substantially impact the results. As can be seen in Exhibit 2-5, the response for breakeven (including the desired 15 percent Profit or Contribution) has *increased* to 2.74 percent.

The Dynamic Effect of Different Response Percentages on Profits

The cost per order (CPO) is *the amount you have spent or plan to spend* for promotion divided by the number of sales or customers you have achieved or expect to achieve.

Like attrition, the effect on profit of different CPOs—no matter which media are used for the promotion—is profound.

The chart in Exhibit 2-6 shows clearly that *as the cost per order decreases as the result of increased percentage response* (shown here in .25 percent increments from 1.5 to 2.5 percent on a mailing), *the profit rises dramatically.* Even when the CPO is higher than the allowable—at 1.5 percent and 1.75 percent—there is still a profit because of the 15 percent "contribution and/or profit" that has been taken as a cost.[5]

Of maximum importance is understanding how the ACPO works and how this number is critical in determining your marketing strategy.

Sometimes It Is Better *Not* to Promote to Everyone

The ACPO impacts many other aspects of marketing programs as the following example demonstrates.

In developing a card recuperation program for a credit card company, a marketer decided to target *all* the former cardholders whose cards had expired and not been renewed since the launch of the card a number of years before. There were 16 categories of

Exhibit 2-6 Effect on Profit of Variable Costs Per Order

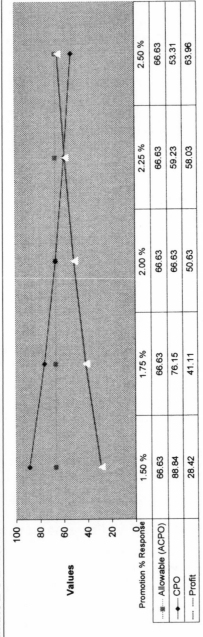

Promotion % Response	1.50 %	1.75 %	2.00 %	2.25 %	2.50 %
Allowable (ACPO)	66.63	66.63	66.63	66.63	66.63
CPO	88.84	76.15	66.63	59.23	53.31
Profit	28.42	41.11	50.63	58.03	63.96

······✳······ Allowable (ACPO)   ──◆── CPO   ······ Profit

previous customers and each was coded accordingly (List A to List P). The marketer determined that his allowable was 265.00 for each recuperated card.

The results (in Exhibit 2-7) show that eight of the lists (Lists A thru H) produced cardholders at CPOs *lower* than or the same as the allowable (the straight line) and eight at CPOs *higher* than the allowable. Those few with the highest CPOs ate disproportionately into the profits generated by the good performers.

> It's a scarier notion to turn clients away than it is to hope against hope that you can make profitable the 500 clients you should get rid of. I call this the "hope springs eternal" way of thinking. . . . A company can't afford to let optimism stand in the way of making a tough decision about customers when it is necessary.[6]

Hard as the decision may be to make, what matters is the profits from loyal customers, not the number of customers you have. Lester Wunderman summed it up nicely when he said: "Your share of loyal customers, not your share of market, creates profits." And he might well have continued by observing that your share of the expenditure of *the right customers* is the springboard to even greater profits. The *right customers* can be defined by two key characteristics:

1. They can be (or have been) acquired for less than the allowable.

2. Their lifetime value is equal to or greater than your minimum assumption.

If the marketer had not mailed the 6 lists (K through P) that had higher CPOs than the 265 allowable, he would have had only 707 less recuperated cardholders—a shortfall of 35%—but he would have saved more than half (56 percent) of his marketing expense. If instead he had decided to make his cut-off *after* those recuperated cardholders whose CPO *averaged* 265, (Lists O&P) the shortfall would have been just 229 cardholders (11 percent) and the marketing saving would have been 20 percent. It is worth noting that the average cost of each of the recuperated cardholders above this cut-off line was 510, just short of *twice* the allowable.

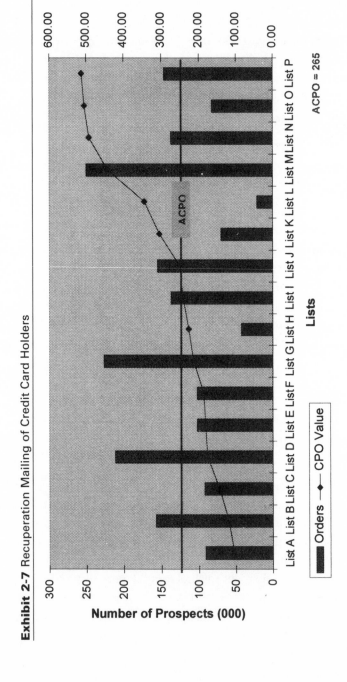

Exhibit 2-7 Recuperation Mailing of Credit Card Holders

Of course it is *always* easy to be wise after the fact. But had this marketer tested carefully and used the available planning tools with an understanding of the ACPO concept, he could have saved substantial cost without losing significant revenue.

Saving cost through careful ACPO planning can be as profit-effective as increasing revenues. While our instincts (and egos) almost always drive us to go for the highest possible sales to the largest number of customers, the risk rises exponentially when we do not exercise the proper level of caution. That caution is essential.

It Is Almost Always Possible to Test

One aspect of direct marketing that differentiates it from "image" and "brand" advertising is the range of testing possibilities that exist and the ability to use tests to refine strategies and tactics. No serious DM professional would make a significant promotional investment without first testing and adjusting each step of the economic model for a direct marketing program before committing significant resources. Chapter 5 discusses the funnel process used in the typical direct selling sequence. The principle of "casting the largest net to catch the most fish" applies here as well. Simply put, it means initially promoting to the broadest possible range of likely prospects and narrowing the focus of subsequent promotions as experience dictates.

Looking for the profit dynamic leverage points using models such as this can have a profound effect on strategy and should be included in any strategic analysis. It can inform everything from offers, pricing and sales strategy to media choice.

As we have seen, determining the cost of acquiring a customer depends on the ways the customer is acquired. How much you can afford depends upon the value of this customer over time.

As a rule of thumb, in data-driven marketing as in almost everything else, it is best to take a very conservative view of revenue generation and a relatively pessimistic view of costs. Only when you know that there is more money coming in than is going out can you feel secure that you can meet or exceed your objectives.

Believing the Unbelievable is Dangerous

The ACPO can also add sanity to marketing efforts and help avoid dangerous mistakes. If the actual CPO is above the ACPO, you know you are in trouble. But if it is much, much lower than the ACPO, while often seemingly very good news, it is important to determine why and ascertain whether the market is trying to tell you something important.

In launching a Music Club in Brazil, we became intoxicated with the unbelievably low cost per new member we were achieving—far lower than the allowable—and pushed the accelerator pedal right down to the floor to build club membership. Boy, did our Club take off as thousands and thousands of members rushed to join.

We should have worried about the "unbelievability" of that low cost per member and used the brake instead of the gas pedal on the promotion. It wasn't until later that we found that *an unacceptable number of the members we were recruiting so inexpensively proved to be unwilling to pay for their purchases.* Add to that the fact that the cost per member of the repeated media insertions we were placing was increasing so fast that media expansion became economically impossible.

Recruiting all those members so rapidly destroyed our profitability rather than adding to it. We would have done well to heed the teachings of the Law of Lens that states, "anything outside of a certain comfort level will not be believed" and its corollary, "results within the comfort zone will tend to be accepted, sometimes without the appropriate level of skepticism."[7] The problem was that the results gave us such confidence that we did not look at them with the necessary "level of skepticism."

There is a metaphor about response media that provides excellent litmus. It looks at the number of insertions you plan to make as if you were gazing into a clear glass bottle of milk. At the top is the thick cream, then there is the milk and below that there is water.

The problem is that when deciding how much of a given medium to use, you don't have a clear transparent vision into the bottle. You may skim the cream—low cost responses—the first time out and then go directly into the very deep, dangerous, and expensive water. The only way of avoiding this is to go slowly, watch carefully the cost per order of each insertion, and learn to plot the increments of order cost increase from continued insertions. Combined with adjusting your allowable on the basis of the *actual* attrition and bad pay experience can help you to a healthy combination of cream and milk and avoid drowning you in profitless water.

Determining the Allowable Cost Per Name for a Customer Database

A critical economic question for any marketer desirous of using marketing data is whether to use existing data on the market or build his own database. The answer is almost always to do both.

Building a consumer database from the responses to your promotions is an obvious and important task. In the best of all possible worlds, the cost of selling to the "prospect" list will be covered by the allowable. As in any normal DM activity, the name will simply be added to the "customer" file without the attribution of a specific cost for the name generation.

The economics of renting data from third parties are somewhat more complicated and impact your costs. Usually depending on the number of data characteristics you wish to use, the data provider rents you single or multiple use of files that meet your target criteria at a negotiated cost per file or more commonly cost per thousand. (Costs are frequently stated "per thousand" because the unit numbers for media are too small and unwieldy.) The more specific the targeting and the more detailed the selection, the higher the cost. The data remains the property of the data owner. Only when an order (or sometimes a request for more information) is received by the marketer does the data become his to use as often as he likes in future marketing initiatives without payment to the original data owner. The original data owner keeps his files, but the marketer has now obtained data on the same customer.

Building your own marketing database usually involves merging various lists from a variety of sources. Many companies have captured the names of customers and prospects, responders to sales promotion efforts and the like. Publishers have the names and addresses of their subscribers and often many of their other readers as well. Cell phone operators, associations, credit card companies, other financial service providers and ISPs, all have the names of the customers who use their services.

Distance purchasers—people who habitually transact business with a company by mail, phone or the Internet—are almost always better prospects than customers and/or prospects who do not. These customers have already overcome the "fear" of purchasing products and services, even shoes, at a distance. The meteoric rise of product and service sales on the Internet provides a stunning example of this.

However, there are many cases where promotions are undertaken for the *primary purpose* of generating names, getting prospects to "raise their hands" so to speak, and indicate their interest in knowing more or receiving offers, etc.

Building a list from scratch is a daunting task, but it is sometimes necessary in countries where existing lists are scarce and where a highly professional organization wishes to aggressively enter the market. Companies such as Reader's Digest have approached the problem through doing massive initial promotions to virtually every list they can rent. Their strategy is simple: Initially mail the highest number of names possible with a large and exciting incentive. Offer participation in the incentive (usually a "rich" sweepstakes) to every responder *whether or not* he agrees to purchase the product. Remember that the objective is only partially to sell a subscription. Just as important is to entice a response, even if it is a "No" to the offer, and capture the names of the responders in the database for future promotional use.

This is a perfectly legitimate way of building a prospect file, and it can be argued that it is probably less expensive than renting names over and over from existing list owners. Whether that argument is correct depends on how often the names will be promoted and whether the initial names used can be rented over and over again. It also depends upon the difference in percentage response that will be achieved now that these names are part of a "house" list.

The theoretical "List Generation Model" (Exhibit 2-8) is instructive. It shows us that using the sweepstakes incentive reduced the cost per name from 6.95 to 1.46 (before adding in the cost of the incentive) and 1.77 after the incentive cost has been included.[8] It also indicates that the list generator would have to use the names

Exhibit 2-8 List Generation Model

Input List of Lists, Publications, Broadcast Media or Other Below:	Available Quantity or Circulation	Rental or Media Cost Per '000	Expected Response %	Normal No.of New Names to Database	Cost Per Name	Expected Response %	Incentivized No.of New Names to Database	Cost Per Name
List 1	250,000	120.00	1.80%	4,500	6.67	9.00%	22,500	1.33
List 2	200,000	100.00	2.00%	4,000	5.00	11.00%	22,000	0.91
List 3	350,000	135.00	1.60%	5,600	8.44	8.00%	28,000	1.69
List 4	350,000	120.00	1.40%	4,900	8.57	9.50%	33,250	1.26
List 5	150,000	85.00	1.70%	2,550	5.00	7.00%	10,500	1.21
List 6	275,000	120.00	1.60%	4,400	7.50	6.00%	16,500	2.00
List 7	90,000	125.00	1.80%	1,620	6.94	5.50%	4,950	2.27
List 8	85,000	100.00	1.60%	1,360	6.25	6.00%	5,100	1.67
List 9	140,000	110.00	1.75%	2,450	6.29	6.00%	8,400	1.83
List 10	135,000	90.00	1.50%	2,025	6.00	6.00%	8,100	1.50
List 11				-	-		-	-
List 12				-	-		-	-
List 13				-	-		-	-
List 14				-	-		-	-
List 15				-	-		-	-
List 16				-	-		-	-
List 17				-	-		-	-
List 18				-	-		-	-
List 19				-	-		-	-
List 20				-	-		-	-
List 21				-	-		-	-
List 22				-	-		-	-
List 23				-	-		-	-
List 24				-	-		-	-
List 25				-	-		-	-
List 26				-	-		-	-
List 27				-	-		-	-
List 28				-	-		-	-
List 29				-	-		-	-
List 30				-	-		-	-
TOTAL	**2,025,000**			33,405			159,300	
				Weighted Average 6.96			Weighted Average 1.46	

TOTAL	2,025,000
Sweepstakes or Other Incentive Cost	50,000
Incentive Cost Per Response	0.31
Average Cost Per Name	6.96
Average Cost Per Name Including Incentive Cost	1.77
Average Rental List Cost '000	120.00
Average Rental List Cost Per Name	0.12
No.of Times Name Needs to be used to Recoup Investment	14.8

gathered in the sweepstakes at least 14.8 times to breakeven when compared to renting the names.

But this is only a part of the equation and simply the first step in determining the value of these names. The most important issue is how these names will respond to future promotions. It must be assumed, even though many will *only* have responded to participate in the sweepstakes that they will perform better than the lists from which they were derived. These people have defined themselves as "responders."

The actual "value" is difficult to assess in advance of testing the names and establishing their unique characteristics and purchasing patterns. Thus, developing a rational "allowable" for how much we can afford to spend for each name is largely educated guesswork.

Probably the best course of action would be to assume that you were in the list rental business and that you would derive your revenue from renting these names to third parties at their fair market value, the amount you would expect to pay to rent them. Next, ask yourself how many times you would plan to market to the names in a specific period of time, say one year. Finally, multiply the list rental amount you would be prepared to pay for each thousand names by the number of times you would use them. Now discount the result by an error factor, say 25%. This will give you a "ballpark" value for what you can afford to pay. Exhibit 2-9 illustrates a methodology for valuing a name.

Companies that run major "survey" programs with the objective of building consumer databases for rent derive their revenues from two basic sources:

1. The sale of the responses (on an exclusive basis and sometimes called "sponsorship") to specific questions placed in the surveys by the clients combined with general data from the survey (i.e., the "exclusive" or "sponsored" data may be the dates of expiration of home and auto insurance placed by an insurance company; this would be combined with "general" data such as the location and size of the home and the make and year of the car).

2. The subsequent sale of data derived from the surveys to marketers who wish to target consumers who have given this information.

Exhibit 2-9 Valuing a Name

ITEMS	VALUES	COMMENTS
Potential Quantity of Names	159,300	It is important to conservatively estimate the number of names that will be derived. Estimating too high may drive an expenditure that will make the actual cost per name too high.
Estimated Minimum Rental Value Per 000 Names	100.00	The amount you would be willing to pay to rent the names
Estimated No. of Rentals Per Year	7	The number of times you would be likely to use the names in a 12-month timeframe
Estimated Total List Value	111,510	The result of multiplying the number of names (divided by 1000) by the value to be obtained per thousand by the number of rentals in a given timeframe
Value Per Name	.70	The result of dividing the total value by the total number of names
Discount Percentage for "Error"	25%	An arbitrary discount amount
Final Conservative Value	0.525	The result of applying the discount to the value per name

In determining the allowable for the data derived from the survey programs, these companies tend to use the methodology illustrated in Exhibit 2-9 after taking into account their "sponsorship" revenues from questions pre-sold to clients as described under "Items." The economic model[9] for these companies is that they try to cover all the costs of the survey distribution and premiums (if any) with sponsorship revenues and earn their overheads and profits from subsequent sale of the data derived. The key is a low-cost access to market for the distribution of the surveys.

Publishers with large circulations for their various newspapers and magazines are ideally suited to building this type of database. Their main costs of survey distribution are the cost of printing the surveys and inserting them in their publications plus the costs of receiving, keying and selling the data plus the cost of any incentives offered to stimulate response. Their low-cost access to market combined with their knowledge of their readers gives them a substantial competitive advantage over other marketing database developers.

More than thirty years ago, National Demographics and Lifestyles (NDL) built a very successful business with a somewhat different model. NDL arranged with companies selling appliances and other goods with warranty registrations to include data cards in their product packages as part of the warranty registration process. In return the manufacturer received valuable data on their purchasers. Smaller and with less questions (and thereby less data received) than the larger surveys distributed by publications and other mass-list generators, these cards became the basis for important marketing databases. The process was slower than media-distributed surveys because of the time between the insertion of the cards by the manufacturer, the distribution to wholesalers and retailers and the sell-through and eventual return of the cards by the consumers. But it also made the distribution cost of the surveys much lower than having to pay for access to market.

Some experiments in developing marketing databases of consumers have been undertaken by some of the more progressive postal systems, especially in Latin America. Eager to build their revenue from direct marketing activities but hindered by lack of quality mailing lists that make it profitable for mailers to use direct mail, these systems have experimented in using the postal system for the distribution and collection of surveys. They can do this at marginal or negligible cost while at the same time building an asset that can both add profitable revenue to the post office in its own right and provide the needed data for mailers to use the postal system for their promotions. Having determined the allowable cost of adding data to their databases, they can fine-tune their database development methods.

Incentives definitely increase response, and *relevant* incentives can enhance the quality as well as the quantity of the resulting database. Whether we admit it or not, we are all tempted by incentives.

Making Customers for Life

Having addressed the important question of how much we can afford to acquire a "name" (or data file) for a marketing database, the next step is to understand the value of a customer over time. An understanding of this is critical if we are to truly know how much to invest in customer acquisition and CRM.

The obvious largest economic determinants in making any "customer lifetime value" (often referred to as LTV) judgments are the most difficult:

▶ How much will the individual purchase from you?

▶ Over what period of time?

▶ At what margins?

The only thing that can be said for certain is that *the further out in time you go with your projections, the less likely they are to be correct.* This is especially true today where it may have been less true many years ago when consumers were less promiscuous and had less choice. The increasing focus on building brand and vendor loyalty and the variety of CRM programs to support this loyalty speak eloquently for themselves.

It is for their long-term value that many companies are prepared to "invest" in a customer, sustaining a loss on the acquisition cost in the anticipation of a profit on the lifetime value. If you breakeven or make a profit on the first transaction (a single sale) or series of transactions (a subscriber or continuity buyer), the question becomes moot: The cost of acquiring the customer in the first place has been relegated to the P&L of that first transaction or series of transactions. That's effectively the end of it. The customer is now a paid-up asset of the company.

Interestingly, when DM companies with consumer databases are purchased or sold, the price paid or asked is almost always based more upon the number of active customers on the database than any other factor. There is no doubt that customers are real assets.

But when a marketer wishes or needs to make an up-front investment to acquire customers whose value over time is unknown, he needs to decide just how much he is prepared to spend acquire that customer and how long he is willing to wait to recoup his money.

Making this wager is often easier for insurance and financial service companies or sellers of subscriptions than for product and service suppliers selling a range of products or services to the same customer. These companies know the likely length of the relationship and can project a revenue stream from long experience. They have a good idea of how much Upsell will be possible, and they factor this into their projection of long-term value.

Developing an all-encompassing template for this is almost impossible. It would have to contemplate an infinite future and crystal ball gazing when doing economic planning is a dangerous pastime. To overcome this difficulty, Lifetime Value Calculation, Exhibit 2-10, looks at 36 months as 12 consecutive quarters and increasingly discounts the future revenue assumptions—"Discount % for Future Uncertainty"—the further they go into the future.

Let's look at what's going on here and the economic considerations that govern the model. (See Exhibit 2-10, Lifetime Value Calculation, to develop your own model.) As noted earlier, the model assumes the user defines the program with certain inputs (clear boxed cells) and then the formulae in the model (shaded cells) deliver the outputs:

▶ **Input 1.1:** A description of the product or service being offered—"Input Product or Service Description."

▶ **Input 1.2:** An initial sale with actual payments—"Revenue Assumption"—coming in the 1st, 2nd, and 3rd Quarters.

▶ **Input 1.3:** A "Net Margin Assumption (Excluding Acquisition Cost)" shown as a percentage of revenue.

▶ **Output 1.1:** The model delivers the "Net Contribution" value (Input 2 * Input 3) for each time period and sums them in the first column under the heading "Estimated Total Value."

This first section sets the scene for everything that is to follow. It assumes that a customer has been recruited and has made a purchase. It excludes the cost of having recruited him since one of the principal objects of the exercise is to determine how much the customer *might* be worth over time, *might* because any future lifetime value calculation is based on many assumptions. The other objective is to determine how much we are prepared to invest to attract him in the first place.

The next section concerns the possibility of an "Upsell if Any." Many marketers make a low-end offer in the early stages of the lifetime of a customer to overcome the initial price barrier of the relationship. They then endeavor to migrate the customer to a higher price point or more profitable product or service. The addition of an extended warranty for a low additional price after the purchase of an appliance would be a good example.

While the Upsell module can be ignored without affecting the validity of the final lifetime value calculations, the model takes this into consideration and provides the opportunity to calculate the effect of an Upsell if there is one. However, if there is an Upsell effort, the user must define the program with certain inputs:

▶ **Input 2.1:** Once again we need to input a description of the product or service being offered—"Input Product or Service Description."

▶ **Input 2.2:** The additional revenue that will be generated by the Upsell—"Addition to Initial Revenue Assumption" needs to be input in the periods when it will be earned.

▶ **Input 2.3:** A "Net Margin Assumption (excluding Up Sell Cost)" shown as a percentage of revenue. This will almost certainly be a considerably higher percentage than the initial "Net Margin Assumption" as the customer is simply adding to his original purchase.

▶ **Input 2.4:** To calculate the cost of making the Upsell, the model requires the "Upsell" Promotion Cost Per '000'.

▶ **Input 2.5:** Finally the model needs an estimate—"Percentage Response Assumption"—of the percentage of people to whom the upsell offer is made that will accept it.

▶ **Output 2.1:** The model will derive the "Up Sell Promotion Cost" on a unit basis.

▶ **Output 2.2:** The model also delivers the "Net Contribution" value (Input 2.2 * Input 2.3) for each time period and sums

Exhibit 2-10 Lifetime Value Calculation

	Estimated Total Value	1ST Quaterly Revenue	2ND Quaterly Revenue	3RD Quaterly Revenue	4TH Quaterly Revenue	5TH Quaterly Revenue	6TH Quaterly Revenue	7TH Quaterly Revenue	8TH Quaterly Revenue	9TH Quaterly Revenue	10TH Quaterly Revenue	11TH Quaterly Revenue	12TH Quaterly Revenue

Initial Sale:

[Input Product or Service Description]
- Revenue Assumption
- Net Margin Assumption — 100.0%
- (Excluding Acquisition Cost)
- **Net Contribution**

Upsell if Any:

[Input Product or Service Description]
- Addition to Initial Revenue Assumption
- Net Margin Assumption — 25.00%
- (Excluding Upsell Cost)
- Upsell Promotion Cost Per '000 — 1,000.00
- % Response Assumption — 35.00%
- Upsell Promotion Cost
- **Net Contribution**

Second Sale:

[Input Product or Service Description]
- Second Sale Revenue Assumption
- Net Margin Assumption — 25.00%
- (Excluding Second Sale Promotion Cost)
- Promotion Cost Per '000 — 1,000.00
- % Response Assumption — 10.00%
- Second Sale Promotion Cost
- **Net Contribution**
- Discount % for Future Uncertainty — 20.00%
- **Discounted Net Contribution**

Exhibit 2-10 Lifetime Value Calculation (Continued)

Third Sale:

[Input Product or Service Description]									
Third Sale Revenue Assumption						150.00	150.00	100.00	100.00
Net Margin Assumption	20.00%					30.00	30.00	25.00	25.00
(Excluding Third Sale Promotion Cost)									
Promotion Cost Per '000'	2,000.00								
% Response Assumption	15.00%								
Third Sale Promotion Cost						30.00	25.00
Net Contribution						16.67	20.00	25.00	25.00
Discount % for Future Uncertainty	30.00%								
Discounted Net Contribution						11.67	21.00	16.00	16.00

Fourth Sale:

[Input Product or Service Description]									
Fourth Sale Revenue Assumption						100.00	100.00	100.00	100.00
Net Margin Assumption	25.00%					25.00	25.00	25.00	25.00
(Excluding Fourth Sale Promotion Cost)									
Promotion Cost Per '000	1,500.00								
% Response Assumption	15.00%								
Fourth Sale Promotion Cost						15.00	24.00	15.00
Net Contribution						9.00	9.00	16.00
Discount % for Future Uncertainty	40.00%								
Discounted Net Contribution						9.00	9.00	16.00

Cumulative Revenue
Revenue Cash Flow
Cumulative Lifetime Customer Value
Discounted Contribution Cash Flow

Annual Discount Rate %   10.00%
Quarterly Discount Rate %   2.41%
Net Present Value of Revenue
Net Present Value of Contribution
(First Q is not discounted)
Desired Profit/Contribution   10.00%

Allowable Cost of

them in the first column under the heading "Estimated Total Value," deducting the value of Output 2.1.

Before continuing with the explanation of the model, it is worth noting that, in the example, the sum of the Net Contribution from the initial sale (20.00) and the Net Contribution from the Up Sell (22.14) total 42.14. At this point in time, the marketer has re-couped less than one-third of the calculated allowable acquisition cost.

The next section of the model is labeled "Second Sale." Here we add the next transaction following the same input pattern as de-scribed above in the Upsell. We input the description, the revenue in the periods it will be received and the net margin percentage as-sumption. We then input the promotion cost and the expected re-sponse assumptions. From these is derived the "Net Contribution" for this transaction.

If we could look into the future and predict with certainty how it will unfold, we would all be rich, thin, and famous. But because this "Second Sale" transaction begins further out in time than the first one or the possible Up Sell, there is a new line asking for the input of what we call the "Discount Percentage for Future Uncer-tainty." As the first revenue predicted is nine months in the future, it is prudent to discount it by a generous factor.

Our rule of thumb starts at 20% for Quarters 3 and 4 and adds an additional 10% for each two additional quarters. Thus in the theoretical example above, the revenue stream for the "Third Sale" carries a 30% "Uncertainty" premium and this rises to 40% for the "Fourth Sale" as the revenue begins in Quarter 7. For a longer pe-riod than the three years shown here—a simple task for regular spreadsheet users—it would be advisable to increase the uncer-tainty premium.

Is this the right formula for discounting the uncertainties of the future? The answer can only be that it has been used reasonably ef-fectively for some years: a lot can happen over the period including changes in the degree of attrition and the uncertainty premium is intended to mitigate the economic effects of the unknown.

Since the percentages are user defined, they can be changed on the basis of experience and/or judgment. But once again, it is better

Exhibit 2-11 Allowable Cost of Acquiring a Customer

Annual Discount Rate %	10.00%
Quaterly Discount Rate %	2.41%
Net Present Value of Revenue	1,304.80
Net Present Value of Contribution	181.42
(First Q is not discounted)	
Desired Profit/Contribution	10.00% 130.48
Allowable Cost of Acquiring the Customer	50.94

to be conservative than to indulge in wishful thinking.

Because money costs money and because the cost of acquisition of the customer is paid up-front and the revenue received over time, it is necessary to determine the Net Present Value (NPV) of the revenue flow from all the customer transactions. To do that additional inputs and outputs have been provided as shown in Exhibit 2-11.

First we need to input the annual discount rate for the revenue flow. This is normally the current or projected rate of inflation. Since the model is built in quarters of each year, the NPV is calculated by dividing the "Annual Discount Rate Percentage" by 4. Since the 1st Quarter is current, this is not discounted in the calculation. Next the user needs to input the "Desired Profit/Contribution" percentage—the amount he wishes to make on the customer over the period. The model then calculates the "Allowable Cost of Acquiring the Customer."

Marketers are primarily interested in retaining and enhancing the customers they have and acquiring new ones to whom to profitably sell their products and services. As they better understand the economics of data-driven marketing and use the tools available to them, each of these objectives should be achieved with greater success.

The allowable cost per order and the economic calculations driven by it lie at the heart of all economically successful marketing, especially direct marketing. The data needed to make assessments should be easily extracted from any sophisticated marketing database through mining the gold that is there. Sadly, all too often it lies unappreciated and unused.

Armed with this knowledge we are able to evaluate and plan all types of marketing and CRM programs. We can assess the relative effectiveness and likely success of the media we plan to use and the sales incentives we plan to offer. And we can limit the risk of titanic disasters that can sink great projects and promising careers.

Notes

[1] *Economist Technology Quarterly,* June 12, 2003, Page 12.

[2] " . . . along with improved sales promotion should come an intelligent plan for inviting inquiries in your advertising and for giving your follow-up material just as much careful attention as you give your up-front advertising." *MaxiMarketing,* p. 134.

[3] Since Pampers and many other disposable products are sold in "packs" while other FMCG products may be sold individually, either the "pack" or the individual product data can be entered in the model.

[4] *Retail Takes Stock of Radio Tags,* Republica Report, Oslo, Norway, September, 15, 2003.

[5] Because of the importance of viewing "sensitivities"—results that are better or worse than the projection— many of the Templates contain a tool that allows the user to see the sensitivities on either side of his calculations.

[6] Chris Dallas-Feeny, Senior VP, Booz Allen, quoted in "Dumping Customers for Profit," *RetailWire Digest* (Winter 2003), p. 9: www.retailwire.com.

[7] The Consumer Decision Model/The Incentives Program, Robert M. Kleinbaum; Proceedings of the 1989 Making Statistics More Effective in Schools of Business (MSMESB) Conference: *Statistics Applied to Marketing Management.* University of Michigan.

[8] While this is substantially greater than the more commonly used three-time multiple for catalog purchasers compared with prospects, the circumstances are substantially different. In the catalog example, the figures compared purchasers and prospects. In gaining new names with an incentive, the difference between initial and subsequent performance is likely to be considerably greater.

[9] While it clearly differs from company to company, "Survey" data

developers like to receive approximately 50 percent of their revenues from sponsorship. Since the sponsors have the exclusive rights to the data derived from their sponsored questions, this can be looked at as a "pre-sale" of the data, but whether it is looked at this way or as a different category of revenue makes no difference.

▶▶▶3
The Importance of
Customer Focus

ithout customers you don't have a business, no matter how impressive the business plan or shiny the new technologies. In fact, there are many investment bankers whose decisions to invest or not to invest in a company are driven much more by an assessment of the current customer activity than any "fact-filled" business planning document.

Customers come in all shapes and sizes. Their purchasing decisions may be motivated by need, by want or even by whim. Sometimes they follow the herd towards the latest fads—hula-hoops, pet rocks or the latest fashions as dictated by a conspiracy of fashion houses eager to make each new season's output a compelling reason to replenish a wardrobe. Sometimes they are adventurous, willing to make purchases that are reflective of what they like, not what "everyone" likes. If there is an identifiable trend that has emerged after years or relative conformity, it is that today's consumer is increasingly desirous of being treated as an individual, eschewing the mass. Whether this is expressed by watching narrow-interest cable television channels rather than the networks or by going on carefully planned individual vacations to exotic locations rather than on packaged tours, reaching the individual consumer through his or her interests has become a major marketing preoccupation.

"From the outset, customers are not homogeneous. Their one common characteristic is the relationship or affinity they form with companies they favor with their business—and often their continued loyalty."[1] As we have seen, all customers are not created equal and more and more they act as individuals, not part of a group.

Each has different economic and psychographic characteristics and if we fail to recognize and cater to these differences, we do so at our peril.[2] Many manufacturers, retailers and even political parties still have difficulty in understanding this.

In its "Inside Business" supplement of August 9, 2003, *Time Magazine* wrote:

> Knowing your customer well enough to avoid costly business goofs has always been an elusive goal of marketing strategists. Standard demographic data—age, gender, employment status, income, place of residence—are usually insufficient to forecast consumer behavior with any precision. That's why during the past five years market researchers have been developing more sophisticated tools to get inside consumers' heads. It's no longer enough for companies to know you are a 35-year-old white male making $45,000 a year and have a wife, 2.5 kids and a mortgage. To predict accurately what you'll buy and what you won't, marketers these days are more interested in whether you donate to Greenpeace or if you believe in creationism. Says Dawn Iacobucci, a professor at Northwestern University's Kellogg School of Management and editor of the *Journal of Consumer Research*:

> Companies need to know what's on your mind. What's in your heart? What do you really want to do with your life?
>
> The answers, marketers hope, can be discovered through an emerging quasi-science known broadly as psychographics. Market researchers supplement conventional marketing data with informed assumptions about personality traits and human behavior gleaned from other disciplines, including psychology, sociology and probability theory. Using computers to organize and manipulate vast storehouses of such consumer information, they believe they are getting much better at sorting people into categories of like-minded individuals. And once the sorting is done, they are getting better at predicting how people are likely to behave.

Some Square Meters, Like Some Customers, Are Worth More Than Others

Many years ago—before CRM was the flavor of the decade—I was asked to join a meeting at Bloomingdale's in New York. The discussion turned to what could be done to increase the loyalty of its customers. I suggested that like the airline frequent flyer lounges, the store create a "Bloomies' Club" for the affluent middle-aged women who were perceived to be the department store's best customers. It would be a friendly place where these shoppers could have a cup of coffee, meet their friends and safely leave their belongings while they "shopped 'till they dropped." It was even suggested that the store might find a way to gather the customers' purchases from the different departments and deliver them to the "Club" or to their cars, thus saving them the trouble of carrying them around the store and not incidentally, freeing them to make even more purchases.

At the suggestion of using "valuable floor space" for this kind of customer care, one of the Bloomingdale's executives interrupted the meeting and taking me by the arm led me down a long hallway to a tiny cubicle tucked away on the top floor. Using his office as an illustration, he explained that the very suggestion of "wasting" valuable floor space for a "Club" was totally inconsistent with the prevailing retail wisdom of using every possible square foot of floor space to display and sell merchandise. "What you marketing types don't realize" he said with derision, "is the value of each square foot of retail space."

This executive surely knew the *average* value of each square foot of space but despite the ample tools available, he only knew the *average* value of his customers, not their individual values. He certainly did not understand that "average" is the most dangerous word in accountable marketing.

This is a lesson often ignored by retailers whose mindsets are almost entirely on the value of each square foot (or meter) of merchandise display space or linear measure of shelf space. Each unit of space in a retail outlet like each customer is different. How many retailers have studied the relative value of a unit of retail space and of a customer?

Just visit any department store and compare the paltry number of customers in the furniture department with those hordes flocking around the cosmetic and jewelry counters. Just think how many dining room tables or couches you have ever (or will ever) purchase compared to how many high-value gifts.

If Pareto's Principle applies to the revenue derived from each unit of retail space, some units are worth far more than others. One way of getting to the essence of the economics of this trade-off is to ask how much increased revenue would you need from your best customers to justify giving up some of your least productive retail space?

Calculating the Relative Value of a Square Foot of Retail Space and of a Customer

The hypothetical example shown below illustrates the argument. Exhibit 3-1 explains this process.

Whether the real percentages are 80/20 or some other combination, we know that *neither all square meters nor all customers have the same values*. We also know that our objective is to increase our share of the wallets of our best loyal customers and there are a number of ways to skin this particular cat. Recognizing their value and rewarding them for their loyalty lies at the heart of effective CRM activities. How much we can afford to spend on this reward and recognition is both calculable and essential.

Exhibit 3-2, Relative Value Equation, provides a means of looking at this issue. It assumes a 10,000 Sq. Meter store that does 70 million of sales, 7,000 per square meter. Applying the 80/20 rule, the best 20 percent (2,000) of the square meters produce revenue of 28,000 each compared to the 80 percent that produce only 1,750 each. Applying the same principle to the 35,000 customers, only 7,000 produce 56 million in revenue or 8,000 each while all the rest produce only 500 each. Thus, if you wanted to use 1,000 of the low value meters to enhance the sales of the 7,000 best customers, these customers would only have to increase their spend by 3.13 percent to justify the operation.

The numbers themselves don't matter. What matters is the principle and an understanding that viewing strategic questions in the context of the customer paradigm can make a substantial difference in strategic planning. Things are not always what they seem. Just as

Exhibit 3-1 Calculating Retail and Customer Value

ITEM	VALUE	COMMENT
Size of Retail Outlet	10,000 Sq. Meters	
Total Store Revenue	70,000,000	
Average Revenue Per Sq. Meter	7,000	Divides the total store revenue by the total number of sq. meters
Average Value of Best (Highest Revenue) Sq. Meters, Per Sq. Meter	28,000	Applying the 80/20 rule (Pareto's Principle) to the average value per sq. meter
Average Value of Other (Low Revenue) Sq. Meters, Per Sq. Meter	1,750	Applying the 80/20 rule (Pareto's Principle) to the average value per sq. meter
Number of Customers	35,000	
Average Value Per Customer	2,000	Divides the total store revenue by the total number of customers
Average Value of Best Customers Representing 80% of the Sales	8,000	Applying the 80/20 rule (Pareto's Principle) to the average value per customer
Average Value of Other Customers Representing 20% of the Sales	500	Applying the 80/20 rule (Pareto's Principle) to the average value per customer
Number of Sq. Meters for Proposed "Club"	1,000	Obviously, the "Club" would be located in space where the revenue per sq. meter was traditionally low
Revenue Loss as a Result of Conversion to Non-Revenue Producing Space	1,750,000	Calculated by multiplying the number of sq. meters needed for the "Club" times the average value of the low revenue sq. meters
Increase in Revenue Per Customer Among "Best" Customers to Re-Coup Revenue Loss From Selling Space	2.5	Calculated by dividing the revenue loss by the 20% "best" customers
Percentage Increase in Needed Revenue from Best Customers to Justify the "Club"	3.13%	Derived by calculating the percentage increase of the "best" customer revenue

Exhibit 3-2 Relative Value Equation

	%	Sq.Feet/ Meters	Number	Value
Average Value of Retail Space in Revenue Terms Per Sq.Foot/Meter				7,000.00
No. Sq.Feet/Meters		10,000		
TOTAL Value				70,000,000.00
% of Sq.Feet/Meters	20.00%	2,000		
	80.00%	8,000		
% of Value	80.00%			56,000,000.00
	20.00%			14,000,000.00
Value Per Sq.Foot/Meter Best				28,000.00
Value Per Sq.Foot/Meter Other				1,750.00
TOTAL Revenue Value				70,000,000.00
No. Customers			35,000	
Average Value Per Customer				2,000.00
Best Customers	20.00%		7,000	
Other Customers	80.00%		28,000	
Best Customers	80.00%			56,000,000.00
Other Customers	20.00%			14,000,000.00
Average Value of Best Customer in Revenue Terms				8,000.00
Average Value of Other Customer in Revenue Terms				500.00
Need for a Club of		1,000		
Loss of Revenue from these Meters				1,750,000.00
Increase Revenue from Best Customers Needed to Justify				250.00
% Increase	3.13%			

"Case Rate" needs to be viewed from the perspective of "Customer Rate" so too, the value of a square foot of retail space might be compared to the value of a customer. Using these different viewpoints helps to creatively evaluate strategic alternatives as the basis for the development of innovative marketing strategies.

The Marketing Database: Much More Than a List of Names

The marketing database is key to understanding and managing customer relationships on a one-to-one basis. It is here that the cumulative knowledge about the customer resides. Properly designed and managed, it is the closest thing we have to the totally integrated customer knowledge that was the historic asset in the head of the small retailer.

Once bitten by the marketing database bug, there is a certain tendency to want to put every bite of available data into the database, oblivious of its future use or cost. If data is power, so the argument goes, the more power you have the better. This thinking is very expensive[3] and largely misses the point about using the knowledge the data can impart to drive the marketing process. Wrote Lester Wunderman "Data is an expense. Knowledge is a bargain."[4] The database does *not* need, as some people suggest, "everything you can find out about the customer."

What do we really need in the database? We need only that information that will allow us to better target our customers with *relevant* and timely promotional messages, data that will allow us to communicate on a truly *personal* level, data that will provide us with more profitable business at less marketing cost.

As can be seen in Exhibit 3-3, the data needs (essential) and wants (desirable) are divided into four categories:

▶ Contact Data

▶ Demographic Data

▶ Lifestyle and Psychographic Data

▶ Transaction Data

How can we use all this data and how can it drive the marketing process? There are a number of answers that will be discussed below. "The first step in leveraging an organization's core group of loyal and profitable customers is to *understand their motivations*" [author's italics], write Bob Stone and Ron Jacobs in *Successful Direct Marketing Methods*. "Some customers are easily predictable, preferring long-term stable relationships. Other customers may spend more, pay their bills more promptly, or require less maintenance. Others may value the organization's products or services over all others."[5]

Data: Understanding and Insight

Understanding the motivations of people you have probably never met sounds harder than it is. How we live and how we act, what we like and don't like, the things we own and how we use them define

Exhibit 3-3 Data Needs and Wants

DATA CHARACTERISTICS	ESSENTIAL	DESIRABLE	COMMENT
Contact Data:			**Contact Data** is the driver of all communications, shipments, etc. It must be accurate and up-to-date. *The user must also have the recipient's limited or unlimited permission to make contact.*
• Name	Yes		
• Address	Yes		
• Telephone		Yes (if given)	
• Email		Yes (if given)	
• Permission	Yes		
Demographic Data:			**Demographic Data** while extremely valuable is not essential. Economic worth, for example, can be inferred from address data. Age by birth date of principal householder and family members is useful, especially for targeting "birthday" and age sensitive promotions.
• Economic worth		Yes	
• Age (birth date)		Yes	
• Married or single		Yes	
• Partner's name and birth date		Yes	
• Children (names and ages)		Yes	
Lifestyle & Psychographic Data:			**Lifestyle and Psychographic Data** including home and car ownership provide a context for promotional activity as well as specific opportunities and can also be used to infer other data. Previous direct marketing purchases inform willingness to purchase at a distance. Preferences for media allow tighter targeting. Payment preferences inform economic perspective and credit. *Relevant* product ownership and recreational preferences inform lifestyle type and likely categories of purchase.
• Previous "direct" purchaser		Yes	
• Home ownership or rental		Yes	
• Car ownership, type, and year		Yes	
• Media preferences		Yes	
• Payment preferences (credit card, check, etc.)		Yes	
• Relevant product ownership		Yes	
• Recreational preferences		Yes	

Exhibit 3-3 Data Needs and Wants (Continued)

DATA CHARACTERISTICS	ESSENTIAL	DESIRABLE	COMMENT
Transaction Data:			**Transaction Data** on current customers is of critical importance. It allows you to assess the critical economic components of your interaction with customers and builds valuable data that will drive all future promotional efforts.
• Source and date of first transaction	Yes		
• Recency of last transaction	Yes		
• Frequency of transactions	Yes		
• Value of transactions	Yes		
• Form of order (Tel., Email, etc.)	Yes		
• Mode of payment	Yes		
• Incentives taken	Yes		
• Complaints			

us all. And like it not, our characteristics have certain similarities to other people. In that sense, customers are no different than we are.

If we have all the essential and desirable data we can gain important insight into our customers and prospects and target with a great deal of precision. But if we only have some of it, we can still infer characteristics and motivations that will help our targeting.

Looking Glass[6] provides an excellent illustration in their "Cohorts" cluster called, "Danny and Vickie." It is described in very personal terms: "Being good parents and raising great kids are top priorities for Danny & Vickie, which means they get little time for themselves. . . . Although somewhat conservative, they'll take calculated risks and be spontaneous when they get the chance. When they get time to relax it's often spent at home with the kids and a movie, or grilling out back with the neighbors. . . . who have their own kids in tow." That gives us a general picture but a more specific one comes from looking carefully at the data. Looking Glass describes them as follows:

> **Do they carry plastic?** Not a lot. They try to keep their debt in check because they're paying off a mortgage, a home-equity loan and a car loan. They carry store cards like JCPenney and Sears, as well as a Visa or MasterCard Gold. They prefer something that rewards an organization or affiliation, like a school or charity.

> **Are they wired?** Well, Danny & Vickie like to think they're Internet savvy. But, as in most households, it's the kids who are teaching their parents how to surf the web. It's the primary source of entertainment for the family—the kids are playing online games, mom is looking for recipes and dad is gambling. Their house looks like the inside of a Radio Shack . . . with a computer, CDs, tons of videos and DVDs, a Nintendo Game Cube and a cell phone for everyone. Welcome to the 21st century family!

> **Shop-a-holics?** Honestly, a trip to the mall is a night out for this family. They're not very brand loyal because their kids have a huge impact on what they buy, which is influenced by what is hot in the high school hallway or on MTV. Vickie

might pick up something for herself when she's buying the latest teen trends at American Eagle Outfitters, Old Navy or Abercrombie & Fitch. But her shopping vices lean towards Target, Sears, JCPenney and Wal-Mart.

Glued to the tube? They'd rather spend a quiet evening at home than go out, and that usually means watching TV or a movie from the comfort of their couch. They own a wide variety of videos and DVDs, and they order pay-per-view about once a month. *ABC Family, Animal Planet, Cartoon Network* and *Disney* are favorites. But they also like *A&E, Bravo, Comedy Central, ESPN* and *Cinemax*. What's interesting is that they're really into reality TV: "*Big Brother,*" "*The Mole,*" "*Survivor,*" you name it! Perhaps these shows are more exciting than their own lives?

Bitten by the travel bug? Not really—they don't have time! If they go out of the country, it's to an all-inclusive resort in Mexico or the Caribbean. Most don't have a passport or belong to any frequent flyer programs, so they tend to do things closer to home like camping or going to an interactive theme park . . . Wet n' Wild, Great America, Sea World, Nickelodeon Studios and Six Flags are just a few of their favorites.

Motivated by a combination of raising their kids and restricted by the cost of taking care of their family, this profile certainly tells us quite a lot about the kinds of things this family is likely to purchase and how they are likely to purchase them. Combined with actual transaction data the marketer should be able to fashion offers with direct appeal even if some of the desirable specific data is missing.

The Most Likely Prospects Are Almost Always Better and Less Expensive

It is an industry maxim that your best prospect is the customer who bought from you yesterday (recency). The next best prospect is the customer who has purchased from you a number of times in the past (frequency) and the next best, the customer who has spent a lot of money with you (monetary value). These three characteristics, "recency," "frequency," and "monetary value"—often referenced simply as "RFM"—are foundation blocks for selections of prospects from any marketing database of customers.

But many other characteristics can also impact the best selection of prospects from a marketing database, especially one that has been rented. Our marketing job is to turn as many prospects into customers as possible and to do so with a minimum amount of waste. Marketing disposable contact lenses to people with perfect 20/20 vision is extremely shortsighted.

Today's marketing databases often contain a considerable depth of data that has been compiled from a wide range of sources. This data allows the marketer to search for the most likely prospects and to do substantial modeling to try and sharpen the focus as much as possible. In a perfect world, we would be able to target with such accuracy that every prospect would become a customer. But we don't live in a perfect world.

The entire segmentation and modeling process is intended to field the largest number of prospects "able," "willing," and "ready" to become customers. The reverse triangle (Exhibit 3-4) may add insight to the segmentation process.

▶ Every prospect should be *able* to purchase what you are offering. That means they should have enough resources to be able to afford it.

Exhibit 3-4 The Segmentation Process

▶ A lesser number of prospects will be *willing* to purchase what you are offering. They may have the economic resources but no interest in the offer.

▶ Even fewer will be *ready* to purchase what you are offering. They may be able and willing but for dozens of reasons, not ready now. *But they may well be ready next time you make the offer.*

There is a continuous debate within the direct marketing community about the worth of the cost of customer and prospect segmentation. Segmentation and data modeling are expensive, although decreasingly so. The list owner or a database operator needs to work on the data and this is often both time and resource intensive. Companies supplying lists usually charge for each "level" of selection over and above the cost of the name, address and basic attributes. For the list supplier, it is often more profitable (at least in the short run) to rent as many names as possible rather than receive additional revenue for undertaking the segmentation process. While this is in direct conflict to the trend towards extensive segmentation and modeling, it is a reality nonetheless.

How much is the segmentation worth and how much is too much? The first question that has to be asked is: if I pay additional per thousand costs for segmentation, how much will each increase my response rate? And ultimately, how much of a saving on the unsegmented total mailing cost will I achieve by mailing less to obtain the same number of orders, as I would have with the original mailing quantity and response percent rate? The answer lies in looking carefully at the cost/benefit analysis of the segmentation and modeling process.

"Prices vary between 'Response' and 'Compiled' files, between 'B-to-B' and 'Consumer' and the available 'selects' (segmentation) vary widely within those four categories depending on certain market conditions" according to Peter Jupp, President of Infocore.[7]

The following table (Exhibit 3-5) built from Infocore data provides some guidance on segmentation costs and should serve as a good benchmark when assessing these costs. The "lifestyle" data

Exhibit 3-5 Data Types

DATA TYPE	PRICE PER THOUSAND $US
Base List	70.00
Additional for Selections:	
Email Addresses	85.00
US $65,000 Average Income	15.00
Credit Card Holders	6.50
Bank Card Holders	10.00
Dwelling Type	5.00

available from one supplier is priced for the one-time use of the basic list and additionally for selections.

Just name and address alone costs US $70.00 per thousand. Assuming a mailing *without* the use of the Email selection (an additional US $85.00 per thousand) but including the highlighted selections for *income* ($15.00), credit card holders ($6.50) and the *type of dwelling* in which the prospect lives ($5.00), the total cost comes to $96.50 per thousand and is estimated to increase the response by .75 percent from 1.6 percent to 2.35 percent as illustrated in Exhibit 3-6.

As we can see in Exhibit 3-6, while the addition of the "selects" increases the cost per thousand, we promote to less thousands (148,148 instead of 250,000) to attain the same 4,000 orders. The total saving is $86,111 or 34 percent of the original total *without selections.*

"The major cost of a mailing campaign" writes Doug Sacks, Infocore's Senior VP International

> is the mailing (postage, printing and lettershop). Lower these by selective list selection and modeling and your overall savings can be significant without impacting your response rate negatively. . . . Is "smart" and targeted direct marketing only a function of cost? In the age of increasing privacy legislation, consumer backlash, over-mailing, Spam and abusive and intrusive telemarketing tactics, this needs to be a major consideration for all direct marketers, even if it weren't a money-saving exercise.

These comments are right on the money. Had the costs of segmentation been greater or the likely difference in response percentage

Exhibit 3-6 Segmentation Economics

Cost Per '000 of Communications Package (Excluding Lists): 600.00

Lettershop Costs Per '000: 75.00
Mailing, E-mail or Other Distribution Cost Per '000: 200.00
Other Mailing Costs Per '000: 75.00
TOTAL Promotion Costs Per '000 (Excluding Lists): 950.00

Basic List Rental or Usage Cost Per '000: 70.00

TOTAL Basic Promotion Costs Per '000: 1,020.00

TOTAL Unsegmented Mailing Quantity: 250,000
Estimated % Response Without Segmentation: 1.60%

Orders	Cost Per Order	Mailing Size Needed	Total Promotion Cost	Saving	% Saving on Promotion Cost
4,000	63.75	250,000	255,000		

List Segmentation & Modelling:

	Addtl. % Response	Addtl. Cost Per '000	Cost Per Order	Mailing Size Needed	Total Promotion Cost	Saving	% Saving on Promotion Cost
Segmentation 1: [Describe]	0.20%	25.00	58.06	222,222	232,222	22,778	8.93%
Segmentation 2: [Describe]	0.30%	35.00	51.43	190,476	205,714	49,286	19.33%
Segmentation 3: [Describe]	0.40%	35.00	44.60	160,000	178,400	76,600	30.04%
Segmentation 4: [Describe]	0.20%	25.00	42.22	148,148	168,889	86,111	33.77%
Segmentation 5 [Describe]			-	-	-	-	-
Modelling 1 [Describe]			-	-	-	-	-
Modelling 2 [Describe]							
Modelling 3 [Describe]							
Modelling 4 [Describe]							
TOTAL	1.10%	120.00					

smaller, the segmentation might not have been *economically worthwhile* but that is seldom the case. By using the template (or a similar set of calculations) the marketer could have assessed these variables with considerable ease. By using good judgment and respect for the customer, the marketer can avoid, as Doug Sacks puts it "alienating their prospective or existing customers with poorly targeted direct marketing campaigns."

The "Household": A Better Marketing Unit Than the "Individual"

The variable that he could only judge by instinct is the negative effect on consumers of receiving multiple communications that don't interest them and turn them off to the sender company. I have an image I can't get out of my head. It is a photo of a family group, father, mother, two kids and a dog. Each has received an identical mailing for the same product at the same time. What could they be thinking about the sender company? The answer is probably that the company is sloppy and inefficient and certainly not the kind of company with whom to do business. It wouldn't be at all surprising.

But that is exactly what happens in many campaigns where the marketer is unwilling to pay for the costs of de-duplication, a minimum segmentation technique.[8] Applying it to the family who received five identical mailings and assuming that each communication costs 1.00, not only was 4.00 totally wasted but the principal intended recipient is probably well on his way to becoming an attrition casualty if he hasn't become one already.

There are many "cultural" traps that should be avoided. Credit card companies, for example, often hold their data by credit card number. But communicating with these "numbers" almost assures a level of duplication among cardholder families. Holding the data in an integrated database *organized by "household"* can eliminate this costly and annoying duplication without inhibiting the necessary administrative and operational functions.[9]

In terms of the total cost of the marketing effort, the extra cost of de-duplication, segmentation and modeling is proportionally small. These procedures almost always more than pay for themselves by reducing the total size and cost of the promotion without reducing the result. *The concern with the cost per thousand of a marketing effort should be less important than the total cost and effect of the initiative after the elimination of as much waste as possible.*

Attrition: The Enemy of Profit

Keeping your good customers is less expensive and more profitable than finding new ones. Yet there is an understandable tendency among marketers to do everything they can to minimize costs. All too often however, costs are cut that in fact end up costing more money than the saving. And all too often, it is *the customer* who gets left out of the equation. *The rule should be: Promote only to those people who offer the best chance of purchasing, testing all the time for additional purchasers who can be acquired for less than the allowable. These are first and foremost likely to be your former best customers.*

If it is true that "a penny saved is a penny earned" then think how many pennies are saved by keeping your good customers. That's why marketers interested in accountability are so concerned with attrition: as we know, it almost always costs more to acquire new customers than to treat the ones you have well so they stay.

Determining the cost of attrition starts from understanding its effect. Put simply, if you have one hundred customers who purchase the first of a six product sequence[10] and you have the same one hundred customers buying the second, third, fourth, fifth and sixth items, then you have a total sale of six hundred units. But as you lose customers through attrition, the total sale diminishes and the investment in acquiring those customers is lost.

If we look a snapshot from the Attrition Table (Exhibit 3-7), we see the dramatic effect of customers leaving.

The illustrations show 1,000 customers as the starting quantity through their fifth shipment. With perfect fidelity, the cumulative number of purchases would have been 5,000 (1,000 customers times five purchases) compared to just 4,095 as shown in Exhibit 3-7 where there is an attrition of 10% of the customers leaving after each shipment. If each product made a profit contribution of 15.00, the loss of profit from the effect of attrition would be 13.574 or 18 percent of the 75,000 that would have been earned if there had been no attrition. A growing understanding of this equation has been the most powerful driver of Customer Relationship Management. No

Exhibit 3-7 Attrition Table

Starting Quantity	1,000
Revenue Per Unit	100.00
Estimated % Profit Per Unit	15.00

15%

Number Purchased — Initial Offer
% Cancelling after Shipment No.

Shipment Number	%	% Remaining	Number of Purchases	Cumulative Number of Purchases	Cumulative Revenue Value	Cumulative Profit
1	100%	100.00%	1,000	1,000	100,000.00	15,000.00
2	10%	90.00%	900	1,900	190,000.00	28,500.00
3	10%	81.00%	810	2,710	271,000.00	40,650.00
4	10%	72.90%	729	3,439	343,900.00	51,585.00
5	10%	65.61%	656	4,095	409,510.00	61,426.50

wonder that marketers are increasingly concerned with minimizing attrition.

Understanding attrition is easier than doing something about it or even of knowing how much we can afford to spend to minimize it. The place to begin is with calculating the level of attrition, whether for a continuity product or any customer base.[11]

The illustration in Exhibit 3-8 assumes that there is a sequence of 36 products and that 10 percent of the customers leave after each of the first six shipments, and 5 percent after each additional shipment. The profit from the sale of all 36 of the products to 100 percent of the initial customers would have been 540,000. The profit derived by the model after attrition is 202,452. The cost of attrition in this example is 337,548 in lost profit or 62.51 percent of the potential.

The attrition calculation is also the key to another significant economic factor, the amount of inventory needed for a marketing program. If we assume that on a 36 shipment program we will ship 36 of each piece, we are in for a big and expensive shock. Using the attrition table to help plan production and inventory is essential. In Exhibit 3-8 we see that starting with 1,000 units for the first shipment, the number of products needed falls to only 127 for shipment 36. That's a large drop but not unusual. Using the attrition table can help avoid overstocking.

The Best Time to Stop Attrition:
At the Beginning of a Purchasing Sequence

Planning for the level of attrition is the best way to mitigate it. The earlier efforts are made to reduce it, the greater the effect. Having calculated the negative effect of the likely attrition, the marketer must decide how much of that could be reasonably applied to CRM activities aimed at reducing the attrition, what these activities would be and whether they would pay for themselves.

As indicated, it seems only logical that the highest level of attrition in any customer's purchasing sequence would come near the beginning of that sequence—customers who keep purchasing build up a momentum and a loyalty over time and are less likely to quit. One of the key strategies to combat this is to make promotional initiatives at the outset with the objective of lowering the effect of attrition early when the percentages are highest.

Exhibit 3-8 Attrition Table

Starting Quantity	1,000
Revenue Per Unit	100.00
Estimated % Profit Per Unit	15.00 — 15.00%

Shipment Number	Number Purchased Initial Offer / % Cancelling after Shipment No.	% Remaining	Number of Purchases	Cumulative Number of Purchases	Cumulative Revenue Value	Cumulative Profit
1	100.00%	100.00%	1,000	1,000	100,000.00	15,000.00
2	10.00%	90.00%	900	1,900	190,000.00	28,500.00
3	10.00%	81.00%	810	2,710	271,000.00	40,650.00
4	10.00%	72.90%	729	3,439	343,900.00	51,585.00
5	10.00%	65.61%	656	4,095	409,510.00	61,426.50
6	10.00%	59.05%	590	4,686	468,559.00	70,283.85
7	5.00%	56.10%	561	5,247	524,655.55	78,698.33
8	5.00%	53.29%	533	5,779	577,947.27	86,692.09
9	5.00%	50.63%	506	6,286	628,574.41	94,286.16
10	5.00%	48.10%	481	6,767	676,670.19	101,500.53
11	5.00%	45.69%	457	7,224	722,361.18	108,354.18
12	5.00%	43.41%	434	7,658	765,767.62	114,865.14
13	5.00%	41.24%	412	8,070	807,003.74	121,050.56
14	5.00%	39.17%	392	8,462	846,178.05	126,926.71
15	5.00%	37.22%	372	8,834	883,393.85	132,509.08
16	5.00%	35.35%	354	9,187	918,748.47	137,812.27
17	5.00%	33.59%	336	9,523	952,335.54	142,850.33
18	5.00%	31.91%	319	9,842	984,243.27	147,636.49
19	5.00%	30.31%	303	10,146	1,014,555.60	152,183.34
20	5.00%	28.80%	288	10,434	1,043,552.32	156,532.85
21	5.00%	27.36%	274	10,707	1,070,709.21	160,606.38
22	5.00%	25.99%	260	10,967	1,096,698.25	164,504.74
23	5.00%	24.69%	247	11,214	1,121,367.63	168,205.14
24	5.00%	23.46%	235	11,448	1,144,842.94	171,726.44
25	5.00%	22.28%	223	11,671	1,167,125.30	175,068.79
26	5.00%	21.17%	212	11,883	1,188,293.53	178,244.03
27	5.00%	20.11%	201	12,084	1,208,403.35	181,260.50
28	5.00%	19.10%	191	12,275	1,227,507.69	184,126.15
29	5.00%	18.15%	181	12,457	1,245,656.80	186,848.52
30	5.00%	17.24%	172	12,629	1,262,888.48	189,434.77
31	5.00%	16.38%	164	12,793	1,279,278.04	191,891.71
32	5.00%	15.56%	156	12,948	1,294,838.64	194,225.80
33	5.00%	14.78%	148	13,096	1,309,621.21	196,443.18
34	5.00%	14.04%	140	13,237	1,323,954.64	198,643.70
35	5.00%	13.34%	133	13,370	1,337,005.91	200,550.89
36	5.00%	12.67%	127	13,497	1,349,090.12	202,452.02

Average Number of Purchases	13.50		
TOTAL Number of Purchases	13,497		
TOTAL Revenue		1,349,680	
TOTAL Profit			202,452

Attrition Effect:

			%
Revenue & Profit if No Attrition	3,600,000	540,000	
Actual Revenue & Profit with Attrition	1,349,680	202,452	
Cost of Attrition	2,250,320	337,548	62.51%

As we have seen in Exhibit 3-8, with attrition of 10 percent after shipments one through 6 and 5 percent thereafter, the average number of products purchased over the 36 product sequence is 13.5. Just by concentrating on reducing the attrition after the sixth shipment by half, to 2.5 percent, the average rises to 16.94 and delivers an additional profit of 51,644.

Marketers frequently develop incentives ("You can have a piece of candy if you are good child") to fight attrition and announce them early on in the customer relationship.[12] One is the "points" systems based on the successful airline bonus miles awards to frequent travelers. It is characteristic of the genre. What makes these particularly useful is it allows the marketer to effectively create a "currency" that has whatever value he wishes to give to it and to use this currency with great flexibility. In an effort to reduce attrition, for example, a marketer giving away points could have a big bonus point give-away after a certain number of transactions, incentivising the customer to keep buying so that his points would be able to be used for a big prize.

Other incentives also work well and do not need the complicated mechanics that are a part of the "points" plans. Special merchandise offers available only to customers who have passed certain purchasing thresholds can sometimes work wonders in arresting attrition. That's the good news. The bad news is that once started, these programs take on a life of their own and are very hard to stop.

Whatever we do, it has a cost and it is necessary to know what that cost is and whether it is "allowable" before embarking on expensive and potentially economically counter-productive exercises.

Using the "Attrition Reduction Calculation" facility[13] (Exhibit 3-9), we can make some educated guesses. If we are able to reduce attrition sufficiently to increase the average number of purchases by say, 40 percent (the input used in the Exhibit 3-9 example) the new average will be 22.50. This would increase the profit by 66.69 percent or 135,019. Dividing this by the 1,000 customers, would give us an *additional maximum* of 135.02 to spend for the CRM program. It will be the "maximum" because if exactly this amount is spent, there will be no difference with the result if it had not been spent. Since this would be a senseless exercise in wheel spinning, it only

Exhibit 3-9 Attrition Reduction Calculation

Attrition Reduction Calculation		
Cost of Attrition Per Customer		337.55
Increased Average Number of Purchases if Attrition is reduced by %	40.00%	22.50
Increased Profit from Attrition Reduction		135,019.19	66.69%
Maximum Allowable Investment Per Customer in Attrition Reduction		135.02
Proportion to be allocated to CRM	60.00%	
Conservative Investment Per Customer in Attrition Reduction		81.01

makes sense to spend less than this maximum. The question is how much less?

The template provides a mechanism "Proportion to be Allocated to CRM" allowing the *input of a percentage that would be prudent to allocate* and delivers a recommended "Conservative" investment per customer to reduce attrition.

It is important to understand that the results of any CRM activity of this kind can only be evaluated over time as experience is accumulated and the existing data enriched. Unless that experience is in place, the initial figures included in the model will only be "guesstimates" and should be taken as no more than benchmarks to use for planning purposes. These calculations can also inform the amount you can afford to spend for CRM activity discussed in Chapter 4 and "Investing in Customer Relationship Management," Exhibit 4-2.

Keeping the Customer Happy, Well Served, and Fulfilled

There are lots of reasons we lose customers. They see a more attractive offer from a competitor or they may just lose interest in what we are selling. Some move away and some even pass away. But the biggest reason must be that we don't take proper care of them: they feel, as it were, unfulfilled.

In my early days in the industry, I used to have to go regularly from my home and workplace in New York City to Marion, Ohio to visit the wonderfully named, Fulfillment Corporation of America. "Only in America," broadcast one of the early radio talk-show hosts Gene Shepard, "could you have fulfillment supplied by a corporation."

Fulfillment, however it is supplied, can be the unseen hero or villain of all your efforts to reduce attrition and more positively, enhance your customer relationships. It is the essential back-office of direct marketing, neither glamorous nor terribly exciting but absolutely essential.

At its worst, fulfillment is simply an impersonal and mechanical service function that handles the logistics of accepting orders, processing them and getting the goods shipped and delivered to the customer and sometimes, providing customer service. *At its best, fulfillment is a totally integrated partner of the marketing effort, dedicated not only to serving the customer superbly but also enhancing the customer relationship.*

According to one of the great DM professionals, "Fulfillment should be concerned . . . with not only fulfilling the order but also fulfilling the customer's expectation. Good fulfillment practice, including prompt shipment, can significantly affect conversion and acceptance rates. The subject is, technically, a matter of operations rather than marketing. . . . "[14] Nonetheless, its impact on the total marketing effort can be profound.

Since fulfillment expenses are a major factor in determining the costs of any direct marketing initiative, understanding the many steps in the fulfillment process and costing them as accurately as possible is critical to the overall economics of any program. What we need to know is shown in Exhibit 3-10.

With these costs in hand, figuring out the actual fulfillment and distribution costs for a single product sale or a sequence [15] using the Template, "Fulfillment and Distribution" (Exhibit 3-11) should be relatively simple. The key is to be as accurate[16] as possible and if in doubt, use conservative numbers (higher costs, lower revenues).

While Exhibit 3-11 is designed to illustrate the fulfillment cost build-up for a sequence of shipments the Template can be used just as well for a single shipment.

There are a number of items in this Template that may need some explanation:

Exhibit 3-10 Factors in Order Fulfillment Costs

ITEM (S)	WHAT'S NEEDED	COMMENT
Incoming "Initial" Order Costs, Estimated Response Rates, and Percentage of people who purchase	• Each medium (post, telephone, email, etc.) by which orders are received • The percentage of the total number of orders that are expected from this medium • The cost of handling each order from each medium • The number of people who make contact but in the end do not purchase	"Initial" Orders come in through various media, and handling these orders has different levels of cost. Handling telephone orders is, for example, more expensive than those that come by email. Some people make contact (especially by telephone) and then decide not to order. The cost of handling the non-orders is often as much as the orders and must be accounted for. The Template "Fulfillment and Distribution" delivers as an output both the "Weighted Average" for incoming order costs and the costs of "non-conversion"—the non-orders.
Incoming "Subsequent" Order Costs, Estimated Response Rates, and Percentage of people who purchase	The same data as above	The Subsequent order costs are relevant where there is a selling sequence. Often, however, there will be no additional incoming order costs.
Costs for all "Initial Fulfillment" activities such as Order Handling, Data Entry, Welcome Letter, and any "Other Fulfillment" items	Specific costs for each of the initial fulfillment functions	These need to be developed and used to build the fulfillment model. Some may differ from those applying to "subsequent" fulfillment functions.
Costs for all "Subsequent Fulfillment" activities	The same data as needed for the initial fulfillment should be input	If there is a sequence, the fulfillment tasks and costs may change for the subsequent shipments, and these differences must be reflected in the model.

Exhibit 3-10 Factors in Order Fulfillment Costs (Continued)

ITEM (S)	WHAT'S NEEDED	COMMENT
Costs for all "Initial Distribution" activities such as Picking & Packing, Dispatch Document Preparation, Invoice Preparation, Postage and/or Other Delivery Costs, and miscellaneous other distribution costs	Specific costs for each of the "initial" distribution functions	Like the fulfillment costs, these need to be carefully developed and input into the model.
Costs for all "Subsequent Distribution" activities such as Picking & Packing, Dispatch Document Preparation, Invoice Preparation, Postage and/or Other Delivery Costs, and miscellaneous other distribution costs	Specific costs for each of the "subsequent" distribution functions	As above. Note that these costs are often different than those expended in the initial shipment.
Customer Service Costs	Specific costs for handling all aspects of customer service including in-bound and out-bound telephone costs	This is a significant cost category and needs careful assessment. While hard to plan due to the unknown of how many customer interactions will be necessary, it is essential to generously cost this activity.

▶ When inputting the costs for incoming orders for the initial fulfillment, you are asked to estimate the percentage of people responding by each medium, the cost of handling this response and the percentage of people *who actually purchase*. This allows the template to amortize 100% of the costs for handling the incoming orders against the lower percentage that actually buy. When inputting this information for subsequent purchases, the assumption is that everyone buys and therefore the user is not asked for the percentage of people who purchase.

Exhibit 3-11 Fulfillment and Distribution

Fulfillment

	Initial			Subsequent	
	Estimated % Responding	Cost Per Unit	% Who Purchase	Estimated % Responding	Cost Per Unit
Incoming Order Postage	30.00%	1.00	100.00%	100.00%	1.00
Incoming Order Telephone	30.00%	4.00	60.00%		
Incoming Order Fax					
Incoming Order Internet	40.00%	0.50	80.00%		
Incoming Order Email					
Incoming Order Other					
Weighted Incoming Order Costs		2.13			1.00
Non-Conversion Costs		0.52			
Order Handling		1.50			0.50
Data Entry		2.50			
Welcome Letter					
Other Fulfillment 1					
Other Fulfillment 2					
TOTAL Initial Fulfillment		**6.65**			**1.50**

Distribution Costs

	Initial Cost Per Unit	Subsequent Cost Per Unit
Picking & Packing	1.00	1.00
Dispatch Document Preparation	0.50	0.50
Invoice Preparation	0.25	0.25
Postage and/or Other Delivery Costs	4.50	4.50
Other Distribution Costs 1		
Other Distribution Costs 2		
TOTAL Distribution Costs	**6.25**	**6.25**
Fulfillment & Distribution Costs	**12.90**	**7.75**

Customer Service Costs

Estimated Number of Customer Service Calls:

	Initial Order		Subsequent Order	
	Number	Cost Per Unit	Number	Cost Per Unit
Incoming	2	3.00	1	3.00
Outgoing	1	4.00	1	4.00
Other Communications Costs [Specify]			2	2.00
TOTAL Cost		**10.00**		**11.00**
No. of "Subsequent" Shipments Net of Attrition			5.0	
TOTAL Customer Service Cost				**21.00**

TOTAL Fulfillment & Distribution Cost **72.65**

Some incoming order mechanisms will have lower percentages of "buyers" than others. Telephone orders are likely to be the highest as well as the most expensive. When using a toll-free number, each lost call has a cost. If you believe you will have a substantial number of lost calls, it is recommended that you lower the "% Who Purchase" figure to provide for this.

Only experience will guide you on this and if you do not already have experience as a reference, it is advisable to input conservative percentages and then to carefully track the actual as the basis for the next project.[17]

▶ Data entry (the first time a new customer is added to the file), order handling (specific costs related to the fulfillment of the first or subsequent orders), the preparation of a "Welcome Letter" or other communications, all make up parts of the initial fulfillment process as do postage (or other distribution means) and shipping costs.

▶ As "Customer Service Costs" can be a significant expense, within the Template there is a section to help determine these costs. In the example in Exhibit 3-11, they total 21.00, more than a quarter of the "Total Fulfillment & Distribution Cost" of 72.65.

▶ A distinction is made in the Template between "fulfillment" and "distribution" costs. This is done because while it is usually a "fulfillment" operation to distribute the product, distribution costs are quite separate from fulfillment costs.

Building the fulfillment costs in this way allows us to see them clearly and minimize any nasty surprises. It also allows us to evaluate each of the fulfillment and distribution steps and search for economies and/or alternative procedures.

Our concentration must be on satisfying not only the customer need but his expectations as well. What we want is a customer who feels fulfilled, who is happy that he is doing business with us and who will not become an attrition casualty. And we want to do this within the tight economic parameters that assure us a generous return on our promotional investment.

Notes

¹ Bob Stone and Ron Jacobs, *Successful Direct Marketing Methods* (Seventh Edition) (Chicago: McGraw Hill, 2001), p. 55.

² This applies not only to "customers" in the commercial sense. The *Economist,* in its issue of August 16, 2003, reported (p. 27) that "Some White House political operatives believe the role of independents in elections is overrated: that is, people whose votes are really up for grabs rather than those who profess independence but usually vote along partisan lines may be as low as 7% of the electorate." This suggests that the most likely person to vote for one party or another is the person who voted for them last time.

³ While following Moore's Law—that data density [of integrated circuits] has doubled approximately every 18 months, always bringing down the cost—data storage and associated costs still make the holding of data for which there is no likely use wasteful of corporate assets.

⁴ Wunderman, Lester. *Being Direct,* New York: Random House, 1996.

⁵ Stone Jacobs,*Successful Direct Marketing Methods* pp. 56 & 57.

⁶ An American research and marketing company, Looking Glass, developed a highly successful system of targeting branded "Cohorts." They discovered that by the aggregation of certain demographic and psychographic data into named Cohort clusters, they could better understand the prospects and provide insight for their clients.

⁷ All names have been de-duplicated and checked against the US Postal Service's National Change of Address file to verify addresses.

⁸ Many companies who rent lists now insist on paying only for "Net Names." As the same name is often found on more than one list, the buyer only wants to pay once, normally for the first time it appears. The issue of "Net Names" is covered in detail in Chapter 9.

⁹ Standard practice dictates that when you are using more than a

single list, a de-duplication routine is followed. However, it is not unusual to have considerable duplication within customer lists held by a single company when the files are not held at a "household" rather than an individual level. A single company achieved mailing savings in excess of US $6 million per year simply by avoiding this duplication and creating rules that prevented the same household from receiving more than one communication in any promotional effort.

[10] The expression "sequence" is used in this chapter to describe a series of customer purchases that may be a "continuity" or simply a number of purchases resulting from regular promotional activity over a wide product range.

[11] The Template, "Attrition Table," allows for the input of the loss of customers after each shipment by inputting the estimate of the percentage to be lost. The difference of the numbers between the column labeled "Shipment Number" and the previous column which permits the input of the percentage loss of customers is that only after we know how many we lose as a result of attrition can we know how many should be shipped next. The template also calculates the actual *"Number of Purchases,"* a critical marker for product production and/or inventory control.

[12] Incentives are covered in detail in Chapter 7.

[13] This facility is an integral part of the Attrition Table template.

[14] Edward Nash, "Back-end Promotions," *Direct Marketing: Strategy, Planning, Execution,* Fourth Edition (New York: McGraw Hill, 1982), p. 369.

[15] The Template: Fulfillment & Distribution does not provide for any "Cycle Promotions" for "Club" marketing, as these are included separately in the Template: Clubs.

[16] While strict accuracy is always the best policy, it is sometimes difficult to get the exact cost of each item when developing the initial plan. It is recommended that when this problem arises, you input the best guess based on previous experience and indicate it in such a way that when you have the exact number it can be used to replace the "guesstimate."

[17] There is another important aspect to be considered: it is almost always worthwhile to develop a special promotional piece or action to try to get firm orders from those who showed interest but did not make the purchase. If the call center is good enough to get informa-

tion that will allow you to reach these prospects again, you will have a very special and specific list of people who have already demonstrated interest in your product or service and you should expect a very high "Response and/or % Who Purchase" rate if you promote to them. In that case, only a few media can be used: Direct Mail, Outbound Telemarketing, or Emails.

► ► ►**4**

Customer Relationship
Management

No aspect of the marketing continuum has received more hype in the past decade than Customer Relationship Management (CRM). The resurrection of CRM from its small retailer origins to the flavor of the decade is one of the great comebacks of marketing history. And the millions and millions of dollars that have been spent on integrated marketing database technology to support CRM activities evidences the seriousness with which this most important function of marketing is being viewed by companies in every sector.

With all the interest and investment in CRM, it is ironic that there have been so many failures compared to so few successes. It is imperative that we ask whether the theory is better than the practice, at least up to now, and what can be done about it?

"It is impossible to state precisely what customer relationship management (CRM) means to everyone," wrote Randy Harris.[1] "The term has been applied to almost every element of business that even remotely interacts with a customer."

Customer relationship management (sometimes called "Customer Relationship *Marketing*") is nothing more or less than the sum of a series of actions and initiatives designed to reinforce the customer's initial purchase decision—the decision that made him a customer in the first place—and sustain his relationship with the seller. These relationships might take the form of a formal "loyalty" program, such as those run by the airlines, or something as simple as a restaurant headwaiter who makes sure his regular customers are not only greeted by name and taken to their favorite table but also invited to taste the chef's new creations or have an aperitif "on the house." CRM shrinks the distance between a purely commercial and a one-to-one relationship.

Wrote John G. Sanchez, President & CEO of Zunch Communications, Inc. of Dallas in an important 2001 "White Paper on Customer Relationship *Marketing*":[2]

> Marketers started the new millennium in one of two groups: those who practice Customer Relationship Management, and those who do not. Those who do are reorganizing their marketing programs to create and strength brand loyalty. They put as much emphasis on retaining customers as they do on attracting customers. . . . Those who do not practice CRM may not have to—yet. But they will. They will if they are to survive . . . if they are to sustain profitable growth in the face of diminishing returns from the marketing waves that preceded CRM.

What's surprising is why it took companies so long to recognize a simple truth that had been around since Eve propositioned Adam to try that apple: Keeping the customer happy lies at the heart of successful commercial relationships between sellers and buyers. And what is even more surprising is that with all the talk about CRM, there are so few companies whose embrace of CRM is strong enough to change existing product-centered cultures.

The Location of the Most Effective and Efficient Integrated Marketing Database

That database is located between the ears of a good merchant. In the 1840s, long before CRM had a designer label, the great department store pioneer Adam Gimbel laid out a CRM credo: "If anything done or said in this store looks wrong or is wrong, we would have our customers take it for granted that we shall set it right as soon as it comes to our knowledge. We are not satisfied unless our customers are."[3] Before the existence of all of today's expensive technology designed to keep, mine and model customer data, good merchants knew instinctively and by experience that understanding and serving their customers' needs and wants lay at the core of their businesses.

They knew that the customer was queen or king. They knew that Mrs. Jones liked red dresses and that by putting some new ones aside and telling her they were "reserved for you" was likely to lead to a happy, grateful and loyal customer and profitable sales time and time again. But those were simpler days.

As discussed in Chapter 1, the tremendous choice available to today's customer and the high volume of seductive selling messages to which we are all exposed has made us more commercially promiscuous than we were even a generation ago. In Michael Treacy's book, *Double-Digit Growth: How Great Companies Achieve It–No Matter What*,[4] the author writes:

> Customer loyalty is a contradiction in terms—an oxymoron. . . . If there ever were any customers who would never abandon you for a competitor's product–as we were all told at our father's knee—they are nowhere to be found today. Sentimental loyalty doesn't exist. Companies that have committed to complicated schemes for customer loyalty management don't have much to show for it.

Nonetheless, if it is true—and there is a lot of evidence to support it—as propounded by Jack Schmid and Alan Weber in *Desktop Database Marketing*, " . . . that a 5% increase in current-customer business can translate into as much as a 50% increase in the bottom line,"[5] it is not surprising that CRM is looked upon as something of a chastity belt to keep other suitors at a safe distance.

An increasing body of research with impressive figures from the mid-1990s supports this finding:

> Loyalty can have more to do with a company's profits than scale, market share, unit costs, and many other factors usually associated with competitive advantage. As a customer's relationship with the company lengthens, profits rise. And not just a little. Companies can boost profits by almost 100 percent by retaining just 5 percent more of its customers.[6]

What has changed in this new millennium is both our ability *to measure* the value of CRM, make it accountable, and to plan our CRM activities based on a foundation of economics and our in-

Exhibit 4-1 The Economics of Reducing Defections

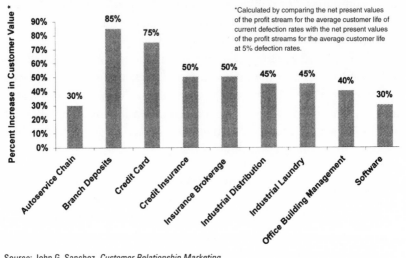

REDUCING DEFECTIONS 5% BOOSTS PROFITS 25% TO 85%

*Calculated by comparing the net present values of the profit stream for the average customer life of current defection rates with the net present values of the profit streams for the average customer life at 5% defection rates.

Source: John G. Sanchez, *Customer Relationship Marketing.*

creased understanding of the enormous impact on profits that arise from brand loyalty.

Exhibit 4-1, reproduced from the Sanchez "White Paper," demonstrates how the reduction in defections boosts profits over a wide range of both consumer and business-to-business applications. This is supported by the author's comment that echoes Schmid and Weber:

> Reducing defections by just 5 percent generated 85 percent more profits in one bank's branch system, 50 percent more in an insurance brokerage, and 30 percent more in an auto-service chain. [Credit-card company] MBNA America has found that a 5 percent improvement in defection rates increases its average customer value by more than 125 percent.[7]

Business literature is replete with success stories that demonstrate how putting the customer's interest ahead of the company's interest—providing outstanding service—is the best way of producing growth and profit. If you are happy with what the merchant is selling you and the service he is providing, why go anywhere else? Retailers–the closest point of contact with customers–have been an obvious incubator for the development of CRM strategies.

Wal-Mart has a "greeter" program with customer-service personnel greeting regular customers by name. Prada's loyal customers carry a sleek Prada loyalty card with an imbedded Radio Frequency ID chip that allows a sales associate to identify a shopper upon greeting them:

> Sales associates are armed with PDA's on steroids that have color screens and a wireless connection to their shopper database and product database to be able to pull up information on the shopper's life, style interests and prior purchases . . . in order to provide an extremely personalized, creative shopping assistance service that matches the shopper's needs to the merchandise available.[8]

How Much Can We Afford to Spend for CRM?

The strategic economic issue for all CRM initiatives must be their cost/benefit relationship. Put simply: How can we determine how much we can afford to spend on CRM activities for a single customer or group of customers to produce what level of loyalty and/or incremental business? And can we justify the huge technology expenditures that are needed to develop truly integrated marketing databases?

Putting the technology investment to the side for a moment, the first consideration is how much we can afford to spend on CRM for an individual customer. This is best considered by focusing on three factors:

▶ An estimate of the revenue and profit likely to be earned from the customer *without* any CRM activity.

▶ An estimate of the *incremental revenue and profit* likely to be earned from the customer *with* CRM activity and at what cost.

▶ An estimate of *how much it would cost to replace this customer* with a similar one.

Exhibit 4-2 Investing in Customer Relationship Management

Allowable Cost of Acquisition for Mandated Contribution and Profit	80.00	
Initial Cost of Acquisition	60.00	
Difference Between Actual & Allowable	20.00	
Estimated Number of Orders in a Period	4	**Total**
Average Order Value	100.00	400.00
Estimated % of Contribution or Profit	20.00%	80.00
Lifetime Contribution or Profit		
Assumption **without** CRM Program	100.00	
Estimated Number of Orders in a Period with CRM Program	7	**Total**
Average Order Value with CRM Program	130.00	910.00
Estimated **Contribution or Profit** with CRM Program	20.00%	182.00
Increase of Revenue with CRM Program	510.00	
Incremental Contribution or Profit of CRM Program	102.00	
Lifetime Contribution or Profit		
Assumption with CRM Program	202.00	
Cost of Acquiring a **Replacement** Customer	60.00	
Amount Available for CRM:		
% of Incremental Profit to be Used for CRM	40.00%	
Difference Between Actual & Allowable	20.00	
Amount of Incremental Profit to be used for CRM	40.80	
Amount Available for CRM Program	60.80	

	Revenue	Profit	% Profit
Without CRM Program	400.00	100.00	25.00%
With CRM Program	910.00	141.20	15.52%

While the inputs for these calculations demand a number of assumptions, these can be modeled (see Exhibit 4-2, "Investing in Customer Relationship Management") to produce, if not a flawless formula for CRM economics, at least a powerful analytical tool that should inform decision-making and permit the consideration of a wide range of "what ifs."

In Exhibit 4-2, we start, as usual, with the original ACPO. That's what the marketer paid to acquire this customer in the first place and should include a mandated rate of contribution and profit. Next are the *actual* acquisition cost and any difference from the ACPO. A positive difference (in this case 20.00) is important because it adds to the bottom line over and above the mandated rate of contribution and profit. Adding this into the total profit *without the CRM program* elevates the percentage of profit on this customer from an assumed 20 percent to 25 percent.

The next task is to calculate the estimated revenue from the customer over a number of time periods. It is always wise to be conservative in estimating revenue—guessing low only enhances the final profit if you have been overly conservative. Since the marketer expects to make a profit on this incremental revenue, it is necessary to input the desired percentage. In this example we have used 20 percent, which has been entered as the input for "Estimated Contribution or Profit with CRM Program."

If this were all there was to the calculation, we would have a lifetime "Contribution or Profit Assumption" of 100.00 (the sum of the 80.00 of profit on revenue of 400.00 at 20% plus the 20.00 positive difference between the ACPO and the CPO) and that would be that.

The economic purpose of CRM activities is to enhance the customer relationship, resulting in increased revenue and profit. In Chapter 6, we look at the costs of reinstating a "lapsed" credit card holder and how to make a judgment as to whether it is better to keep investing in retaining the cardholder or whether the money could be better spent acquiring a new one. This same issue conditions all CRM investments.

What we are trying to determine here is *how much to invest in CRM activities to gain how much additional sales and profit.* And is this expenditure likely to deliver a greater benefit than going out and acquiring a new customer,[9] a cost we have estimated at the same level as the initial acquisition, 60.00, although experience should dictate whether this figure should be higher or lower.

To arrive at the CRM expenditure determination, we now have to make some further assumptions. With a successful CRM program, incremental revenue and profit *should* be generated from the customer both from *a longer-term relationship than without CRM* and from *an increased level of sales during the initial period in excess of the non-CRM forecast.*

Without CRM, we estimated four Revenue Periods, each producing 100.00 of revenue. Our CRM assumption adds an additional three periods. But as a result of the CRM activities, we also estimate a rise in revenue of an average of 30.00 per period for each of the seven periods. If we further assume that the profit on this incremental revenue will be 20 percent, we add an additional 82.00 to the 100.00 we had without the CRM program, giving a total of 202.00.

Exhibit 4-3 Lifetime Contribution

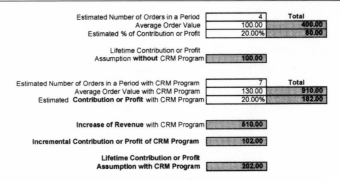

Is It Better to Keep the Customer You Have or Get a New One?

To have a CRM program costs money and anything we spend will reduce the 202.00 "Lifetime Contribution or Profit Assumption with CRM Program" shown in Exhibit 4-3. Thus, the decision of how much we can *afford to spend*, stated as a percentage of the 102.00 *incremental* contribution or profit, is dependent upon whether this will provide enough money to mount an effective CRM program or whether we would be better advised to use the money to acquire new customers.

For the purpose of this example, we have assumed we'll spend 40 percent of *the incremental profit* of 102.00 or 40.80. Since we also have a 20.00 positive difference between the ACPO and CPO, it is reasonable to use it all for additional CRM funding. This gives us a total of 60.80 per customer to spend on CRM and reduces the profit from 202.00 to the 141.20 as shown in Exhibit 4-4. If all our assumptions are correct, the comparison of the initiative with and without a CRM program (Exhibit 4-4) shows increased revenue and profit

Exhibit 4-4 Sensitivities (+/−) to Target Response Percentage

Amount Available for CRM:			
% of Incremental Profit to be Used for CRM	40.00%		
Difference Between Actual & Allowable	20.00		
Amount of Incremental Profit to be used for CRM	40.80		
Amount Available for CRM Program	60.80		

	Revenue	Profit	% Profit
Without CRM Program	400.00	100.00	25.00%
With CRM Program	910.00	141.20	15.52%

with the CRM program, although the *percentage* of profit is lower with the CRM program than without it.

Since we are seeking to determine whether it is better to invest in CRM (and if so, how much to invest) or, alternatively, to invest in the acquisition of a new customer, we need to review the sensitivities in Exhibit 4-5.

The key is the percentage of the "Incremental Profit" that can be economically used for CRM. The graphic makes it obvious that, below 40 percent, using the "Amount Available for CRM" to fund a CRM program is a better bet than trying to acquire a new customers and above 40 percent, the acquisition of a new customers is economically better.[10] This applies only to the example and might be a very different percentage given other inputs.

If the performance of all customers were equal, then our next step would be to try and determine how much of a CRM program we could mount for approximately 60.80 per person.[11] However, we know that this is too simplistic. We therefore need to divide our customer base into value segments and apply the same methodology to each segment.

As can be seen in Exhibit 4-6, the total base of 100,000 customers has been divided into five segments. For each segment, the percentage of customers assumed to be in each segment is entered

Exhibit 4-5 Sensitivities (+/–) to Target Response Percentage

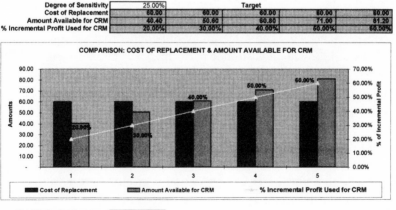

in the "% of *with* CRM Target Profit" boxes. The assumption here is that a certain percentage of the customers will perform better than the average computed in the model: the best segment is allocated 30 percent of the calculated average amount available for CRM—and at descending percentages the other segments receive less, with the last two segments getting no investment at all.

The result shows a total 6,080,000 available to spend for CRM but much more interesting is the amount available to spend for each segment and the "Amount Avail. For CRM Per Customer." Deducted from this amount is the total amortization of 250,000 for fixed technology applied to each customer.[12] The final column shows us the amount of money available for the tactical CRM actions for each segment: 182.40 for the best customer segment, 10% of the customers, 60.80 for the next 20%, 40.53 for the third segment of 20%, for the rest *if* the marketer decides to spend it. The decision to spend money on the rest of the customers is based on determination of value.

With both the macro and micro view of the CRM economics, it should be possible to fashion a tactical program for all or some of the customers or at the very least, determine if there is enough money available to make such a program worthwhile.

Segmentation: The Key

It should not be surprising to see that this is exactly what the airline "miles" programs and other "points" based CRM incentive or loyalty programs do. While the total CRM program technology and infrastructure uses a portion of the available CRM program money, the lion's share goes to fund a hierarchy of benefits that are awarded on the basis of individual customer performance: The more you fly, the more you spend, the more points you get and the richer the benefit program for your segment.[13] Obviously, the more we have to spend per person in each segment, the more benefits we can offer.

> Frequent-flyer, frequent-visitor, frequent-buyer, programs are a regular fact of CRM life. Brand Loyalty Marketers know that it is better to reward brand loyalty than to exploit brand loyalty while diverting resources in trying to attract the indifferent. Knowing, serving and indulging one's loyal

Exhibit 4-6 Sample Segments

Number of Customers	100,000
Fixed Technology Investment	250,000
Technology Amortization Per Customer	2.50

	Number in Segment	% of Customers in Segment	% of "with CRM Target Profit"	Amount Available For CRM Including Technology	Amount Available For CRM Per Customer
[Input Segment 1 Name]	10,000	10.00%	30.00%	1,824,000	182.40
[Input Segment 2 Name]	20,000	20.00%	20.00%	1,216,000	60.80
[Input Segment 3 Name]	30,000	30.00%	20.00%	1,216,000	40.53
[Input Segment 4 Name]		0.00%		-	-
[Input Segment 5 Name]		0.00%		-	-
Available For Other Segments	40,000		30.00%	1,824,000	45.60
TOTALS	100,000		100.00%	6,080,000	

customers is the best way to serve consumers and it is the best way to serve shareholders.[14]

If the planned economic result were the only consideration as to whether or not to mount a CRM initiative, using this methodology would make the decision relatively easy. But as noted above, there is also the issue of the needed IT infrastructure and how much technology is the *right* amount.

Small Is Beautiful

The *right* amount is a movable feast and obviously highly dependent on managements' appetite for risk and its CRM objectives. However, small, is almost always beautiful. Reporting on interviews with a wide range of experts, Jim Dickie of *destination CRM* wrote:

> The common point of view of these visionaries seems to be that CRM is merely a part of some bigger picture, and that if you want it to add any value to what your organization does, you need to commit to implementing intergalactic systems that will blot out the sun in their complexity and grandeur, and take four or five years to fully implement.[15]

Many companies have gone this route and made massive investments in all-singing, all-dancing, sun-blotting CRM technology. At this writing, there are unfortunately few real success stories and for many companies who invested too much without understanding the cultural dynamics of CRM, this has taken the bloom off their rosy projections. "I've yet to find a company that will acknowledge that they've achieved their expected ROI on any large CRM investment, " said Cathie Kozik, CIO at Tellabs, Inc. in an interview. "The most successful seem to have focused on delivering CRM functionality in meaningful pieces rather than going for a full blown implementation."[16]

In assessing the needed technology investment for a CRM program, overcoming the temptation to build "intergalactic systems" is good advice. However sophisticated we might wish the system to be, its cost will have to be amortized over the total program. If we can determine how much we can afford to invest for each customer and customer segment and multiply this amount by the number of customers in each segment, we should be able to develop a global estimate of how much we have available for technology and how much for tactical operations.

Making Choices

If a choice has to be made, *marketing tactics that have a direct interface with the customer's wants and needs should always take precedence over technology expenditure.* If the culture of customer-focus has supplanted the more traditional product-focus culture, there is almost always a way to keep the investment small and to enjoy impressive results. The Paris department store that *guaranteed parking space for its best customers* or the news magazine publisher who *guaranteed home delivery of subscription copies* of its weekly publication by Sunday afternoon are just two examples that underline the point. Another is the "Private Bank" unit of a large international bank who had their client service people put their *home or private telephone numbers on their business cards* as a means of demonstrating to their high-value customers that these customers were so special they could contact their private bankers 24/7.

The parking spaces were there anyway: Making them available to the best customer segment cost virtually nothing but the identification of these customers and providing them with information about the availability. The incremental sales to this segment were extraordinary. The guaranteed home delivery did have a cost—not so much "high tech" as "low tech"—(lots of young people on motorbikes), but it was recouped many times over in a substantial increase in the renewal rates from these subscribers compared to people who simply received their subscriptions in the post. It was impossible to measure the direct effect of the private telephone numbers on the private bankers business cards except anecdotally. One happy client looked at the card and said: "You mean I can really reach you outside bankers' hours. That's amazing!"

How would an expensive high tech system have helped in any of these cases? It's difficult to imagine. In each, what drove the success was CRM management thinking simply about what they could do to make the customer or client's life easier and better. In fact, the lesson is that by stepping back and asking yourself what you as a customer would really want to enhance the relationship, whether or not it is current policy or practice, will frequently generate "out-of-the-box" solutions that are both effective and economical. The secret is thinking of yourself as a customer, not as a marketer, and acting accordingly.

The low cost of using email and the Internet to communicate with customers about their loyalty programs makes this the communications medium of choice for CRM marketers. However, the industry has seen an alarming rise in the number of customers who do not wish to provide their email addresses, fearing that by doing so will only add to the already horrific SPAM problems. Marketers are therefore increasing their incentives for receiving and getting permission to email customers.[17]

Another useful way to make a "back-of-the-envelope" assessment of any CRM program is to ask the question: *If, instead of spending money on a fancy CRM program, the customer is refunded his share of what would have been spent, in more product for the same price or less price for the same product, would it have the same effect on his loyalty?*

The *London Evening Standard* newspaper ran an article on retail loyalty cards with this ominous headline: "Consumer Backlash Threatens Store Cards."[18] "Shoppers," said the article, "regard the tiny savings[19] offered by loyalty cards as Tesco Clubcard or Nectar [offered by supermarket chain Sainsbury's] as not worth switching stores for, . . . " Citing a survey by retail think-tank IGD, the article went on to say: " . . . only eight percent of shoppers would change stores to take advantage of a loyalty card compared to 58 percent who would move for lower prices."

Exercising Judgment

The costs of sophisticated CRM technology are significant and must, as we saw in Exhibit 4-6, be allocated against each customer. It is therefore wise to look at the total cost of any technological investment in terms of how much of that investment can be recouped per customer CRM activity as a benchmark for determining if the investment is justified or if there is a simpler (and less expensive) solution.

Customers have a lot more sense than some marketers think they have. If the loyalty program benefits are insignificant or too complicated, they not only don't foster loyalty; they create a negative image of the company trying to create loyalty. If the benefits are not there, perhaps simply giving more value in the product is the best way to go. However, if you can add more real and/or perceived value through a well-organized program—especially one that offers to make dreams come true and that you can afford—then a CRM initiative will almost certainly make sense.

A large multidivisional communications company began its CRM investigation like most others. How, management asked, could all the data on subscribers to its many magazines, buyers of its large range of general book and CDs and subscription data for its pay TV service and ISP be integrated and made available in real time so that the incoming telesales people would be able to personally identify and proactively handle each customer? The proposed answer was a totally new software infrastructure and the investment of many millions of dollars.

There was no lack of hungry systems providers and consultants eager to start work immediately and share a slice of this very tasty cake. Fortunately, one of the managers forced the team to address the key question that defined the problem: If you had everything on the very long "wish list," he asked, how would you use it and how would it earn back its cost? How, he wanted to know, would you *use* the information that someone had been a pay TV subscriber for three years in selling a magazine subscription? Or just because someone had three different magazine subscriptions, why would he be a good prospect for the ISP service?

Team members struggled with the task of putting real opportunities against the wish list functionality and ended up agreeing with the simple rule that says: If you don't need the technology and can't see a definite short-term use and payoff, don't make the investment.

Following the dictum that a relatively small improvement in the performance of the best customers would have a major effect on profits, the company used a simple in-house developed program to aggregate its customer data and determine their multiple subscribers and product customers. They then sent each of these customers a letter thanking them for their loyalty to the company's products and offered each two *free* tickets to a theatrical performance in which the company had an interest and available tickets. All the customers had to do was phone an 800 number to register the date they wanted their tickets.

The response was enormous, even if some people called the company's hotline to ask: "what's the catch"? When they found out there was none, they were full of enthusiastic thanks. One year out, the retention level of the segment *offered* the tickets (including those who did not, for one reason or another, take their tickets) was more than 20 percent better than a carefully chosen control group.

CRM: Caring, Not Technology

Anyone who has ever made an *unexpected* gift to a loved one knows that these are the most cherished gifts of all.[20] It doesn't need a sophisticated system. It just needs *imagination* and *caring*.

The most sophisticated "system" won't assure the retention or loyalty of your clients. In fact, as stated previously, *"recognition" is often as or more important than "reward."* No wonder we hear over and over: "it's the thought that counts." We know that after a short time, employees look on the regular Christmas bonus as part of their salary, and it does little to create loyalty. Likewise, loyalty program participants can be persuaded to migrate their "loyalty" to another program with a richer or sexier reward system.

Timing is a critical factor in building and sustaining any relationship. Ask anyone who has met the potential "love of their life" at a party, exchanged telephone numbers and then waited eagerly for the promised call the following day. When it doesn't come that day or the day after or the day after that, the positive anticipation turns increasingly negative. While we all understand this as it affects our private lives, we often seem unable to transfer this knowledge to the heart of our CRM efforts. Any psychologist will tell you that once the seeds of dissatisfaction have been planted in a relationship, it is extremely difficult, often impossible, to eliminate them. Things go wrong in any relationship, but anticipating what can go wrong and taking timely remedial action before the situation has gotten out of hand can often both eliminate the fallout and strengthen the relationship at the same time.

A London-based senior executive of a large music company flew first class to monthly Board meetings on the other side of the Atlantic. At least a dozen first-class round trips per year to New York as well as many other journeys made him a very valuable customer to the airline. On one particular return to London, Murphy's law that states when something goes wrong, everything goes wrong, lengthened his normal seven and a half hour journey to nearly twenty-four hours. With his fellow high-flying passengers, the subject of conversation was whether they could sue the airline and the certainty they would take their lucrative business to another carrier.

One half-hour after arriving at his home in London there was a ring on his doorbell. The visitor was a representative of the airline who personally apologized, handed the executive a magnum of vintage champagne and an envelope with a personal letter of apology from the Chairman of the airline, a voucher for two first-class 'Round the World tickets and a check for five hundred pounds. Instead of spreading a virus about the airline, this executive lost no opportunity to tell his friends and colleagues how wonderfully he had been treated "after an unfortunate delay." Perhaps the champagne, the check and the visit cost the airline a total of seven hundred pounds: the flight tickets effectively cost nothing. That's not a lot to spend on a customer whose value to the airline was more than one hundred times that each year.

Sensitivity Is Central

Conversely, *a lack of sensitivity can undermine even the best-intentioned effort at building loyalty.* This is spotlighted by this real research interview with a customer:

Question: *How long have you been a customer at Bank A?*
Answer: Twelve years

Question: *What caused you to close your account and move it?*
Answer: Bank X was right around the corner and paid higher rates.

Question: *Were Bank X's rates always higher?*
Answer: Don't know. I just noticed recently.

Question: *What made you notice?*
Answer: I was a little irritated at Bank A and saw an ad for Bank X.

Question: *Why were you irritated?*

Answer: I was turned down for a credit card

Question: *Had you ever been turned down before?*

Answer: Yes, several times, but in this case the bank solicited me and gave me a big come-on about being a preferred customer and then turned me down with a form letter.

Exhibit 4-7 lists a few important "Rights" and "Wrongs" of establishing and sustaining loyalty.

Recognition of the importance of the individual customer to the company, caring for his or her individual wants and needs in a sympathetic and proactive manner is what keeps customers loyal and justifies the expenditure on systems and technology to facilitate the handling of thousands or millions of seemingly *individual* initiatives. The phrase "How can I help you?" from a service attendant only has meaning if that attendant demonstrates that he or she will go the extra mile to help overcome the customer's problem. Otherwise, it is as meaningless as the ritual "have a nice day" spoken by many people who really couldn't care less whether you have a nice day or not. It's the combination of courtesy and real recognition of the customer that makes CRM a reality, not a mechanical

Exhibit 4-7 The Rights and Wrongs of Loyalty

WHAT CAN GO RIGHT	WHAT CAN GO WRONG
• Customer can feel he is recognized and important	• Belief that a loyalty program is in itself a solution to all problems
• Incentives are appropriate to his needs and desires	• Creation of inappropriate incentives and benefits
• He is always treated with courtesy	• Treating the loyal customer just like you would treat a prospect
• Anticipation of problems and avoidance of them	• Not making good on mistakes
• Making good when things go wrong	

marketing effort: It's the difference between having sex and making love.

Where Do We Want to Go and What's the Best (and Most Economical) Way of Getting There?

A goal-orientated approach almost always works best. Exactly what do we want to accomplish with our CRM initiatives and is the goal realistic and achievable? Do we want more customers to come into a retail outlet, higher sales volumes, more repeat purchases, etc.? If the primary and secondary objectives can be tightly defined and strategies and tactics developed, they will almost certainly inform what technology is needed to implement the plan.

By breaking the CRM program into its component parts, the cost of each can be estimated and the likely ROI on each can be determined. The job is then to test a representative sample group from each segment (or, to be more economical, those that appear to offer the likely best result) and see how the actual result measures up against the plan.

This takes time and probably an up-front technology investment as well (another reason to try and keep the initial investment limited). That large investment in time and money is the reason that some CRM technology vendors and consultancies are prepared to install their systems on *a contingency basis*—you only pay if the system works for you and after it has been proven. The problem with this is defining the metrics on which the contingency is based. These must be extremely clear.

Failing a contingency deal, the recommended course of action is to invest in an expandable modular system that has the functionality that meets your primary needs. Spend the necessary time getting the specifications for a complete system right. Then identify a supplier who can provide you with the initial modules but whose system is expandable to meet all (or most) of your longer-term needs and use that for the tests.

Is Corporate Management *Really* On-Board for CRM?

Despite the lip service given to the need to keep customers longer and to making them more profitable, corporate managements in all industries have been slow to accept the fact that a customer-centric focus may mean major changes in both existing organization and process. These changes do not come easily.

In a very useful article, "The Top 10 Misconceptions About CRM Revealed," Rene Litalien gathers together many of the pitfalls that have plagued CRM projects and provides useful solutions.[21] " . . . the process of implementing a CRM program often goes wrong because of hurried projects that are implemented simply for technology sake with unrealistic project timelines and poorly documented goals." Gaining top-management support is critical. This support and commitment can best be obtained by demonstrating that automation:

▶ "Supports the business strategy (e.g., automation delivers the information required to make the key decisions, which in turn enables business strategy to be realized).

▶ "Measurably impacts and improves results (e.g., improved win rates, improved margins, higher sales revenues, and higher customer satisfaction ratings).

▶ "Reduces costs (e.g., lower general sales costs) and thereby pays for itself over a specified time period. It is best if you can document your case for automation based on business impact."

While the support is important, *commitment* is essential. And it does not come easily:

Creating a loyalty-based system in any company requires a radical departure from traditional business thinking. It puts creating customer value—not maximizing profits and shareholder value—at the center of business strategy, and demands significant changes in business practice. . . . While senior executives may be daunted by the time and investment required to engineer an entire business system for high retention, they may have no alternative. Customer loyalty appears to be the only way to achieve sustainable superior profits.[22]

Customer relationship management is a detail intensive activity that can easily lose senior management attention if the managers are faced with too many trees and lose the overall view of the forest.

The forest is growth and profitability derived not only from a customer-centric focus but also from reengineering of traditional marketing activities to scale each initiatives to individual customers based on their performance.

There is no question that Customer Relationship Management—the fourth pillar of the marketing continuum—will play a growing role in the future of all marketing, even if it is undergoing some teething problems. It moves marketing from monologue to dialog, serves both marketer and customer and meets the standard of accountability demanded by modern management.

Notes

[1] Question 65 from David R. Laube and Raymond F. Zammuto, editors, *Business Driven Information Technology: Answers to 100 Critical Questions for Every Manager.* © 2003 by the Board of Trustees of Leland Stamford Jr. University, Stanford University Press.

[2] John G. Sanchez, *Customer Relationship Marketing,* 2001. Sanchez, as do a number of other commentators, uses "Customer Relationship Marketing" instead of "Customer Relationship Management" to describe CRM.

[3] George Anderson, "CRM Leaves Out the Customer," *RetailWire Digest,* (Winter 2003), p. 9 from *www.retailwire.com.*

[4] Portfolio 2003

[5] Jack Schmid/Alan Weber, *Desktop Database Marketing,* (Lincolnwood, IL: NTC Business Books, 1998).

[6] Frederick Reichheld and W. Earl Sasser Jr., "Zero Defections: Quality Comes to Service," *Harvard Business Review* and quoted in Sanchez's White Paper, "Customer Relationship Marketing."

[7] Ibid.

[8] Anderson, "CRM Leaves Out the Customer," p. 8 from *www.retailwire.com.*

[9] One issue that has not been factored into this methodology is the chance that promoting to acquire new customers may be more or less successful than anticipated. If less successful, the cost of acquiring a "replacement" customer will obviously rise.

[10] A further consideration, although not one dealt with in the Tem-

plate is the Net Present Value (NPV) of the money used to acquire the customer in the first place or to acquire a new one. Since few customers return their acquisition investment in a short period of time, an added factor must be the financial cost of this investment.

[11] For the purposes of the modeling, no amortization of the necessary technological investment has been made at this point.

[12] The technology investment issue is examined later in this chapter.

[13] The concept of segmentation of benefits is hardly new: manufacturers, goods producers and others in the business-to-business arena have long given their customers "quantity discounts," a lower price to large purchasers than to smaller ones.

[14] Sanchez, John G., *Customer Relationship Marketing*, 2001. Page 27.

[15] "ForwardBusinessSolutions," June 5, 2003.

[16] Thomas Hoffman, *ROI Report Urges Wary Approach to CRM Projects Computerworld*, February 24, 2003.

[17] DM News, *Spam Fears Affect Loyalty Marketing*, November 18, 2003.

[18] Jonathan Prynn, Consumer Affairs Editor, *London Evening Standard*, January,6,2004, Page 15.

[19] Savings described in the article varied by on average. A shopper at Harrods or Marks & Spencer, for example, would have to spend 5,000 pounds to save 50 pounds in the loyalty scheme.

[20] Many years ago in its heyday, the advertising agency Saatchi & Saatchi had a tradition of rewarding exceptional staff work with a "brown envelope"–a personal letter and bonus from the Saatchi brothers, thanking the employee for his or her contribution. There weren't many of them but their very existence kept staff defections in a traditionally volatile business well below industry averages.

[21] Rene Litalien, Founder & President of TASK Management Consulting in *CRM Magazine*, "Destination CRM, Viewpoint," October 20, 2003; http://www.destinationcrm.com/print/default.asp?ArticleID=3468.

[22] Frederick Reichheld, "Loyalty-Based Management," *Harvard Business Review*, quoted in Sanchez's White Paper, "Customer Relationship Marketing."

▶▶▶ 5

The Economics of Different
Direct Selling Sequences

W e have seen that the allowable cost per order informs our marketing efforts throughout the continuum. Nowhere does this manifest itself with greater importance than in the different direct marketing selling sequences that put us in one-to-one relationship with our customers and provide a regular channel for sales.

Whether we are selling a single unit of merchandise or attracting customers for a complex sequence of purchases, an essential task is to understand the different economics and carefully work from these as our point of departure.

The analogy of the diamond and the wheelbarrow as the best and worst products to sell using direct marketing methods should condition our thinking. If a product has too low a value or price point or is unsuited to convenient shipping and home delivery, it is unlikely to be profitable to sell it through direct marketing methods, especially as a stand-alone item. The reason for this is quite simply because the cost of using the direct marketing sales channel will be out of proportion to the revenue received.

All selling sequences have their own peculiarities and economics. Choosing the most appropriate for any marketing project is a high priority. That choice will be driven by a number of factors but the *most important is finding a careful balance between the needs of the marketer to use a particular selling sequence and the receptivity and willingness of the consumer to accept it.* Some consumers will be happy to be "committed" to a sequence while others will not wish to make any commitment no matter how limited or amorphous.

Choosing the Right Selling Sequence [1]

Why should a person join and accept the commitment of a "club" rather than purchase the same product or service through a subscription or on a single purchase basis? Why should he buy from a catalog instead of from single offerings? Every sequence demands that we answer these questions for the consumer and that we understand that there will always be a trade-off between the benefits the selling sequence offers and the drawbacks, real or perceived.

The following are the principal marketing forms.

Selling a single product (or multiples of that product) through response advertising (using any media) is the simplest. An offer is made, an order received and paid for, the product is delivered to the purchaser and the loop is closed. Examples might be a cell phone, a book, CD, garment or any other product category. All good direct marketers will wish to retain the history of this transaction[2] and promote buyers with additional offerings at a later time. But this should not be considered here.

Single products (or "one-shots" as they are sometimes called) can be paid for in a single payment (the most usual method) or in a number of installments.

Selling a sequence of products on a "Continuity" basis is employed when the product offering:

▶ Is for products that lend themselves to being received by the consumer as a series delivered over time.

▶ Does not require the consumer to receive the entire series at the same point in time.

▶ Has a high price for the entire series that, as a whole, would act as an inhibitor to purchase while periodic delivery with monthly or some other periodic pricing overcomes this difficulty.

An offer is made to start the continuity series and the cost of acquiring the customer is amortized over the purchase period. The buyer receives regular shipments until the end of the series (where there are a set number of units as there would be if you were selling a set of eight china place settings or all the James Bond videos).

There are also "open-ended" continuities (such as Reader's Digest Condensed Books) that are shipped until the consumer indicates he does not wish to receive any further titles.

The key difference between "continuity" and installment sales—where the consumer receives the product at one time but pays over an extended time—is the ability of the customer to stop the process and only pay for what he has received. History has proven that many consumers prefer this somewhat more flexible system to installment payments.

Selling products through a "Club" is yet another selling form that spreads the customer acquisition cost over a series of purchases. Club structures normally make an introductory offer (purchase a mixed fruit basket) with a *commitment* to continue purchasing on a regular basis a new basket of seasonal fruit on a regular basis (e.g., each month) unless you indicate you do not wish to receive it ("'til forbid") or on receipt of a "cycle" promotion. Clubs, because of their structure have very different economics than other forms.

Retail Stores without Walls: Selling through Catalogs has a long history. Some, such as the original Sears catalog, contained everything from wheelbarrows to underwear and met the myriad needs of families living outside of major cities where large varieties of most goods were scarce. Today's catalog offerings include a few mega-catalogs but are more often product-group-specific, from fashion or upscale electronics to garden seeds and plants.

The key economic determinants in addition to the cost of acquiring the customer in the first place are the average order value derived from each catalog customer and the return on each size catalog page unit.

Subscriptions provide products or services on a regular delivery basis. Whether to a magazine or some other product, which is shipped (or provided[3]) on a regular basis, subscriptions are characterized by an agreement to purchase a specific number of units over a predetermined time period.[4] Some subscriptions are sold for a fixed term (and need consented "renewals" to continue the shipments) and others are on a "'til forbid" basis with an initial term and then an open-ended cancellation.

Insurance policies, credit cards, even institutional memberships are variant forms of subscription selling but subscription programs nonetheless. Just as in calculating the long-term value of a customer, in continuity, clubs and subscriptions, *attrition*—the loss of customers who start purchasing but cancel or just stop for one reason or another—is a critical factor and plays a significant part in planning. It also impacts *how many products* will be needed for each cycle of shipment so that product inventories are neither too large nor too small for total needs.

Each of these selling forms as they apply to data driven direct marketing is discussed in some detail below, and templates are provided to help prepare calculations for each.

Selling Single Items

Although the economics of single product sales have been discussed in Chapter 2, it is worth revisiting this most widely used direct marketing form in greater detail.

As we have seen, the single sale is the simplest data driven direct marketing form. It does not have the problems that come with attrition, nor does the fulfillment of the orders require complicated procedures. Providing that there is sufficient revenue to cover the basic mailing or other media costs, promotion of single items can be the basis for an excellent and profitable business.

Cost of Access to Market: A Key Factor in DM Pricing

Unless the product or service you are selling has very special characteristics and a clearly identifiable market with a low-cost access, there are certain minimum requirements to have the best chance of success (Exhibit 5-1).

Philip Kotler sets forth six steps in developing pricing[5] These steps depend upon a number of objectives that inform the needs of direct marketers as they do for all marketers. The most important for our immediate purposes is "Estimating Costs" because they condition whether or not the single sale direct marketing strategy is applicable. Direct marketers know that *the lower the price of the product to the consumer, the greater the need for a high multiple between the actual product cost and the revenue.*

The first imperative is to know the cost of access to market. Together with a conservative estimate of the minimum response per-

Exhibit 5-1 Cost of Access to Market

Cost of Access to Market Per 000	1,000
Conservative % Response	1.50%
Cost Per Order	66.67

centage and the other cost items, we should easily be able to calculate how much this multiple needs to be and, from that, the selling price.

That doesn't mean that the "selling price" will be a price that consumers will "buy." If the price is too high, few of the many potential customers who beat a path to your door will make a purchase—even if you have invented a better mousetrap.

Conversely, and all too often, desirous of making sales, marketers delude themselves that additional sales will make up for very low margins and end up with a situation in which the more they sell, the more they lose. They would obviously be better off to cry over the model that shows they will not make a profit on the initiative than over the expensive spilled milk of additional losses.

The first essential calculation is the Cost of Access to Market. This is the marketing cost of reaching the prospects (normally stated as a cost per thousand) and assumes in this example that to reach 1,000 prospects there is a cost of 1,000.00. The further assumption is a response rate of 1.5 percent. Before we even consider the cost of the product and its fulfillment, we know that we have to provide 66.67 solely for marketing.[6] Obviously, the lower the cost of access to market and the higher the predicable response rate, the lower this amount will be. But it is a necessary starting point.

The next step is the cost of the product. For the purpose of this model we have assumed this cost to be 60.00 for each unit.

Now we must consider the percentages of the as yet undefined selling price that will be necessary to meet the costs of taxes included in the price, fulfillment (including credit card charges), bad pay, returns, any premiums or incentives, miscellaneous items and our desired profit or contribution. We need to know (or should be able to guess from past experience) the normal percentages for these activities. As a start, to turn these percentages (which, in this example add to 30 percent without the actual product cost) into numbers, we need at least a *target* selling price. This price must be high enough to cover the cost of the product (60.00) and the cost of the marketing (66.67) and have enough left over to pay the variable costs and generate a profit or contribution.

To arrive at that price, it is a relatively simple matter to test any Target Selling Price greater than the sum of the access to market and product cost and then to assess the sensitivities on both the plus and minus sides.

The Exhibit 5-2 ("Product Pricing Evaluation Model") shows what happens if we start with 230.00 as the target price and run the sensitivities at 20 percent increments. We see that we could have a selling price as low as 184.00 and still make a profit of 16 percent.

It is of more than casual interest that at 230.00 the actual ratio of the selling price to the product cost is 3.8 to 1. This is an acceptable ratio but a bit on the low side. For mid-range products a ratio of product cost to price should be more than 4:1.

Looking at the component parts of the single product sales model we see that in this example, the access to market eats the lion's share of the revenue. The reason for this is the *relatively irreducible cost of the marketing.* If the price were to drop substantially, (product price to 200.00 with product cost still at 60.00) while the *actual cost of the access to market* would remain the same, the percentage would change dramatically from 29 percent to 33 percent and profits would be diminished accordingly.

The Necessity for Price Testing

Once we know the economics are right, we have to evaluate whether the price we wish to charge is one that our prospects will accept. As Tofler points out, we need to look carefully at competitive pricing of similar products and perceived values. Only when we are convinced that what we are offering has a strong competitive chance in the marketplace does it make sense to go ahead. And "going ahead" means rigorous testing[7] and evaluation. A primary function of that testing is to determine the relative merits of different prices—whether a lower price generates more sales and profits than a higher price (Exhibits 5-3 amd 5-4).

One of the advantages of direct mail and email as media for direct marketing is the ability to offer the same product at *different* prices to small list segments and then to compare the results. Because these media are highly discreet, it is unlikely that the com-

Exhibit 5-2 Product Pricing Evaluation Model

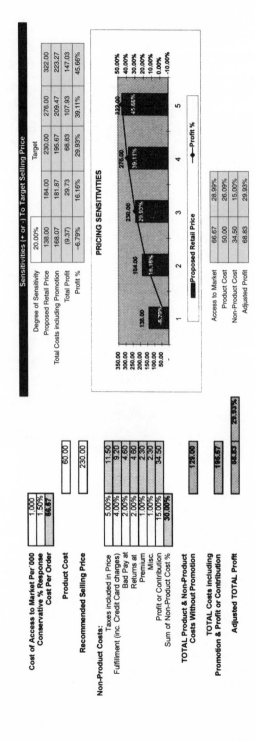

Cost of Access to Market Per '000	1,000
Conservative % Response	1.50%
Cost Per Order	66.67

| Product Cost | 60.00 |

| Recommended Selling Price | 230.00 |

Non-Product Costs:

Taxes included in Price	5.00%	11.50
Fulfillment (inc. Credit Card charges)	4.00%	9.20
Bad Pay at	2.00%	4.60
Returns at	2.00%	4.60
Premium	1.00%	2.30
Misc.	1.00%	2.30
Profit or Contribution	15.00%	34.50
Sum of Non-Product Cost %	30.00%	

| TOTAL Product & Non-Product Costs Without Promotion | 129.00 |

| TOTAL Costs including Promotion & Profit or Contribution | 195.67 |

| Adjusted TOTAL Profit | 68.83 | 29.93% |

	Sensitivities (+ or -) To Target Selling Price					
				Target		
Degree of Sensitivity	20.00%					
Proposed Retail Price	138.00	184.00	230.00	276.00	322.00
Total Costs including Promotion	168.07	181.87	195.67	209.47	223.27
Total Profit	(9.37)	29.73	68.83	107.93	147.03
Profit %	-6.79%	16.16%	29.93%	39.11%	45.66%

PRICING SENSITIVITIES

350.00
300.00
250.00
200.00
150.00
100.00
50.00
-

138.00 -6.79%   184.00 16.16%   230.00 29.93%   276.00 39.11%   322.00 45.66%

1   2   3   4   5

50.00%
40.00%
30.00%
20.00%
10.00%
0.00%
-10.00%

■ Proposed Retail Price   ◆ Profit %

Access to Market	66.67	28.99%
Product Cost	50.00	26.09%
Non-Product Cost	34.50	15.00%
Adjusted Profit	68.83	29.93%

Exhibit 5-3 Sample Distribution of Costs and Profits

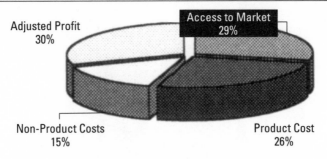

Adjusted Profit
30%

Access to Market
29%

Non-Product Costs
15%

Product Cost
26%

petition will receive one of the test promotions and see what you are doing. This can provide a significant competitive advantage. If there is a certainty, it is that at the beginning of any planning or operational process, the best thing you can do is keep the selling program as simple as possible.

Exhibit 5-4 Sample Distribution of Costs and Profits

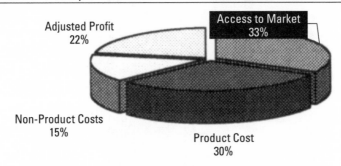

Adjusted Profit
22%

Access to Market
33%

Non-Product Costs
15%

Product Cost
30%

Just Start Dating

As indicated earlier, the single sale can be the first step to building a relationship with the customer and the beginning of a series of transactions that taken together will give value to this customer over the purchase lifetime. The belief that to have a lifetime value a customer must make a commitment (through "continuity," a "club," or a subscription) is often over-stated. Jerry Shereshewsky, a direct marketing guru from Yahoo!, makes the analogy with dating. It can start with a drink and develop naturally into more intense interactions, even the commitment that comes with marriage. Dating is not a bad place to start.

Some consumers are prepared to commit to a proposition, and some like to retain their freedom, even if this freedom comes at a price.[8] Those prepared to commit are more likely to accept the offer of a club structure or a subscription for a fixed or open-ended term. Those who want the ultimate freedom of choice, tend to purchase their magazines at the newsstand and shun clubs, perhaps following Groucho Marx's famous dictum that he wouldn't want to join any club that had such low standards it would accept him as a member.

Companies like consumer commitment. What could make a brand-loyalty advocate happier than knowing—like Proctor & Gamble would like to know for Pampers—that his consumer would continue to purchase for a predictable period (preferably forever) and he could carefully plan his product, his marketing, and his profits accordingly? It is convenient and has the potential for the maximum economic efficiency. But many consumers, like many bachelors, avoid tying the knot and find alternative ways of purchasing what they desire.

For those who see the many advantages in "committed" purchasing structures, there exist three principal forms of direct marketing commitment: continuities, clubs and subscriptions.

Continuity Sales

Assume for a moment that you are marketing a publication series of 20 volumes. Assume further that, as an incentive to get the prospect to start purchasing the series, you are prepared to give the first volume as a free gift with the purchase of the second. Thus two volumes will be delivered in the first month and then one each month for the following 18 months at a price of 25.00 each with an additional postage and handling charge of 2.00 for each volume. The consumer has no commitment to continue purchasing; he can quit at any time.

The key data assumptions (theoretical) that will drive the allowable cost per order can be seen in Exhibit 5-5.

When all these items have been calculated, we find that on *each first volume* we ship we *lose* 11.77 and on *each subsequent volume* we have net revenue of 7.55 for *a total net margin per customer of 66.64.*

Exhbit 5-5 Key Assumptions Regarding ACPO for Continuity Sales

ITEMS	VALUE	COMMENT
First Unit Price	00.00	No charge is made for the first unit. It is the Free Offer.
Distribution or Postage Charge Back on First Volume	00.00	
Subsequent Volumes	25.00	Each of the 19 additional volumes carries a price of 25.00.
Distribution or Postage Charge Back on Additional Volumes	2.00	Each of the 19 additional volumes carries a distribution or postage charge of 2.00.
% Returns	4.00 %	Four percent of the people who receive a volume return it.
% Bad Pay	4.00 %	Four percent of the people who receive a volume keep it but do not pay for it.
Manufacturing Cost of each Volume	5.00	All volumes have the same manufacturing cost.
Packaging Cost of each Volume	.50	All volumes have the same packaging cost.
Royalty Costs	7.00 %	Each volume except the first, which the copyright holder has allowed to be given away without a royalty payment, carries a royalty of 7% of the price received.
Fulfillment Costs	2.70	The sum of all the handling and fulfillment costs is 2.70 for each volume, including the free first volume.
Average Number of Purchases Per Customer (Attrition)	11.1	Assumes that 100% of the customers take volumes 1 & 2 and 20% cancel after volume 3, 15% after volume 4, 10% after volume 5, 5% after each of volumes 6–9, and 2% after each of the other volumes.
Cost of Payment Options	3.5 %	Cost of paying credit card company commission and other charges on payments.
% Contribution or Profit Expectation	20.00 %	The marketer wishes to have a 20% profit or contribution to his overheads.

This 66.44 is the allowable cost per order—the amount that the marketer can reasonably spend to attract a customer who will perform according to the given assumptions and produce a given percentage of Contribution or Profit.

Thinking of "Contribution and/or Profit" as a "Cost" Is Essential

Remember that we have taken *as a cost* an expectation of 20 percent of revenue as a contribution and/or profit.[9] Thus, if the actual cost of acquiring the customer is exactly 66.64, the marketer will have a profit and/or contribution of 20 percent of the revenue at the end of the effort. If the cost per order is lower, the entire difference will flow to the bottom line. Conversely, if it is higher, it will flow out of the bottom line—less than 20 percent will be derived as profit and there could potentially be a loss.

At first glance it may seem unusual to take the profit and/or contribution as a cost. Profit is normally what's left over at the end of the exercise. But seen as a means of determining how much you can spend to attract one customer to make a purchase or series of purchases, the reason becomes obvious. Had we not provided for the profit in determining the "allowable" and then achieved as the *actual* cost per order, exactly the allowable amount, we would have been left without a profit. We would have spun our wheels at great speed and gone nowhere.

Of course, hitting the actual cost per order target exactly on the bull's eye almost never happens. That's not particularly important.

We may be able *to afford* to spend 66.64 (the allowable in the continuity book program) to obtain an *average* customer who will perform according to our previous assumptions. But how much better it would be if we could attract fewer customers at less cost who would purchase more volumes with less attrition.[10]

The table in Exhibit 5-6 compares the Net Margin before Customer Promotion, using the original attrition assumption (Value No. 1) and a lower attrition assumption resulting in a greater number of purchases (Value No. 2).

As a direct result of a 32 percent improvement (decrease) in the rate of attrition we gain an increase of more than 40 percent in the Net Margin.

Exhibit 5-6 Net Margin before Customer Promotion Calculations

ITEM	VALUE NO. 1	ASSUMPTION	VALUE NO. 2	ASSUMPTION
Average Number of Purchases Per Customer (Attrition)	11.1	Assumes that 100% of the customers take volumes 1 & 2 and 20% cancel after volume 3, 15% after volume 4, 10% after volume 5, 5% after each of volumes 6–9, and 2% after each of the other volumes	14.6	Assumes that 100% of the customers take volumes 1 & 2 and 10% cancel after volume 3, 5% after each of volumes 4&5, 3% after each of volumes 6–9, and 2% after each of the other volumes
Net Margin Per Customer Before Promotion	66.64		93.66	

The novels of the 19th-century author Charles Dickens were so popular that it was impossible for the publisher to print a sufficient number of entire copies fast enough to meet demand. As a result, chapters—each ending with a "cliff-hanging" event to assure continued reader interest—were produced on a periodic basis and sold in "parts" to an eager public. This served the publisher and the public nicely. The publisher didn't have the large front-end investment in paper, printing and inventory, and as each chapter was sold, he received his revenue. The readers paid a relatively low price for each new install-ment, making the stories "affordable." The material wasn't delivered through the post or the Internet but directly by newsdealers.

Whether this was the inspiration for either the "part-work" of "fascicle" business[11] is unknown, but many of the same economic factors drive continuity selling.

Probably the most prominent form of continuity selling has been in the information and recording (music and video or CD) cat-egories. Housewares and "collectibles" have also used the system with great success. When the series is completed, the customer has the "full" work, whether it is a complete set of dishes on a multivolume encyclopedia.[12]

The formats and the offers vary widely, but the key characteristics are these:

▶ The promotion offers a "series" type product delivered on a regular basis (normally monthly) for a specific period of time (until the series is completed) or open-ended with no defined completion.

▶ The customer normally receives an incentive to start "collecting" the series, often the first item in the series free or at a substantial discount.

▶ The customer commits either to:

- Purchase and pay for a specified minimum number of the units in the series or,

- Simply examine each shipment for "N" days with no obligation to purchase and the right to return individual items and/or cancel at any time.

▶ Where the series is finite, after a certain time has passed and a good purchase and payment record been established, the customer is often offered a "Load-Up," the opportunity to purchase and receive all the units to complete his set or collection in a single shipment, either:

- For a substantially discounted single payment (sometimes allowed in installments) or,

- On the same monthly payment terms until the series is finally paid up.

The template in Exhibit 5-7 assumes the sale of a limited edition collectible series of commemorative plates with a maximum of 30 plates in the series. On the left-hand side are all the required inputs, on the right hand the derived results.

As we can see, we need to know all our revenue sources and costs. For example, in addition to the prices we are going to charge for the first and subsequent units, we also need to input any

Exhibit 5-7 Continuity Selling and Load-Ups

CONTINUITY SELLING

Product Description: Commemorative Plate Series

Input:

	%	Items
No. of Units in Series (or assumed maximum number of units)		30
Price of First Unit		29.90
Charge for Postage/Shipping		4.00
Price of Subsequent Units		34.90
Charge for Postage/Shipping		5.00
Anticipated Number of Purchases Discounted for Attrition		12.20
First Unit Product Cost including Packing & Any Royalties or Licenses		6.27
Subsequent Unit Product Cost including Packing & Any Royalties or Licenses		6.65
First Unit Fulfillment including Shipping		5.61
Subsequent Unit Fulfillment including Shipping		4.65
First Unit Payment Option Costs		0.82
Subsequent Unit Payment Option Costs		0.94
Costs of Premiums & Points		11.20
Anticipated % of Returns from Customers	1.50%	
Anticipated % of Bad Pay	1.00%	
Desired Contribution or Profit	20.00%	
Average Media Cost Per '000		1,000.00
Estimated % Response to Promotion	1.00%	

Revenue:

	Currency Amount
Product Sales Over Period	420.78
Less:	
Postage & Distribution Charge Back	60.00
Net Revenue Over Period	480.78

Costs:

	Currency Amount
Production of Product (Include Packing)	80.73
Fulfillment (Include Shipping)	57.69
Costs of Premiums & Points	11.20
Payment Option Costs	11.35
Anticipated Returns	7.21
Anticipated Bad Pay	4.81
Desired Contribution or Profit	96.16
TOTAL Costs Before Promotion	269.15

	Currency Amount
Margin Per Customer	211.63
Allowable Marketing Cost Per Continuity Buyer	211.63
No. Orders Per '000 necessary to Breakeven Before Contribution & Profit	4.73
% Response necessary to Achieve Breakeven Before Contribution & Profit	0.47%
Estimated Profit (Include Contribution & Profit Provision)	207.73

additional charges we plan to make for postage and distribution because these will increase the total revenue. The actual cost of this distribution will be picked up in the "costs" section and added to total fulfillment. Because some marketers charge more (or less) postage and distribution than the actual cost, the inputs have been designed to cater for this possible difference.

Calculating the estimated "attrition" is a complicated but necessary task. A detailed discussion of attrition and calculatng its effect is given in connection with Exhibit 3-8. Using the attrition model for this example, we can calculate that the average sale will be the first plate (free) plus 11.2 additional plates for a total of 12.2.

A word should be said here about bad pay, people who take the product and do not pay for it. One aspect of continuity selling is that the marketer has excellent control over whether or not to ship any item in the continuity sequence. Thus, if there is a delay in the receipt of payment, he can delay the next shipment or stop shipping altogether. How much leeway he is prepared to give—shipments made before payment is received—depends upon his policies, and it would be normal to continue shipping to a customer who has paid regularly in the past, even if recent payments have been slow. However, remember that the amount of bad pay in continuities can be "controlled," and therefore the percentage of total revenue related to bad pay is or should be relatively low.

When all the inputs have been completed, we see a useful overview of the project, which provides critical strategic planning information as a baseline for doing "what if" sensitivities:

▶ Margin Per Customer

▶ Allowable Marketing Cost Per Continuity Buyer

▶ No. Orders Per '000 Necessary to Breakeven before Contribution & Profit

▶ Percentage Response Necessary to Achieve Breakeven before Contribution & Profit

▶ Estimated Profit (Including Contribution & Profit Provision)

Now the sensitivities are easy. What would happen if you changed the pricing or incentives? If the media cost per thousand is higher or lower, how will this difference impact the strategies? Calculating these is simply a matter of changing the inputs to reflect the sensitivities and then deciding on the best combinations to test.

Careful and thorough planning of the entire process becomes increasingly necessary as the forms of the marketing become more complex. If there is to be accountability when you analyze your campaign results at the end of the process, the template model will provide the benchmark for the analysis.

Enhancing Continuity Selling with Load-Ups

As noted above, one of the ways continuity marketers enhance their total profits and reduce (or eliminate attrition) is through the process called "Load-Ups." This enables the purchaser to commit to receive the whole series either in a single shipment or through regular periodic shipments at a highly beneficial price. The Load-Up is almost always offered after the customer has already demonstrated his desire to build his collection and has made and paid for a number of purchases. Choosing the right moment to offer the Load-Up is important and marketers almost always try and make the Load-Up offer *before* attrition eats too deeply into total sales.

Exhibit 5-10, the extension of Exhibit 5-8 ("Calculating Load-Ups") allows the user to project the effect of the anticipated Load-Up program and to determine the most appropriate pricing. This template requires some further explanation.

As can be seen in Exhibit 5-8, the point of departure is the number of units in the total series. This is derived from referencing the appropriate cell in "Continuity Selling" (Exhibit 5-7) or simply by inputting a new number.[13] Next is the need to define at what point in the series ("Number of Shipments before Load-Up") the Load-Up promotion will take place. This will determine the number of units

Exhibit 5-8 Calculating Load-Ups

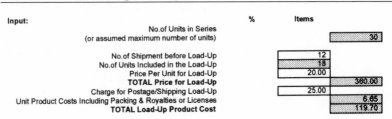

Input:	%	Items
No.of Units in Series (or assumed maximum number of units)		30
No.of Shipment before Load-Up		12
No.of Units Included in the Load-Up		18
Price Per Unit for Load-Up		20.00
TOTAL Price for Load-Up		360.00
Charge for Postage/Shipping Load-Up		25.00
Unit Product Costs Including Packing & Royalties or Licenses		6.65
TOTAL Load-Up Product Cost		119.70

Exhibit 5-9 Sample Estimated % Response to Load-Up Promotion

Load-Up Fulfillment Costs	35.00
Load-Up Payment Option Costs	25.00
Costs for Any Additional Incentives	-
Anticipated % of Returns from Customers	5.00%
Anticipated % of Bad Pay	10.00%
Desired Contribution or Profit	20.00%
Load-Up Average Media Cost Per '000	1,000.00
Estimated % Response to Load-Up Promotion	15.00%

included in the Load-Up, in this case 18, the number of units left after the first 12 to make the original total of 30.[14] Estimate of the percentage of response then follows (Exhibit 5-9).

As the pricing for each unit in the Load-Up is almost always considerably lower than the individual units sold on the normal continuity basis, the next step is to address this issue. The original pricing used in the example was 29.90 plus 4.00 packing and shipping for the first unit and 34.90 plus 5.00 packing and shipping for subsequent units. For the Load-Up, the assumed pricing would be 20.00 for each unit, and there would be a total distribution charge of 25.00 for the whole shipment. The "Total Price for Load-Up" has been derived as a multiple of the 18 units times 20.00 each. Should the user wish to modify this and chose an arbitrary total amount, it can simply be input in the "Total Price for Load-Up" box.

Developing the total Load-Up cost model is a relatively simple matter of copying the initial inputs from the Continuity Selling template or using new data. Since the fulfillment will have different parameters for the Load-Up and the percentage of returns and bad pay may rise reflecting the larger amounts involved, these percentages need to be estimated and entered, as does the desired Contribution or Profit percentage.

Finally we need to calculate the promotion cost of achieving the Load-Up. Just as we calculated this for the initial continuity sale, we need to know the cost per thousand of the load-up promotion and the expected percent response of purchasers accepting the offer. This is a key driver and the likelihood is that this response percentage should be significant because the only people to whom the promotion will be made are people who are already serious collectors of the series. How high this percentage should be will be a product of both the richness of the offer and the quality of the promotion. Previous experience and history must inform the assumption.

From a strategic point of view, what we want to determine is whether it makes economic sense to offer a Load-Up rather than continue the normal continuity sequence.[15] The issue is: How many additional normal shipments would be necessary to achieve the same economic results as the Load-Up?

Getting to that result demands that we first revisit the revenues and costs associated with the sales before the Load-Up. While driven in the continuity model by the rate of attrition, since the Load-Up will only be offered to purchasers who are still receiving their regular shipments, attrition no longer applies and the revenue and cost figures have been recast in the template to reflect this.

What we find in this example (Exhibit 5–10) is that to achieve the same level of profit as the Load-Up, the number of non-Load-Up sales would have to increase from the originally contemplated 12.2 to 14.6. That's a big jump or put another way, that is a big reduction in attrition.

Those drivers that will have the most significant impact on the total are:

▶ The number of units in the Load-Up.

▶ The price for the Load-Up.

▶ The estimated percentage response.

To review this we need only change the inputs.

For example, if we assume that we can charge more than 20.00 each for the plates in the Load-Up—say 25.00 each—the number of normal shipments to achieve the same profit would rise from 14.61 to 19.10. If the Load-Up using the 20.00 price came later than after shipment 12—say after shipment 15—the marketer would have to have shipped 15.29 units to have the same profit. Using the original figures (with a price of 20.00 each) but reducing the percentage response from 15 percent to 5 percent, the number of shipments to achieve the initial profit would fall to 13.82.

Continuity selling sounds more complex than it is. With the right product and good fulfillment and delivery systems, it can be a highly effective system for delivering a "series" product over a reasonable time period at costs to the consumer that make it less economically burdensome than having to pay for everything at once.

Exhibit 5-10 Calculating Load-Ups

Input:

	Items	%	Revenue:	Currency Amount
No. of Units in Series (or assumed maximum number of units)	30			
			Revenue from Sales before Load-Up	472.80
			All Costs of Sales before Load-Up	364.92
			Margin Before Load-Up	107.88
No. of Shipment before Load-Up	12			
No. of Units Included in the Load-Up	18			
Price Per Unit for Load-Up	20.00		**TOTAL Load-Up Revenue**	385.00
TOTAL Price for Load-Up	360.00		**Less:**	
			TOTAL Load-Up Costs	314.45
Charge for Postage/Shipping Load-Up	6.65			
Unit Product Costs Including Packing & Royalties or Licenses	25.00			
TOTAL Load-Up Product Cost	119.70		Load-Up Margin Before Load-Up Promotion Cost	70.55
			Cost of Promotion Per Load-Up	6.67
Load-Up Fulfillment Costs	35.00			
Load-Up Payment Option Costs	25.00		**Net Margin from Load-Up**	63.88
Costs for Any Additional Incentives	-		**TOTAL Margin from Normal Sale and Load-Up**	171.76
			TOTAL Profit	248.76
Anticipated % of Returns from Customers		5.00%	(Including Contribution & Profit Provision)	
Anticipated % of Bad Pay		10.00%		
Desired Contribution or Profit		20.00%	**Number of Non Load-Up Sales**	
			Necessary to Achieve the Same Profit	14.61
Load-Up Average Media Cost Per '000	1,000.00			
Estimated % Response to Load-Up Promotion		15.00%		

Club Selling

Recent years have seen a major change in the "Club" playing field with the advent of Amazon.com and other similar companies. These Internet entrepreneurs compete directly against the commitment demanded by clubs by offering competitive prices without any need for "joining." Just go to the site, search, and purchase. And for the hesitant who welcomed the clubs' choice of books or records as a cultural guide and one of the reasons for membership, Amazon and its competitors provides recommendations and reviews that serve the same purpose.

Amazon and Groucho Marx notwithstanding, "Clubs" continue to have substantial appeal to certain customer segments and for certain types of products ranging from books and records to fruit, flowers and even beef. They serve the purpose of providing the customer with a regular product selection at preferential prices and normally give him the opportunity to:

▶ Receive the selection and/or other products on offer.

▶ Reject the selection and chose other products on offer.

▶ Reject all the offerings.

Most clubs operate on a *negative option basis*—sending a notice of the "selection"[16] choice and other offerings in advance of the shipment and *shipping and billing for the selection if no instruction is received from the customer before a certain specified date.*

Membership terms vary depending upon the nature of the club. However, there is usually:

▶ An *extensive front-end offer* of premium product at a low introductory price.

▶ A commitment on the part of the member to purchase a minimum number of products during a certain period of time.[17]

While the economic parameters resemble those of the continuity selling system, there are significant differences. Principal among these is the cost of the regular "cycle" promotions and a substantial fulfillment cost of handling the various options given to the customer. Because of the number of variable club options, economic planning is extremely complicated.

In developing a template for Club Memberships, we need to know:

▶ The *unit price of the premium product* which may be charged for or may be given away free as an incentive for membership. For example, if the best offer is three units for only 9.95 the club only receives 9.95 while the actual cost may be much higher.

▶ Any *distribution or postage charge-backs* for this first shipment.

▶ The *estimated average order value* per purchase per cycle for subsequent shipments. Since members may purchase more than a single product and since products often carry variable prices, this needs careful consideration.

▶ The *number of units purchased* in each cycle. This is necessary to accurately drive the revenue and cost equations.

▶ Any *distribution or postage charge-backs* for these further shipments.

▶ The *"bonus" offers*: Some clubs give a free unit for say, every four purchases after the first one. These must be calculated in the costs.

▶ The *number of cycles per year that will be offered* and *the maximum number of years the member may stay* with the club.[18]

▶ The *average cycle promotion cost* per member.

▶ The *percentage of members purchasing* in each cycle.

▶ The *percentage of product shipped and returned* per cycle.

▶ The *percentage of bad pay*.

▶ The *likely attrition* after each cycle.

▶ The *desired percentage Contribution or Profit*.

Exhibit 5-11 contemplates negative option clubs whose members were recruited with an offer of 3 units for 9.95 and who receive a monthly cycle promotion. Forty percent of the members purchase each month. The average order value for each purchase is 36.50, which represents 1.3 units of product. Members receive a bonus of one unit free for every four paid purchases.

On the basis of this analysis, the club looks to be a profitable proposition delivering a profit as a percentage of total revenue of 29.35 percent. But the question is always what happens if the response percentage is below the estimate or perhaps even more importantly, the average order value is below the estimate.

Using the template, we can calculate these and other sensitivities. For example, if the average order value drops from 36.50 to 30.00 then the profit comes down from 72.27 to 37.07 or 17.76 percent, still marginally above the 15 percent set as the management expectation.

If the average order value stays at its initial level of 36.50, but the actual response percentage drops from 2.0 percent to 1.0 percent, then the total profit drops to 22.27 or only 9 percent. For each increase in the number of cycles per member (a reflection of lower attrition), the profit goes up 8.79 or 1.54 percent.

Planning the economics for clubs is a detailed business and requires developing a broad range of sensitivities and then making adjustments so as to maximize efficiencies and profits. Without a model, understanding the interplay of the variables would be almost impossible.

The very nature of the template is that it is something of an oversimplification and while a useful tool to summarize the data, it does not demand the amount of detail that would be preferable to fully understand the economic workings of the club structure and specific club initiatives.

Take, for example, the fulfillment and distribution costs.[19] The template input asks for total costs for the area, but these assume that every aspect of the fulfillment and distribution costs have been measured. Just what it takes to measure them can be seen on the accompanying screen from the ACPO model (Exhibit 5-14). When planning have we considered such important issues as the "real" cost of incoming telephone orders where some of the calls do not

Exhibit 5-11 Clubs

Key Inputs

General:

Number of Premium Units given as Membership Incentive	3
Number of Promotion Cycles Per Year	12
Maximum Number of Years	3.00
% of Total Members Purchasing in Each Cycle	40.00%
Average Number of Units in Purchase in Each Cycle	1.30
Average Number of Cycles Per Member Before Cancellation	15.40
Number of Bonus Units Per Member Per Purchase Unit	0.25

Revenue:

First Unit Price	9.95
Distribution or Postage Charge-back - First Unit	3.00
Average Order Value Per Purchase Per Cycle	36.50
Distribution or Postage Charge-back - Subsequent Units	4.00

Costs:

First Unit Product Cost (Inc. Royalties, if any)	3.20
Subsequent Unit Product Cost (Inc. Royalties, if any)	4.60
Fulfillment & Distribution Cost of Initial Shipment	6.40
Fulfillment & Distribution Cost of Subsequent Shipments	4.60
Cycle Promotion Cost Per Member	1.60
% of Returns of Product Shipped Per Cycle	4.00%
% Bad Pay	2.00%
Contribution or Profit Expectation	15.00%

Promotion:

Estimated Cost Per '000 for Media	1,000.00
Estimated % Response	2.00%

Estimated Life Time Revenue Per Member:

Initial Purchase & Postage/Dist.Charge-back	12.95
Subsequent Purchases & Postage/Dist.Charge-back	233.26
TOTAL Revenue	246.23

Estimated Membership Cost Per Member:

First Unit Product Cost (Inc. Royalties, if any)	9.60
Subsequent Unit Product Costs	34.44
Fulfillment & Distribution Costs	32.90
Cycle Promotion Cost Per Member	23.04
Returns Costs Per Member	9.85
Bonus Units Cost	9.21
Bad Pay Per Member	4.92
Contribution or Profit Expectation Per Member	36.93
TOTAL Costs	160.90

Net Margin Per Member Before Promotion	85.33
No. of Members Per '000 Necessary to Breakeven	11.72
% Response Necessary to Breakeven	1.17%

Estimated Promotion Cost Per Member	50.00
TOTAL Profit Per Member	72.27
with Contribution & Profit Add-back	
TOTAL Profit as a % of TOTAL Revenue	29.35%

Exhibit 5-12 Total Profits as a Percent of Revenue

Net Margin Per Member Before Promotion	85.33
No.of Members Per '000 Necessary to Breakeven	11.72
% Response Necessary to Breakeven	1.17%
Estimated Promotion Cost Per Member	50.00
TOTAL Profit Per Member with Contribution & Profit Add-back	72.27
TOTAL Profit as a % of TOTAL Revenue	29.35%

result in sales, but whose costs must be considered in the total fulfillment expense? Underestimating the fulfillment can have a devastating effect on the total profitability and on the strategic decisions arising from an examination of the options.

Despite the difficulties, club structures for certain products are often best for the customer and for the marketer. While it could be assumed that the appeal of clubs would be primarily to people who lived at substantial distance from retail outlets, the reality is that many members live in large metropolitan areas and feel well served by the mechanisms of club distribution.

Exhibit 5-13 Total Profits as a Percent of Revenue

Net Margin Per Member Before Promotion	88.33
Number of Members Per '000 Necessary to Breakeven	11.72
% Response Necessary to Breakeven	1.17%
Estimated Promotion Cost Per Member	100.00
TOTAL Profit Per Member with Contribution & Profit Add-back	22.27
TOTAL Profit as a % of TOTAL Revenue	9.04%

Catalogs: The 24/7 Store in the Home

When we go to the mall or shopping center or just wander down a shop-lined street, we often have no specific purchases in mind. But when something attracts us, we take a look, possibly try it on and often end up with a shopping bag under our arm. Even if there may still be truth in the old adage that "Christmas is the time women stop shopping and start buying things," the catalog and/or the Internet are home shopping opportunities enjoyed and used by both sexes. The ubiquity of what the British call "wish books" is profound.

The catalog differs from the retail model only to the degree that the catalog is in the home on a 24/7 basis and catalogers, knowing the details of past purchases and having names and addresses of their customers are able to precisely target them and offer appropriate merchandise on a timely basis. Perhaps that's why 2002 US catalog sales amounted to $126 billion, approximately 4 percent of the

Exhibit 5-14 Fulfillment and Distribution

INITIAL FULFILLMENT COSTS	Estimated %	$ Per Unit	% Who Purchase
Incoming Order Postage	30%	1.00	100%
Incoming Order Telephone	50%	2.00	85%
Incoming Order Fax	20%	0.80	100%
Incoming Order Internet			
Incoming Order Email			
Incoming Order Other			
Weighted Incoming Order Cost		1.46	
Non-Conversion Cost		0.18	
Order Handling		1.00	
Data Enty		0.41	
Welcome letter			
TOTAL INITIAL FULFILLMENT		3.05	

INITIAL FULFILLMENT COSTS		$ Per Unit	
Picking & Packing		0.40	
Dispatch Document Preparation		0.70	
Invoice Preparation		0.25	
Postage or Other Delivery Costs		2.00	
Other Distribution Costs			
TOTAL INITIAL DISTRIBUTION		3.35	

SUBSEQUENT FULFILLMENT COSTS	Estimated %	$ Per UNIT
Incoming Order Postage	50%	1.00
Incoming Order Telephone		
Incoming Order Fax	50%	0.80
Incoming Order Internet		
Incoming Order Email		
Incoming Order Other		
Weighted Incoming Order Cost		0.90
Order Handling		
Data Entry		
TOTAL SUBSEQUENT FUFILLMENT		.90

SUBSEQUENT DISTRIBTION COSTS		$ Per UNIT
Picking & Packing		0.95
Dispatch Document Preparation		0.50
Invoice Preparation		0.25
Postage or Other Delivery Costs		2.00
Other Distribution Costs		
TOTAL SUBSEQUENT DISTRIBUTION		3.70

Exhibit 5-15 Catalog Sales

Market	1997	2001	2002	2003	2007	97–02
Total	$76.849	$118.195	$125.720	$134.392	$169.400	10.3%
B-to-B	$29.711	$45.620	$48.511	$52.134	$66.678	10.3%
Consumer	$47.138	$72.575	$77.209	$82.258	$102.722	10.4%

$3.2 trillion in total US retail spending. Figures from the US Direct Marketing Association (in billions of US$) demonstrate the importance of the catalog market (Exhibit 5-15).

Along with magazine subscription marketers, catalogers are the most sophisticated segment of the direct marketing community. Each company has models and methods to maximize its catalog sales and, like good retailers who measure the value of every square foot or meter of shelf space, make each part of each catalog page work as hard as possible. In fact, the driving forces for all catalogers are:

▶ The value of each catalog page (and part of each page).

▶ The product range and average margin.[20]

▶ The value of each catalog customer expressed as the average order value.

▶ The LTV value of each catalog customer.

▶ The cost of acquiring the customer.

Rarely do catalogers make a sufficient margin on the first sale to a new customer to recoup the cost of acquisition.[21] A recent US DMA study reported that catalogers' in-house customer files produced response rates of 4.08 percent compared with 1.62 percent for catalog mailings to prospects. Jack Schmid, a leading American expert in catalog marketing, has written: "It usually takes a new catalog three years to break even and about five years to recapture its initial investment."[22] Because he is referring to *new catalogs*, not *new catalog customers*, this doesn't mean that each new customer is a loss for three to five years. But they are seldom profitable right away.

Establishing the Right Balance Between Catalog Customers and Prospects

The established cataloger has a competitive advantage on the new entrant because he can balance his new customer acquisition cost deficit with his profitable sales to existing customers and grow his business accordingly. Or if he doesn't wish to invest in new customers at any given time, he can promote only to his known good customers with the reasonable assurance that he can make a profit on that investment. In fact, good catalogers carefully concentrate their marketing efforts on various customer segments to enhance their overall profits.

Calling attention to the fact that "all customers are not created equal," Schmid counsels the building of a simple segmentation system to prioritize purchasers and to study " . . . what customers buy, how they respond (phone/fax/mail/email), how they pay (check/cash/credit card/purchase order), and how and why they return merchandise. . . . " He sums it up with this sage advice, "when you discover your best customers, mail them more often, and treat them like good friends."[23]

There are two key variables in catalog marketing that drive profitability:

1. The percentage response from each catalog.

2. The average order value.

As we have seen, a substantially greater percentage of former customers purchase from each catalog than first-time purchasers. Handled properly, the new customer's value increases over time both in *the percentage of times he purchases* and in *his average order value.* Thus, successful catalogers make a substantial effort to enhance the order values of new customers both to recoup their initial acquisition costs and to enhance the total profits. And they do this by careful collection and use of data about the *source*[24] of the catalog customer and his first purchase.

Like retailers, the cataloger want as many people to visit his "store" as possible and to buy as much as possible on each visit. To stimulate this, they use the same sales promotion tools, discounts, incentives, etc., to push that order value upwards.

Exhibit 5-16 (Catalogs) looks at a theoretical 48-page catalog being distributed to one thousand people, 70 percent existing customers and 30 percent new prospects. The catalog has 200 items (SKUs) and a weighted average selling price per item of 60.00. The

Exhibit 5-16 Catalogs

Key Input Data

Per '000 Catalogs

Number of Pages in Catalog	48
Number of Catalog Items (Including all SKUs)	200
Weighted Average Selling Price Per Item	60.00
Weighted Average % Margin Cost Per '000 of Catalogs (Including Distribution)	70.00%
Average Order Value Per Existing Customer	2,000.00
Average Order Value Per New Customer	200.00 / 50.00
Average % Response Per Existing Customer	4.00%
Average % Response Per New Customer	1.60%
% of Existing Customers	70.00%
% of New Customers	30.00%

Existing Customers Revenue	5,600.00
Product Margin	3,920.00
Less:	
Non-Product Costs	990.00
Catalog Cost	1,400.00
Existing Customers Net Margin	1,540.00 / 27.50%
New Customers Revenue	240.00
Product Margin	168.00
Less:	
Non-Product Costs	42.00
Catalog Cost	600.00
New Customers Net Margin	(474.00) / -197.50%
TOTAL Profit (Loss)	1,066.00 / 18.25%
Catalog Revenue Value Per Page	121.67
Net Acquisition Cost Per New Customer	98.75

Non-Product Costs

Taxes included in Price	2.50%
Fulfillment (inc. Credit Card charges)	5.00%
Bad Pay at	2.00%
Returns at	5.00%
Premiums	2.00%
Misc.	1.00%
TOTAL Non-Product Costs	17.50%

Calculating Incremental Values

Number of Catalogs to Reach Existing Customer Order Value: 5

	Initial Order Value	Second Order Value	Third Order Value	Fourth Order Value	Fifth Order Value	Sixth Order Value
Incremental Value of Changing New Customer Purchases	50.00	87.50	125.00	162.50	200.00	200.00
% Response	1.60%	2.20%	2.80%	3.40%	4.00%	4.00%
Incremental Value of Changing % of New Customer Purchases						
% Response	1.60%	2.20%	2.80%	3.40%	4.00%	4.00%
Profit Contribution	(474.00)	(296.81)	(48.75)	270.19	660.00	660.00
Number of New Customers	4.8	4.8	4.8	4.8	4.8	4.8
Profit Contribution Per New Customer	(98.75)	(61.83)	(10.16)	56.29	137.50	137.50
Cumulative Profit Contribution Per New Customer	(98.75)	(160.59)	(170.73)	(114.45)	23.06	160.56

average percentage margin (revenue less the cost of the product) is 70 percent, and the per-thousand cost of printing and distributing the catalog is 2,000 or 2.00 per person.[25]

The average order value from existing customers is 200.00; 4 percent of them purchase while only 1.6 percent of the prospects to whom the catalog is distributed become first-time purchasers, (*New* Customers). Their average order value is only one-quarter of the regular customers, 50.00.

Not surprisingly, looking at the data on the right-hand side of the model, we find that the regular customers produce a significant profit (27.5 percent) while the new customers show a significant loss of 197.5 percent on revenues.[26] This is stated as the "Net Acquisition Cost per New Customer" and amounts to 98.75 for each of the 16 new customers.

The question that arises is: If it is true that these new customers will increase their percentage of purchase and average order values for future catalogs, how long will it take for them to become profitable and the acquisition cost to be recouped?[27]

Exhibit 5-17 is a section of Exhibit 5-16 (the total Catalog template) and can be used to help calculate the incremental values.

Starting from the data derived in the early sections of the template and allowing the user to define the increments he wants to review, the template can be used to calculate the profit contribution for the group of new customers or, more importantly, for each one.

In the example, with an incremental increase in average order value of 50 percent with each new catalog and an increased percentage of purchase of 25 percent, the new customer becomes profitable on the fourth catalog and, with care, should stay that way. How many catalogs per year are sent to which customer depends upon the particular marketer. Too few will likely have as negative an effect as too many.[28] The question is similar to another that is raised at many direct marketing meetings: How often should a marketer mail to a given list before "list fatigue" sets in? The answer (derived after millions of dollars of expenditure over many years by a variety of marketers) is that while frequent mailings to the same list reduce response, as long as using the list is profitable, it's best to keep mailing.

Each catalog has its own unique economics. And like all direct

Exhibit 5-17 Calculating Incremental Values

Calculating Incremental Values

Number of Catalogs to Reach
Existing Customer Order Value: 5

	Initial Order Value	Second Order Value	Third Order Value	Fourth Order Value	Fifth Order Value	Sixth Order Value
Incremental Value of Changing New Customer Purchases	60.00	87.50	125.00	162.50	200.00	200.00
	% Response	% Response	% Response	% Response	% Response	% Response
Incremental Value of Changing % of New Customer Purchases	1.66%	2.26%	2.86%	3.46%	4.06%	4.06%
Profit Contribution	(474.00)	(296.11)	(48.75)	270.19	550.00	550.00
Number of New Customers	4.8	4.8	4.8	4.8	4.8	4.8
Profit Contribution Per New Customer	(98.75)	(61.2)	(10.16)	56.29	137.50	137.50
Cumulative Profit Contribution Per New Customer	(98.75)	(161.19)	(170.4)	(114.45)	23.04	160.54

marketing forms each is accountable. With no need for commitment, a catalog makes an excellent place to shop for many customers and "wishes" often turn into purchases.

Selling by Subscription

Subscriptions are another form of commitment that has become the backbone of the magazine business in many countries where adequate delivery and payment systems exist,[29] and they serve many other products and services as well. For the consumer, subscriptions are a form of convenience providing regular delivery. For publishers, knowing the foundation circulation in advance, receiving prepayment and not having to aggressively market at the retail level all have significant benefits.

To properly plan subscription selling, it is helpful to keep in mind that there is frequently a series of steps (Exhibit 5-18) in the subscription sequence. It normally moves from a "trial" or "introductory" offer through conversion to a regular subscription offered with various term and price options. Each of these leads to first and then subsequent renewals.

The profitability of subscriptions seldom comes prior to the first renewal and sometimes much later. What we can afford to spend to acquire a subscription is the sum of the amounts we spend for mar-

Exhibit 5-18 Steps in Subscription Sequencing

STEP 1: TRIAL OR INTRODUCTORY OFFER

STEP 2: CONVERSION FROM TRIAL TO
REGULAR SUBSCRIPTION

STEP 3: SUBSCRIPTION OPTIONS

STEP 4: FIRST RENEWAL OF SUBSCRIPTION

STEP 5: REGULAR RENEWAL OF SUBSCRIPTION

keting at each step. Therefore, managing the economics of each of the steps in the sequence is essential, and judgements are required at critical points in the sequence if the subscriptions are to deliver the maximum return on the promotional investment.

The work begins with the construction of the "trial" offers. These are almost always "loss-leaders"—promotion-driven offers made at an economic loss to the marketer and intended to make it easy for the potential subscriber to try the proposition before making a significant commitment. It's rather like a test drive for a new car: You wouldn't want to buy it before you have driven it.

We need to start from the normal magazine subscription.[30] Let's assume:

▶ A monthly publication with an annual subscription price of 60.00 (5.00 per copy). This is also offered for different time periods:

- Six months for 40.00 (3.75 per copy).[31]

- Twenty-four months for 80.00 (2.22 per copy).

▶ Trial Offer

- Four issues for 7.50

- Conversion (to one of the above subscription options) is assumed to be 45 percent.

- Average cost of conversion promotion is 4.00, an average of 1.8 efforts at 1.00 each, adjusted for the trial subscribers who do not convert.

▶ General Inputs

- The desired contribution and/or profit is 15 percent.

- The estimated bad debt is 2 percent. Four additional issues are sent before a cut-off of shipping is instituted if payment is not received.

▶ Renewals

- The renewal price is 60.00 per year. This may rise with inflation or other factors but that has not been considered for the purpose of the model.

- The assumption is that there will be an annual renewal program (four mailings offering renewal at .80 each) for each of the years after the trial. A value of 2.3 renewal efforts per year reflects the average after factoring subscribers who renew on the first, second and third efforts. The publisher will seek to get subscribers to allow automatic renewals on a negative option basis thus saving renewal costs but for the sake of being conservative, renewal costs are assumed as necessary for all subscribers.

- Attrition each *year* is assumed to be 20 percent after the first year and 10 percent for each of the next three years. Thus, the average number of years (including the first) will be 3.8. (The "Attrition" template can be used to help calculate this number.)

▶ Costs

- The product cost of each magazine is estimated to be 1.00. If using the subscription mechanism for another service (i.e. an Association) the annual cost of providing the service should be divided by 12 months and the result entered as the "product cost".

- Additionally, there is a royalty payable for externally sourced content of .07 for each issue of the magazine.

- The fulfillment and distribution costs are made up of a number of elements combined together in a fulfillment model similar to the one shown in Chapter 3, Exhibit 3-13.

- There is a planned incentive promotion that will cost 20,000, and this amount must be spread over the estimated number of new subscribers, in the case of this example, 5,000.

Using the template (Exhibit 5-19) as a basic tool, we can evaluate various offers and their impact on the ultimate "Margin for Acquisition" (ACPO). In this example, the "Margin for Acquisition" is 78.10 if the publisher hopes to make a 15 percent Profit or Contribution of

Exhibit 5-19 Subscriptions

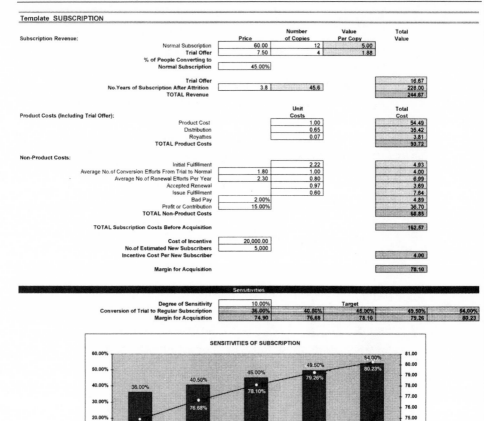

Template SUBSCRIPTION

Subscription Revenue:		Price	Number of Copies	Value Per Copy	Total Value
	Normal Subscription	60.00	12	5.00	
	Trial Offer	7.50	4	1.88	
	% of People Converting to Normal Subscription	45.00%			
	Trial Offer				16.67
	No.Years of Subscription After Attrition	3.8	45.6		228.00
	TOTAL Revenue				244.67

Product Costs (Including Trial Offer):			Unit Costs		Total Cost
	Product Cost		1.00		54.49
	Distribution		0.65		35.42
	Royalties		0.07		3.81
	TOTAL Product Costs				93.72

Non-Product Costs:					
	Initial Fulfillment		2.22		4.93
Average No.of Conversion Efforts From Trial to Normal		1.80	1.00		4.00
Average No of Renewal Efforts Per Year		2.30	0.80		6.99
	Accepted Renewal		0.97		3.69
	Issue Fulfillment		0.60		7.64
	Bad Pay	2.00%			4.89
	Profit or Contribution	15.00%			36.70
	TOTAL Non-Product Costs				68.85

TOTAL Subscription Costs Before Acquisition					162.57
	Cost of Incentive	20,000.00			
	No.of Estimated New Subscribers	5,000			
	Incentive Cost Per New Subscriber				4.00
	Margin for Acquisition				78.10

Sensitivities					
Degree of Sensitivity	10.00%			Target	
Conversion of Trial to Regular Subscription	36.00%	40.50%	45.00%	49.50%	54.00%
Margin for Acquisition	74.90	76.68	78.10	79.26	80.23

SENSITIVITIES OF SUBSCRIPTION

- Conversion of Trial to Regular Subscription
- Margin for Acquisition

36.70. Any lower percentage he is willing to take–and he still has his advertising revenue to add profit and contribution—adds to the acquisition margin, although publishers do not like to factor in advertising revenue with circulation revenue. Also, as the percentage of people "converting" to full subscriptions and the "No. of Years of Subscription after Attrition" change, the impact on the "Margin for Acquisition" (ACPO) changes accordingly.

The sensitivities indicate that even with a conversion percentage as low as 36 percent, there would be a 74.90 margin for acquisition to achieve the desired 15 percent profit or contribution.

Following the steps in the subscription process, the user of the subscription form of distribution will find many opportunities to enhance his marketing efforts and to change the economics accordingly.

Handling One-Time Creative and Start-Up Costs

This raises an important issue that applies to all product and service promotional planning.

The front-end creative and associated costs can be extremely heavy. If these costs are entirely loaded against the test results, the actual cost per order for the test will almost always far exceed the allowable. On this basis, marketers would never get beyond the initial planning stage.

The assumption must be that these initial costs will be amortized against the total marketing program *rather than letting them influence the reading of the test results.* Included into the test results these costs create a dangerous distortion. If the test is a failure and the work cannot be used again, then it obviously deserves to be written-off. But the *costs loaded on the reading of the test result must reflect costs as if the test were a rollout.*

The following template, Promotion Amortization (Exhibit 5-20) should put this into some prospective.

Here is a direct mail and media campaign. Those costs, which are fixed and should be amortized against the whole campaign, are defined in the boxed area. They have been amortized against the total mailing and circulation volumes to derive a Total "Mailing" or "Advertising or Insert" cost per thousand. For mailing the amortization per thousand is 90.91: for advertising or inserts it is 30.43. If all these "fixed" costs had been amortized only against the test quantities, the test mailing would have to carry 1,250.00 per thousand and media would have to carry 350.00 per thousand, both totally unacceptable amounts that would badly distort the test results.

Upselling and Cross-Selling

One of the aspects of all direct marketing is the ability to both upsell (persuade the customer to take a higher priced product or service

Exhibit 5-20 Promotion Amortization

Template PROMOTION AMORTIZATION

Media:

DIRECT MAIL

	Amortizable Cost Items	Available Quantity	Test Quantity	Rollout Quantity	Estimated Response Rate	Test Cost	Rollout Cost	Cost Per Order
Creative Costs of Mailing Package(s)	25,000.00							
Initial Production (plates, films, etc.) of Mailing Package(s)	9,000.00							
Agency Fees	10,000.00							
Other	6,000.00							
TOTAL	50,000.00							
List 'A'		200,000	20,000	180,000	2.00%	27,818	250,364	69.55
List 'B'		350,000	20,000	330,000	1.80%	27,818	459,000	77.27
List 'C'								
List 'D'								
List 'E'								
List 'F'								
List 'G'								
List 'H'								
TOTAL		550,000	40,000	510,000		55,636	709,364	

Mailing Package(s) Production Costs Per '000 including List, Addressing, Mailing, Postage etc. 1,300.00

Amortization Per'000 Against Total Expected Volume 90.91

TOTAL Mailing Cost Per'000 1,390.91

PRESS MEDIA

	Amortizable Cost Items	Available Quantity	Test Quantity	Rollout Quantity	Estimated Response Rate	Test Cost	Rollout Cost	Cost Per Order
Creative Costs of Ads and Inserts	25,000.00							
Initial Production (plates,films,etc.) of Ads and inserts								
Agency Fees	7,500.00							
Other	2,500.00							
TOTAL	35,000.00							
Publication 'A'		500,000	50,000	450,000	0.50%	21,622	194,596	86.49
Publication 'B'		650,000	50,000	600,000	0.65%	21,622	259,461	66.53
Publication 'C'								
Publication 'D'								
Publication 'E'								
Publication 'F'								
Publication 'G'								
Publication 'H'								
TOTAL		1,150,000	100,000	1,050,000		43,243	454,057	

Average Media Cost Per '000 including Cost of Inserts if Used 402.00

Amortization Per'000 Against Total Expected Volume 30.43

TOTAL Advertising or Insert Cost Per'000 432.43

than was first offered) or to cross-sell (sell an additional product or service) to the customer. The sequences for both "Up" and "Cross" selling are used by sophisticated marketers to add substantial value to their initial marketing investments.

As noted previously, the best prospect for a new sale is the person who has just purchased from you. Many marketers attract customers with relatively simple and low-cost products and then make concerted efforts either to migrate them upwards or at least sell them something else as well as the initial product or service. This has the effect of not only amortizing the customer acquisition costs over a longer lifetime base but also hopefully increasing revenue and profit.

It is instructive to examine the economics of the upsell and cross-sell sequences and explore how they impact total profitability.

Upselling: Moving the Customer Up the Value Ladder

A good example of an upsell is a customer has purchased a basic "term" insurance product and is then offered more coverage for an additional premium. Feeling comfortable with the coverage he does not have to be entirely re-sold and the percentage of people accepting the increased coverage (and the accompanying increased premium) reduces the selling cost to 25 percent of the original customer acquisition cost.

The key factors are developed in a matrix such as that shown in Exhibit 5-21, which provides the data to feed the Upsell Template in Exhibit 5-22. In this example, what we see is that the initial policy is nicely profitable, delivering a 65.85 percent profit when the 20 percent "Contribution or Profit" initially taken as a cost is written back into the final profit figure, even after a 200.00 cost to acquire the customer in the first place.

What we also see is that for an additional 50.00 in promotion cost per successfully up-sold policy, substantially more revenue is derived from the policy, bringing the total revenue from 1,302.00 to 1,595.00. The combined profit also rises substantially.

If we now revisit this model with a more aggressive front-end offer, we see the power of the upsell as part of a total strategy.

For the purpose of this sensitivity (see Exhibit 5-23), we will assume that the insurance coverage has been lowered to reflect the new premiums and the first month's "Trial" premium has been dra-

Exhibit 5-21 Key Factors in Upsell Matrix

ITEMS	INITIAL COVERAGE	ADDITIONAL UPSELL COVERAGE	COMMENTS
Coverage Amount for Term Policy	100,000	60,000	Total coverage value of policy after Upsell is 160,000.
Monthly Premium (After 1st Month)	120.00	50.00	First month premium for initial coverage is excluded as this is a "premium" month at low cost.
Number of months of coverage before attrition (After 1st Month)	23	10	Upsell takes place after month 10.
Number of months of coverage after attrition (After 1st Month)	20.9	8.5	Note: The likely attrition must be modeled and the result input in the model.
Contribution or Profit Objective	20.0%	20.0%	
Cost of Acquisition	200.00		
Cost of Acquiring Upsell		50.00	Assumes that Upsell will have relatively low selling cost compared to initial cost of acquisition.

matically reduced from 80.00 to 10.00 along with the subsequent month's premiums from 120.00 to 50.00.

This should have the effect of making the policy more attractive and affordable to a wider public and thereby generate a lower the acquisition cost.

The estimated cost of acquisition of the customer has therefore been reduced from 200.00 to 125.00.

The Net Revenue per policy before the upsell but after acquisition shows a profit of 453.00 before the write-back of the Contribution or Profit. After the write-back, the bottom line is 685.00.

The upsell campaign has not been changed from the original

Exhibit 5-22 Upsell

Revenue:	Monthly Up-Sell Amount	50.00
	Estimated No.Months of Relationship (Net of Attrition)	24
	Month Up-Sell Takes Affect	14
	No.Months of Business Before Up-Sell	10

	Without Up-Sell			Up-sell		
	Initial Value	Install-ments	Revenue	Additional Unit Value	Periods	Up-Sell Revenue
Revenue:						
First Payment	80.00		80.00	50.00		
Subsequent Payment	120.00	23	2,760.00		14	700.00
TOTAL Revenue			**2,840.00**			**700.00**
Less:	%			%		
Cost of Providing Product or Service	15.00%		426.00	15.00%		105.00
Contribution or Profit	20.00%		568.00	20.00%		140.00
Administration	10.00%		284.00	10.00%		70.00
Any Additional Cost			48.00			36.00
Any Additional Cost			12.00			6.00
TOTAL Costs for Providing Service			**1,338.00**			**357.00**
Less:						
Cost Per Order for Initial Sale	200.00					
Cost Per Order for Up-Sell				50.00		
Net Revenue Per Customer Before Upsell but After Acquisition			1,302.00			
Net Revenue from Upsell After Upsell Cost						293.00
Combined Net Revenue						1,595.00
Profit After Write-back of Contribution or Profit Cost			1,870.00	65.85%		433.00	61.86%
Combined Profit After Write-back of Contribution or Profit Cost						2,303.00	65.06%

model. It produced business at a promotional cost of 50.00 per up-sold policy and has the effect of doubling the monthly revenue albeit only for the last 14 months of the policy. This generates Net Revenue from the upsell effort of 293.00.

As can be seen in Exhibit 5-23, the combined Profit after the write-backs is now 60.11 percent of revenue, marginally less than the 65.06 percent (see Exhibit 5-21) for the original program but still extremely good business. And the lower price barrier to purchase should mean lots more policies.

Upselling is an established marketing technique for all products and services[32] where appropriate and permits considerable flexibility in initial offer construction as well as in economic planning. What's most important is that any sequence of upsell initiatives be carefully tested to validate all the variable assumptions, especially the actual cost of promotion to achieve the upsell. Also critical is that the upsell component has a healthy margin between the revenue produced and the costs of providing the service even if the initial sale does not.

Cross-Selling: Selling a Variety of Goods

Probably the most significant difference between upselling and cross-selling is that in the first, the customer already has bought the product or service and what you are selling is essentially more of the same. When you are cross-selling, while the customer has already bought some product or service from you, it is not likely to be more of the same[33] and therefore demands a different and often more expensive sales effort.

While the vendor and the customer have established a relationship, it doesn't automatically mean that the cross-sell product will be of interest. America Online's (AOL) purchase of Time Incorporated was intended to produce millions of customers for the ISP, through aggressive cross-selling. It didn't work out nearly as well as had been forecast.

Just read the "synergy" justification for many mergers where the customer bases of the merged companies were *assumed* to want the products offered by the other merger partner and look at the subsequent reality when it turns out they don't. Nonetheless, cross-selling is often highly successful for these simple reasons:

Exhibit 5-23 Upsell

Monthly Up-Sell Amount	50.00
Estimated No.Months of Relationship (Net of Attrition)	24
Month Up-Sell Takes Affect	14
No.Months of Business Before Up-Sell	10

Revenue:

	Without Up-Sell			Up-sell		
	Initial Value	Install-ments	Revenue	Additional Unit Value	Periods	Up-Sell Revenue
First Payment	10.00		10.00	50.00		700.00
Subsequent Payment	50.00	23	1,150.00		14	
TOTAL Revenue			**1,160.00**			
Less:	%			%		
Cost of Providing Product or Service	15.00%		174.00	15.00%		105.00
Contribution or Profit	20.00%		232.00	20.00%		140.00
Administration	10.00%		116.00	10.00%		70.00
Any Additional Cost			48.00			36.00
Any Additional Cost			12.00			6.00
TOTAL Costs for Providing Service			**582.00**			**357.00**
Less:						
Cost Per Order for Initial Sale	125.00					
Cost Per Order for Up-Sell				50.00		
Net Revenue Per Customer Before Up-Sell but After Acquisition			**453.00**			
Net Revenue from Up-sell After Up-sell Cost						**293.00**
Combined Net Revenue						**746.00**
Profit After Write-back of Contribution or Profit Cost			**685.00**	**59.05%**		**433.00** **61.86%**
Combined Profit After Write-back of Contribution or Profit Cost						**1,118.00** **60.11%**

▶ *The seller already has a relationship with the customer,* who will therefore have a greater willingness to listen to any proposition than he might otherwise have had. This should help improve response and lower selling costs.

▶ *The seller has knowledge of the customer performance* as well as some demographic and psychographic data that will help him select his prospects with greater care than might be possible with "cold" names. This should have an even greater positive benefit on marketing costs.

▶ *The actual cost of "access to market"* will be much lower than it would be with cold prospects.

Cross-selling for all types of products or services follow the same economic rules. The key economic variable is *the cost of an order for the cross-sell compared with what it would have been to someone who is not a current customer.*

The figures shown in Exhibit 5-24 (Cross-Sell) demonstrate what might be called the "profit dynamic" of this comparison. This is an extension of the "Single Products" sale model in Chapter 2 (Exhibit 2-3) and uses the same numbers to establish the "Initial" sale profitability. The assumption is that this single unit (with two identical items) can be cross-sold to buyers of other similar products offered by the same vendor.

Starting from here the user need only input a new "Cross-sell Promotional Cost Per Thousand" and a "Cross-sell Percent Response Assumption" in the model on the right "Calculating the Added Value of the Cross-Sell." The model will then deliver the comparison and demonstrate the profit dynamic of the cross-sell.[34]

As can be seen in Exhibit 5-25, the estimated "Contribution or Profit Write-Back as a Percentage of Revenue" decreased from 15.00 percent without the cross-sell to 13.58 percent with the cross-sell although it delivered a combined contribution of 29.88 against an original contribution of 18.53. Although the cost per thousand of promotion used declined to 650.00 per thousand, this would be reasonable since the promotion was to an existing prospect list and there would be no additional cost in obtaining the data. The cost of the promotion could be reduced or made more elaborate for this ex-

Exhibit 5-24 Cross-Sell

Single Unit Sale

Item Selling Price		60.00
No. of Items		2
TOTAL Product Revenue		**120.00**
Less:		
Unit Product Cost		15.00
No. of Items		2
TOTAL Product Cost		**30.00**
Gross Margin before Other Costs		**90.00**
Postage Charge Back for Package		3.50
TOTAL Revenue		**93.50**
Less:		
Taxes included in Price	9.00%	11.12
Fulfillment (inc. Credit Card charges)		15.00
Bad Pay at	3.00%	3.71
Returns at	4.00%	4.94
Premium		6.00
Misc.		5.00
TOTAL Non-Product Costs		**45.78**
Profit or Contribution	15.00%	18.53
Net Margin Before Promotion		**29.22**

If Per '000 Cost of Promotion (including Media and Lists, etc.) Costs	500.00

Initial Promotional Effort:

Initial Promotional Cost Per '000	500.00
Initial % Response for Breakeven	1.71%
Initial Cost Per Order	29.22
Initial Contribution or Profit Write Back	18.53
Contribution or Profit Write Back as % of Revenue	15.00%

No. of Orders Per '000 Needed to Breakeven and make desired Profit Margin is	17
Stated as a % Response	**1.71%**

Calculating the Added Value of the Cross-Sell

Item Selling Price		100.00
No. of Items		1
TOTAL Product Revenue		**100.00**
Less:		
Unit Product Cost		20.00
No. of Items		1
TOTAL Product Cost		**20.00**
Gross Margin before Other Costs		**80.00**
Postage Charge Back for Package		2.00
TOTAL Revenue		**82.00**
Less:		
Taxes included in Price	9.00%	7.38
Fulfillment (inc. Credit Card charges)		15.00
Bad Pay at	3.00%	2.46
Returns at	4.00%	3.28
Premium		6.00
Misc.		5.00
TOTAL Non-Product Costs		**39.12**
Profit or Contribution	15.00%	18.53
Net Margin Before Promotion		**24.36**

Cross-sell Promotional Effort:

Cross-Sell Promotional Cost Per '000	650.00
Cross-Sell % Response Assumption	5.00%
No. of Orders Per '000 Generated by Cross-Sell Promotion	50.00
Cross-Sell Cost Per Order	**13.00**
Cross-Sell Contribution After Profit Write Back	11.36
Contribution or Profit Write Back as % of Revenue	11.36%

Profit Dynamic:

	Initial Sale	Cross-Sell
Contribution After Profit Write Back	18.53	11.36
Contribution After Profit Write Back as % of Revenue	15.00%	11.36%

	Value	%
Combined Contribution	**29.88**	**13.58%**

Exhibit 5-25 Profit Dynamic of the Cross-Sell

Profit Dynamic:		Initial Sale	Cross-Sell
Contribution After Profit Write Back		16.53	11.36
Contribution After Profit Write Back as % of Revenue		15.00%	11.36%
		Value	%
Combined Contribution		29.88	13.58%

penditure. The dynamic combination of initial sale and cross-sell generate a profit more than 60 percent greater than the initial sale.

The Funnel Process

As we have seen, we sell through many sequences and we "up" and "cross" sell within those sequences. Often we are obliged to begin the process by going to a large and often loosely defined audience to find prospects who can then be targeted with increasingly specific promotions. This is often called "lead generation."

At the beginning of the process, lots of people are promoted with a general promotion—poured into the top of the funnel so to speak. Each further step closes in on those people who may become customers and the wide-mouthed funnel at the top is quite narrow at the bottom. Each step has its costs and the sum of these costs determines what it costs to move a few of the general prospects to become customers.

The process of building an economic model and assessing the cost of acquiring a customer through a number of complicated steps becomes an important part of managing distance selling and differs from any of the specific selling sequences described above.

A small company in England offers a computer support service to small and medium sized businesses and was concerned about how much it could spend at each stage of a complicated sales process to sell its service. Analysis indicated that like many other similar companies in a variety of businesses, they had to cast a very wide net to end up with the desired catch.The process had the following steps organized in a funnel (Exhibit 5-26), a large prospect universe reducing through a number of stages until the sale is made.

Exhibit 5-26 The Funnel Process

In the specific case of the computer support service company with the economic profile shown in the matrix in Exhibit 5-27, the three stages had the following costs:

▶ **Step 1** (including the cost of the initial promotion, the premium, and the handling of the responses): *Cost Per Response = 2.50.*

▶ **Step 2** (including the qualification of names by telephone and the seeking of an appointment for the presentation): *Cost Per Appointment for this Step = 23.33.*

▶ **Step 3** (including the face-to-face presentation): *Cost per Completed Contract for Making the Presentation in this Step = 100.00.*

Using weighted averages, the final marketing cost per "Completed Contract" came to 233.33 quite a large sum. But it was perfectly bearable against the estimated minimum 2.3-year *operational profit,*

Exhibit 5-27 Steps in the Funnel Process

STEPS	COMMENT	COSTS
1. A promotion to a wide range of businesses who could potentially use the service.	This was the least specific of the promotions and offered a discount book for other business services to each person who responded. Merchants who wished to "tag along" for the ride, so to speak provided these service discounts without cost to the computer support company.	200.00 Per '000' for outbound communication. .20 per unit for Premium to enhance response. .30 per unit for handling incoming data.
2. Telephone calls to each of the respondents to seek to make an appointment for a sales representative to make a presentation.	These are less than "cold" calls but need some skill. The telephonist's job is to get an appointment for a salesperson and not to sell the service.	3.50 Cost Per Call 50% of Calls Completed 7.00 Cost Per Completed call 30% Appointments made 23.33 Cost Per Appointment
3. The actual sales presentation.	Where the tire hits the road. The salesperson needs to convince the prospect of the good sense of subscribing to the service and complete the sale.	12 Month minimum contract @ 60 per month 2.3 Years estimate of continuation 40% of Revenue Product/Service cost 20% of Revenue misc. costs 25% Profit/ Contribution objective

which totaled 248.40 for a total profit after promotion of 429.07 and a return on the promotional investment of 184 percent.

Understanding the "Profit Dynamic"

Every economic plan contains certain "profit dynamics," points of critical importance where changes can have a major effect on profits. In each of the steps in the example cited above, there are key moments where the profit dynamic changes:

1. In Step 1, the moment of attracting potential customers, getting them to raise their hands and show interest, the profit dynamic is in:

   - The media and communications cost per thousand of the promotion.

   - The percentage of people who respond.

2. In Step 2, the telephone "qualification," the profit dynamic is in:

   - The cost of outgoing telephone calls.

   - The percentage of calls that are possible to complete—reaching the desired person.

   - The percentage of people who will accept the invitation to see a presentation.

3. In Step 3, the presentation stage, the profit dynamic is in:

   - The percentage of people out of those who see the presentation who will complete the agreement to receive and pay for the service.

   - The assumption of the length of time each will keep paying for the service.

Exhibit 5-28 demonstrates the Funnel Process at work for the computer support service company.

What we are always looking for are ways to improve the economic performance at each stage of the data driven marketing process.

For example, in Step 1 we wish to maximize the initial response. Doubling it from 10% to 20% has the effect of pouring more prospects into the funnel and, with all other things being equal, raises the return on marketing investment from 184 percent to 214 percent. Leaving the initial response at 10 percent—but making the "qualification" step more efficient by increasing the percentage of completed calls by just 10 percent (from 50 percent to 60 percent)

Exhibit 5-28 Steps in the Funnel Process

Funnel (Step 1)

	Total Universe (Circulation)	Outward Cost Per '000	Estimated % Response	Estimated Number Responses	Total Cost Per Name	Total Cost
General (Mass) Offer	200,000	200.00	10.00%	20,000	2.00	40,000.00
Premium to Enhance Response					0.20	
Handling of Incoming Data					0.30	
TOTAL Step 1 Cost Per Name					2.50	50,000.00

Funnel (Step 2)

Qualification of Names to Seek Appointment for Presentation	Units	Total Universe (Circulation)		Estimated % Response	Estimated Number Responses	Total Cost Per Appointment	Total Cost
Outbound Telephone Calls:							
Number of Prospects		20,000					
Number of Calls Per Prospect	1						
Cost Per Call	3.50						
% of Calls Completed	50.00%						
Actual Cost Completed Per Call	7.00						
Completed Calls		10,000		30.00%	3,000	23.33	70,000.00

Funnel (Step 3)

Sales Presentations:	Units			30.00%	900	100.00	90,000.00
Number of Presentations		3,000					
Salesman's Cost Per Presentation	30.00						
% Close Rate	30.00%						
Actual Cost Per Completed Presentation	100.00						
Completed Presentations							

Exhibit 5-28 Steps in the Funnel Process (Continued)

Specific Sale:	Months	Monthly Fee
Service	12	60.00

	Years	Annual Revenue
Minimum Annual Revenue		720.00
Likely Number of Years Continuing the Service	2.3	
Estimated TOTAL Lifetime Revenue		1,656.00

Cost of Service Provision:		
Product Costs	40%	662.40
Misc.	20%	331.20
Profit/Contribution	25%	414.00
Total Cost		1,407.60
Service Profit or (Loss)		248.40

		Individual Customer
TOTAL Marketing Cost Per Customer		233.3
Add-Back of Contribution &Service Profit		662.40
(Surplus or Deficit)		
Net Profit Per Customer After Marketing		429.07

		Total Marketing Campaign
TOTAL Estimated Revenue		1,656,400
TOTAL Profit Including Profit /Contribution		891,169
Taken as a Cost Before Promotion		
TOTAL Promotional & Marketing Investment		210,000
Net Profit/Contribution		385,160
Net Profit as a % of Revenue		25.91%
% Return on TOTAL Marketing Investment		183.89%
Allowable Cost Per New Customer		412.00
to Achieve Profit Contribution Target		

and, more importantly, the percentage response (agreement for an appointment to see a presentation) from 30 percent to 40 percent—has the effect of significantly increasing the return on marketing investment to 261 percent.

This suggests that by improving the skills of the telephone sales people—a likely small expense of resources—there could be a dynamic profit increase.[35] In fact, the total profit per contract would have risen from 429 to 479. Finally, for each 10 percent increase in the presentation to contract "close rate," the profit per contract would increase by 45.00.

The converse is also true. A 10 percent drop in the presentation to contract "close rate" would mean that the profit would fall back by the same 45.00. The allowable cost per new customer based on the original model is 414.00 and that leaves a comfortable margin for error.

The different direct selling sequences—single sales, continuities, clubs, catalogs, subscriptions, up-sales and cross-sales and the funnel—offer endless permutations and combinations to the marketer to accomplish his objectives. Choosing the sequence or sequences that work best for a given proposition is the challenge.

Notes

[1] The expression "sequence" is used in this chapter to describe a series of customer purchases that may be a "continuity" or simply a number of purchases resulting from regular promotional activity over a wide product range.

[2] This is an especially important time to capture the "source code"—the specific source (promotional medium employed, promotion content and date are essential).

[3] A pay television service or the uses of an Internet portal are additional "subscription" examples.

[4] The only difference between an "open-ended continuity" and a "subscription" is that most (but not all) subscriptions have a "term" (stated as "one year" or "six months", etc.). But it is worth noting that this is changing as publishers have found that subscribers are

often happy to take subscriptions with an open-ended term. This allows the publisher to periodically bill the subscription to a credit card and to incur minimal renewal costs. It allows the subscribers to "cancel" when they wish.

[5] 1. Selecting the Pricing Objective; 2. Determining Demand; 3. Estimating Costs; 4. Analyzing Competitor's Cost, Prices and Offers; 5. Selecting a Pricing Model; 6. Selecting the Final Price. Philip Kotler: *Marketing Management: Analysis, Planning, Implementation and Control,* Ninth Edition. (Englewood Cliffs, NJ: Prentice Hall, 1997).

[6] This differs from the normal retail model in so far as the marketer through retail channels knows that his distribution cost will be a percentage of the selling price rather than a minimum fixed amount.

[7] Testing is covered in considerably greater detail in Chapter 8.

[8] Magazines tend to sell subscriptions at substantial discounts from the single copy price. Clubs provide the member with a regular flow of product, usually at a substantial discount from what the product would cost outside the club.

[9] The usage of "Contribution and/or Profit" is intended to signify the amount of money needed to contribute to general overheads and to final profit.

[10] The Template CD-ROM contains a template for calculating the attrition on any program and an explanation of how attrition is calculated can be found in Chapter 3.

[11] Launched first in Spain and Italy but soon thereafter in the UK and many other countries, "fascicles" or part works have proven to be extremely popular. Promoted with heavy television advertising, this form of publishing of both editorial and product content has been largely concentrated at the retail level although the sale of ancillary items such as binders and cases has been effectively used to build consumer databases.

[12] It has always seemed a bit strange that alphabetically organized encyclopedia volumes have been successfully sold in this way, as the customer must wait many months longer to look up "zenith" than "aristocrat."

[13] Because the "default" is to reference the data from the "Continuity Selling" template, should you wish to use another starting num-

ber, this is one of the few places in the templates where you might wish to input data in the shaded cell.

[14] For one reason or another, in some cases, the marketer will wish to offer a selection of units taken from the total series but not adding up to the total number. Thus, the "Number of Units to be Included in the Load-Up" can be any number the marketer desires.

[15] Most marketers using the continuity system and offering Load-Ups would do both. They would continue the continuity shipments as long as they were profitable in parallel with the Load-Ups.

[16] Club "selections" are chosen for their maximum appeal, and there are obvious economic benefits to the club if the maximum number of members accept the selection. In some club structures there are divisions (i.e., in music clubs the divisions might be "classical," "easy listening," "pop," and various "rock" divisions.)

[17] Despite the commitment, many members leave before fulfilling it and the costs of trying to get the customer to either fulfill his commitment or pay full price for the premium he received on joining make collection only moderately successful.

[18] This maximum number of years figure is a difficult one as it is impossible to predict the likelihood of the club's lifetime. Nonetheless, a generous guess needs to be made if we are to be able to properly plan the business.

[19] Fulfillment & distribution issues are covered in detail in Chapter 3.

[20] The mix of products offered and the number of SKUs (Stock Keeping Units) complicate this especially where fashion is offered. Each different size and color (or in the case of product variations, each variation) is an additional SKU.

[21] "The objectives of front-end marketing are to acquire new first-time customers, or to acquire leads and inquiries that can be converted into first-time buyers, and to acquire the most names at the least cost. Smart catalogers measure precisely what it costs to acquire a new, first-time buyer and are tenacious about tracking where the name came from." Bob Stone & Ron Jacobs, *Successful Direct Marketing Methods*, (Chicago: McGraw-Hill, 2001), p. 340.

[22] Ibid.

[23] Ibid Page 345.

[24] Catalog marketers use many different media to attract new cus-

tomers. Some produce *better* customers (customers with higher order values) than others. Where these prospects who become customers *came from* is a critical factor in expanding not only the catalog business but all direct marketing businesses.

[25] "Printing and Distribution" costs for catalogs that appear on the Internet are obviously very different from printed catalogs. So too, are response rates.

[26] This is one of the few instances where the "Profit or Contribution" is not taken as a cost although it could be. The reason is that the model would become distorted and the add-backs necessary to understand the new customer acquisition cost would confuse rather than clarify the issue.

[27] No provision has been made in the template for "attrition" as each catalog revenue model is distinct and while there will be people who stop looking at the catalog, this is unlikely to significantly impact the revenue or cost numbers.

[28] Jack Schmid writes: " . . . too often companies tend to under-mail their best customers. During the mid-1970s, for example, Fingerhut was mailing its customer list 20 times a year. By using simple segmentation techniques such as recency, frequency, monetary, and product category, the company was able to test and ultimately increase its mailings to 30 times a year. Most catalogers probably under-utilize or under-mail their customer list."

[29] It is often argued that you need a very response postal system for subscription marketing. Not always! In Brazil, *Veja*, the leading newsmagazine in the country and the fourth largest circulation newsmagazine in the world has approximately one million subscribers. More than 850,000 of them receive their copies each week hand-delivered between 6:00 a.m. on Saturday morning, the time they start to come off press and 3:00 p.m. on Sunday afternoon. It is faster and less expensive than the postal system, which delivers those subscriptions in rural areas.

[30] Although this varies from publication to publication, the normal magazine business model calls for approximately 50% of revenue to come from subscription and newsstand sales and the remaining 50% from advertising. The "allowable" for a subscription *normally* **excludes the advertising revenue** and focuses only on the subscription revenue. However, some publications are prepared to make no

profit on subscriptions because the additional circulation they enjoy increases their advertising revenues. It all depends upon how they do their accounting.

[31] This six-month offer is intentionally unattractive and almost as expensive as the full year. The publisher, while he feels he must make a six-month offer, doesn't wish people to accept it and has priced it high to discourage response.

[32] The principle of Upselling can easily be seen in the 'tiering' of pay-TV and telephone services where the basic service is the minimum and buyers are offered more extensive packages with more features once they have become customers.

[33] The examples given in Chapter 6 for the multi-product electronics company assume a large Cross-sell component.

[34] Obviously, the user will wish to input his own initial data as well as his own Cross-Sell data and make his own assumptions about response levels.

[35] It has been proven time and again that direct sales people are better at face-to-face presentation selling than making telephone calls to get appointments. It is often worth the extra expense to have specialist telephone sales people convert initial leads into appointments and then turn these over to the sales presenters.

▶▶▶6

Complex Products and Services:
Their Special Characteristics
and Economics

I n the previous chapters we examined how accountability could
be applied to all parts of the marketing continuum, the importance of understanding the allowable cost per order and the
unique economic characteristics of various forms of direct marketing. While there is always a strong temptation to group specifics into
generalized packages, the very discipline of direct marketing argues
against this. If nature abhors a vacuum, direct marketing abhors
sweeping generalizations in favor of specific details and micro
models.

The key economic difference between simple products and
complex ones is that with simple products few things change between the beginning and end to the transaction; with complex ones,
prices and many other elements change over an extended time period. Planning thus becomes considerably more complex.

As marketers increasingly seek to enhance the lifetime value of
their customers, one of the means they use is to combine products
and services into "packages" that aggregate value while at the same
time, holding on tenaciously to the customer's revenue flow. Frequently the "up-front" sale is not the main business objective; it is
rather the commencement of a marketing and sales process.

Give Away the Razors and the Cameras:
Sell the Blades and the Film

Gillette looks for a continuing revenue flow from razor blade sales
to justify a low price or even the giving away of razors. Kodak traditionally made most of its money on its film sales and processing,

not on selling cameras. And telecoms are willing to make substantial investments in subsidizing hardware prices (cell phones) to obtain call volume on their networks. If there are no phones out in the marketplace, there will be no calls. In theory at least, all of these efforts were based on a careful economic analysis of the possibilities for success and rigid accountability of the results.

A recent promotion from a major cell phone service provider offered a trade-in of old cell phones for a range of new ones with the continuation of current contracts for their subscribers and a new service contract for nonsubscribers taking advantage of the offer. The new phones offered ranged from basic to top-of-the-line models. For the basic models there was no charge: You gave them your old phone, and they gave you a new one and programmed it for your old number and account while you waited. For the more sophisticated models, there were various prices but even the most expensive represented a tremendous saving on normal prices.

How could the service provider afford this? Obviously, their calculation was that while they would have to carry the considerable costs of the difference between whatever they could recover for the traded-in used units (probably very little if anything), and any payment received for those units for which there was a charge, the lifetime value of the call usage by the current and new customers would be worth it: call usage is where the Telecoms make their money. The queues of people outside the retail outlets where the "exchanges" could be made were ample evidence of the resonance of the offer with current cell phone users. But would the offer make money considering the front-end costs of subsidizing the phones?

Only time will tell. Certainly the service provider knew his margins on call time and the historic longevity of customers. He also knew his current "churn rate"—the number of people who stopped using and paying for the service. He was betting, just as the bank in England that offered the highest interest rate was betting that his offer would have the effect of "buying" customer loyalty and pre-empting competitive initiatives.

The transformation of a product into a service provides significant profit opportunities. Just think about the "extended warranties" sold by manufacturers of many of the higher-priced appliances from washing machines to automobiles or the communications service contracts that come with cell phones or the extended learning opportunities that come with in-school educational courses.

In the case of "extended" warranties, the manufacturer is able to determine the likelihood of the machine needing additional service and the cost of this service. His initial warranty will give the consumer confidence in the product, and the extended warranty will provide "insurance" against any product breakdown after the initial warranty has expired. It has been reliably reported that some companies make more profit on the extended warranties than they do on the sale of the initial item.[1]

The Challenge of "Combination" Transactions

Determining the economics of "combination" transactions such as these, and strategic planning for the maximization of their profits is a classic DM challenge. In Chapter 2 a simple template (Exhibit 2-3: Valuing A Single Unit Sale) is provided for calculating the breakeven on the sale of a single item or multiples of the same item. While the economics of multiple sales are more complicated, they begin from the same point of departure and closely follow the pattern of the Lifetime Value calculations albeit with some significant differences. In searching for real accountability in all our marketing actions, we need to look at each of the many steps in the marketing process and make our judgments carefully.

Let's assume that the starting point is the theoretical sale by a multiproduct consumer electronics company of a "Home Theater" system that combines a TV receiver with a projector, screen, and "surround" sound system. A DVD player is an *additional* option. Normally sold in retail outlets, the company wishes to also use data-driven direct marketing to increase its total market penetration and profitable sales. Naturally, the manufacturer wants to be sure that the economics justify the use of the direct channel.

While the complete Home Theater package is the primary product, the electronics company anticipates that some customers will already have some of the component units, and therefore a certain number will wish only to purchase certain elements rather than the complete system.[2]

What do we need to know?

▶ The *revenue value of the primary unit of sale* and how many units the person will buy plus the revenue from any distribution and shipping charge-backs.

▶ The total product cost for each of the primary units of sale along with the cost of sales or other taxes and fulfillment including distribution, handling, credit card charges, etc., bad pay and returns and any miscellaneous expenses.

▶ The revenue value of each of the subsequent units of sale, how many units the person will buy plus the revenue from any distribution and shipping charge-backs.

▶ The total product cost for each of the subsequent units of sale, along with the cost of sales or other taxes and fulfillment, including distribution, handling, credit card charges, etc., bad pay, and returns and any miscellaneous expenses.

▶ The anticipated promotion costs and response rates for the initial and subsequent offerings.

▶ The margins and profit expectations.

Just as described in the "Lifetime Value" model (Exhibit 2-10), we need to be able to make an estimate of when we are likely to receive revenue from each of the products or services we plan to sell.

The Home Theater consists of the following components shown in Exhibit 6-1. The company's total strategy looks towards the sale of any or all of these additional products (shown in Exhibit 6-2).

In developing the economic plan, there are some important additional elements that need to be considered:

▶ The normal discount to retailers in this example is 23% of retail.

▶ The normal cost of the merchandise, ready to ship, is 56% of retail.

▶ All shipping/delivery charges will be charged back to the customer and therefore constitute a revenue/cost "wash."

▶ Payment will be split evenly between credit card users and checks.

Exhibit 6-1 Home Theater Components

ITEM	CAN BE SOLD AS "STAND-ALONE"	CONSUMER PRICE	COMMENT
TV Receiver without DVD, plus Cassette, Game, PC (Internet) and auxiliary Cable and Satellite inputs and "Wrap Around" Sound System including multiple Speakers, Projector & Screen	MUST BE PURCHASED AS BASIC UNIT OF PACKAGE	1,795.00	Imaginatively, the manufacturer has combined some components to provide a relatively low-priced (middle class) home entertainment center. Marketed as a package it is intended to appear to be greater than the sum of its parts at a cost of less than the sum of the components.
Total System including DVD Player	YES	1,995.00	As many people will already own a DVD, this is not part of the total package.
Total System including DVDokê	YES	2,095.00	
DVD Player	YES	495.00	
DVD Player with DVDokê ^{3} capacity	YES	649.00	

Exhibit 6-2 Total Product Line Strategy

PRODUCT	CONSUMER PRICE	COMMENT
Home Security Basic Hardware (Average depending upon components)	1,000.00	Easy-to-install basic unit
Home Security Service	100.00 (per month)	Monitoring including phone line cost
Cell Phone Hardware	150.00 (Plus "contribution" from Service Provider)	Company is not a service provider and therefore receives only a "contribution" from service provider.
Game Hardware	300.00	Board controller with two handsets
Game Software	45.00 (Per Unit)	15 new units are issued each year but only 3 are likely to be hits.
DVDokê Software	37.50 (Per Unit)	16 new titles per year. Units are issued in each of 4 music categories.

Developing an economic plan can best begin with the construction of some trial scenarios. While not built on numbers, these are intended to help us visualize the selling options. The Multi-Product Promotion Matrix (Exhibit 6-3) is an example of one way of approaching the problem. It is intended to aggregate all the product elements as a means of providing a "control" on the promotional activities.

In looking at this matrix it is important to understand its various elements:

▶ Each product option has a "Promotion Identification Number" that will be used in the planning process.

▶ The product is then described in detail showing what is being offered.

Exhibit 6-3 Multiproduct Promotion Matrix

Input Promotion Identification Number		If Sale Input Next Promotion Number	Input Number of Weeks Before Next Promotion	If No Sale Input Next Promotion Number	Input Number of Weeks Before Next Promotion
HT1	*TV Receiver __without__ DVD, Plus Cassette, Game, PC (Internet) and auxiliary Cable and Satellite inputs and 'Wrap Around' Sound System including multiple Speakers, Projector & Screen*	OPTION FOR DVDOK1 OR DVDPLAY1	INCLUDE PROMO WITH PRODUCT GIVE OPTION FOR DVDOK1 OR DVDPLAY1	DVDOK1	3
HTDVD1	*OPTION TO HT1 INCLUDED IN FIRST OFFER:Total System including DVD Player*	GMHAR1	3	HSBAS1	6
HTDVDOK1	*OPTION TO HT1 INCLUDED IN FIRST OFFER:Total System in cluding DVDoké*	DVDOKSF1	INCLUDE DVDOKÉ SOFTWARE OFFER WITH PRODUCT SHIPMENT	GMHAR1	6
DVDPLAY1	*DVD Player*	HT1	6	HSBAS1	6
DVDOK1	*OPTION TO DVDPLAY1 INCLUDED IN DVD PLAYER OFFER*	DVDOKSF1	INCLUDE DVDOKÉ SOFTWARE OFFER DVDOKSF1 WITH PRODUCT SHIPMENT	GMHAR1	6
DVDOKSF1	*DVDoké Software*	GMHAR1	INCLUDE GAME SOFTWARE OFFER GMSFT1 WITH PRODUCT SHIPMENT	CPHAR1	6
HSBAS1	*Home Security Basic Hardware (Average depending upon components)*	HSSER1	INCLUDE HOME SECURITY SERVICE HSSER1 OFFER GMSFT1 WITH PRODUCT SHIPMENT	HT1	6
HSSER1	*Home Security Service*	HT1	6	CPHAR1	6
CPHAR1	*Cell Phone Hardware*	HT1	6	GMHAR1	6
GMHAR1	*Game Hardware*	GMSFT1	INCLUDE GAME SOFTWARE GMSFT1 OFFER WITH PRODUCT SHIPMENT	HT1	6
GMSFT1	*Game Software*	DVDOK1	6	CPHAR1	6

▶ There are then two "action" options and two "timing" options depending on whether the prospect purchases or does not purchase.

- *If the purchase is made,* the next product to be offered to the customer is indicated so there will be a logical offer sequence.

- The number of weeks *before* the next promotion is input. In this case the next promotion will be packed with the product.

- *If the purchase is not made*, then the next product to be offered is indicated.

- The number of weeks *before* the next promotion is input. In this case the next promotion will be made in 3 weeks.

Using a matrix of this kind helps keep the focus on the total range of products and offers while providing planning management with the tools to make necessary choices.

This is only the first step.

The next in developing the model is to build a spreadsheet with the key numbers so that they can be incorporated into the final model with maximum ease. It might look something like Exhibit 6-4.

A first glance comparing the two right-hand columns suggests that using direct marketing as a distribution channel may not be "worth the candle." In most cases, assuming that the retail distribution costs roughly 50% of the revenue (the 23% retailer's discount plus sales and promotional support costs), the retail delivers a higher profit margin than the direct marketing effort. *The problem with this view is that it makes no provision for the add-on sales that should make a "customer" more valuable than a "sale."*

Using this matrix as a point of departure, each of the options can be modeled to ascertain an allowable marketing cost and assess the value of customers taking certain actions and the resources available to motivate these actions.

Let's look at some of the possible transactions.

In Exhibit 6-5, on page 170, the primary effort is to sell the Home Theater package (HT1) in either its normal or enhanced configuration, which includes a DVD Player. But we have to ask if it will be a profitable sale, and this will depend to no small degree on the marketing cost per unit. That's why we use the template, Multiple Product/Service Breakeven Calculation (Exhibit 6-6 on page 171) *linked as it is to the previous template* to make the economic calculations.

Note that the standard (HT1) and the more expensive (HTDVD1) products have been combined and a weighted average

Exhibit 6-4 Multiple Product Revenue and Cost Matrix

COST MATRIX

Product Code	ITEM (Input Product Descriptions Below)	Price to Consumer	% Cost of Product	Cost of Product	Gross Revenue	Cost of Shipping	Shipping Charge-Back	Net Revenue	Comparative Retail Net Revenue 50%
HT1	TV Receiver without DVD, Plus Cassette, Game, PC (Internet) and auxiliary Cable and Satellite inputs and 'Wrap Around' Sound System including multiple Speakers, Projector & Screen	1,795.00	56.00%	1,005.20	789.80	50.00	50.00	789.80	897.50
HTDVD1	OPTION TO HT1 INCLUDED IN FIRST OFFER:Total System including DVD Player	1,995.00	56.00%	1,117.20	877.80	60.00	60.00	877.80	997.50
HTDVDOK1	OPTION TO HT1 INCLUDED IN FIRST OFFER:Total System including DVDoke	2,095.00	56.00%	1,173.20	921.80	60.00	60.00	921.80	1,047.50
DVDPLAY1	DVD Player	495.00	56.00%	277.20	217.80	30.00	30.00	217.80	247.50
DVDOK1	OPTION TO DVDPLAY1 INCLUDED IN DVD PLAYER OFFER	649.00	56.00%	363.44	285.56	30.00	30.00	285.56	324.50
DVDOKSF1	DVDoke Software	37.50	40.00%	15.00	22.50	6.00	6.00	22.50	18.75
HSBAS1	Home Security Basic Hardware (Average depending upon components)	1,000.00	56.00%	560.00	440.00	85.00	85.00	440.00	500.00
HSSER1	Home Security Service (Month)	100.00	25.00%	25.00	75.00	-	-	75.00	50.00
CPHAR1	Cell Phone Hardware (Including Service Provider 'Contribution' to Cost)	150.00	125.00%	187.50	(37.50)	25.00	25.00	(37.50)	75.00
GMHAR1	Game Hardware	300.00	56.00%	168.00	132.00	30.00	30.00	132.00	150.00
GMSFT1	Game Software	45.00	45.00%	20.25	24.75	6.00	6.00	24.75	22.50

Exhibit 6-5 Transaction: Home Theater Package

HT1	TV Receiver _without_ DVD, Plus Cassette, Game, PC (Internet) and auxiliary Cable and Satellite inputs and 'Wrap Around' Sound System including multiple Speakers, Projector & Screen	OPTION FOR DVDOK1 OR DVDPLAY1	INCLUDE PROMO WITH PRODUCT GIVE OPTION FOR DVDOK1 OR DVDPLAY1	DVDOK1	3
HTDVD1	OPTION TO HT1 INCLUDED IN FIRST OFFER:Total System including DVD Player	GMHAR1	3	HSBAS1	6

established that reflects the anticipated percentage of people assumed to purchase "standard" and the more expensive products.

This shows us that, with a 7.5% return on a 1,800 per thousand promotion cost, there would still be an Initial Net Contribution of 419.80. And this is after making a "cost" provision of 20% of Revenue (390.00) as the Initial Profit or Contribution objective. Note also that the percentage of response from the promotion to achieve breakeven (still reserving 20% of revenue for Initial Profit or Contribution) is only 0.406%—less than one half of one person per hundred promoted. The proposition on its own, without additional sales, appears to be very attractive.

How would the numbers look if, as we can see in Exhibit 6-7, the actual response was only 0.40%, a response below the calculated breakeven of 0.466%? Now we see a marginal loss (- 6.20) on the initial sale. With this as a starting point, we have to determine if the project still makes sense?

The answer depends upon how much additional business—Lifetime Value, if you will—this customer can be expected to deliver.

The marketing plan called for buyers of HT1 or HTDVD1 to be promoted next with GMHAR1, the Game hardware product. The assumption is that if the purchaser has invested in the home theater and he has children in the home, the game hardware will add a significant extra dimension to the family's home entertainment room. Also, the database indicated that 60% of the purchasers had children in their homes in the right age range and that these could be identified.

By completing the next stage of the template (Exhibit 6-8, page 173) with the GMHAR1 and 3 units of its accompanying software GMSFT1, always referencing the Key Data Reference matrix, the picture can be expanded. This is a profitable exercise not least

Exhibit 6-6 Multiple Product/Service Breakeven Calculation

NET MARGIN CALCULATION

FIRST SALE

Code	ITEM	Anticipated % of People Assumed to Purchase	No.Units of Product You Intend to Sell to Single Consumer	Single Unit Revenue incl. Any Postage or Distribution Charge Back	Total Revenue	Net Margin	%
Option 1							
HT1	TV Receiver without DVD, Plus Cassette, Game, PC (Internet) and auxiliary Cable and Satellite inputs and 'Wrap Around' Sound System including multiple Speakers, Projector & Screen	50.00%	1	1,845.00	1,845.00	789.80	42.81%
Option 2							
HTDVD1	OPTION TO HT1 INCLUDED IN FIRST OFFER: Total System including DVD Player	50.00%	1	2,055.00	2,055.00	877.80	42.72%
Option 3							
		0.00%		-	-	-	0.00%

Weighted Average | | | 1,950.00 | 833.80 | 42.76%

Input Profit /Contribution Expectation | 20.00% | 390.00

Input Promotion Cost Per '000 | 1,800.00
Input % Response Assumption | 7.50%
Promotion Cost | 24.00

Initial Net Contribution of Initial Product or Service | 419.80

% Response Needed for Breakeven (Incl. Profit /Contribution Expectation) | 0.406%

Exhibit 6-7 Transaction: Game Product

NET MARGIN CALCULATION

FIRST SALE

Code	ITEM	Anticipated % of People Assumed to Purchase	No.Units of Product You Intend to Sell to Single Consumer	Single Unit Revenue incl. Any Postage or Distribution Charge Back	Total Revenue	Net Margin	%
Option 1							
HT1	TV Receiver without DVD, Plus Cassette, Game, PC (internet) and auxiliary Cable and Satellite inputs and 'Wrap Around' Sound System including multiple Speakers, Projector & Screen	50.00%	1	1,845.00	1,845.00	789.80	42.81%
Option 2							
HTDVD1	OPTION TO HT1 INCLUDED IN FIRST OFFER: Total System including DVD Player	50.00%	1	2,055.00	2,055.00	877.80	42.72%
Option 3							
		0.00%		-	-	-	0.00%

Weighted Average	1,950.00	833.80	42.76%

Input Profit /Contribution Expectation	20.00%	390.00

Input Promotion Cost Per '000 | 1,800.00
Input % Response Assumption | 0.40%

Promotion Cost	450.00

Initial Net Contribution of Initial Product or Service	(5.20)

% Response Needed for Breakeven (incl. Profit /Contribution Expectation)	0.462%

Exhibit 6-8 Game Hardware Matrix

ADDITIONAL SALES

Code		No. Units of Product You Intend to Sell to Single Consumer	Single Unit Revenue Incl. Any Postage or Distribution Charge Back	Total Revenue	Net Margin	%
Product 1						
GMHAR1	Game Hardware	1	330.00	330.00	132.00	40.00%
GMSFT1	Game Software	3	51.00	153.00	74.25	48.53%
			-	-	-	0.00%
TOTAL				483.00	206.25	42.70%

Input Promotion Cost Per '000   1,000.00
Input % Response Assumption   20.00%
Promotion Cost   5.00

Exhibit 6-9 Profit Contribution Matrix: Initial Sale and Subsequent Sale

LIFE TIME ANALYSIS

Average Revenue Per Customer	2,046.60
Average Net Margin Per Customer	875.05
Net Margin Per Customer (After Promotion Costs)	850.58 41.57%

because the response percentage is bringing the cost per sale dramatically downward.

This is the time to look at the lifetime value of this customer based on the sales so far. We see (Exhibit 6-9) that we have accumulated an average Net Margin of 875.05 or more than 41% on sales. And this is *before* the subsequent sales efforts, efforts such as the sale of additional software for the DVDôke, games and other products.

As the sales process goes forward, additional profitable sales should be possible, and the initial investment made in acquiring the customer returned many times over. In the long run, the initiative should be far more profitable than depending solely on retail distribution despite the first impression.

Are You Going to Sell a Product, a Service, or Both?

As noted earlier, the migration of a product into a service or the combination of a product and service can add substantially to the revenue flow and profit. These "services" are almost always "dependent" upon the existence of a primary product: blades for razors, software for hardware, extended warranty for appliances, and a "monitoring" service for home or office security to name just a few examples. The key characteristic of dependent products for subsequent sale through data driven direct marketing is that there is always a previous transaction. With proper data capture methods, the buyers of the previous product should be able to be identified and marketing resources can then be devoted almost entirely to this group.

Looking back at the Home Theater example, there are two particular opportunities worth examining.

1. Software for DVDôke

This software presents the latest popular songs (without the singer) as if they were music videos and allows the DVDôke hardware owner to become the singing "star" of the video:

- No. of New Titles Per Year: 16
- Price to Consumer Per Unit: 37.50
- Net Revenue after Shipping Per Unit: 22.50

2. Software for "Games"

This software is a standard range of "game" software with new action and other titles:

- No. of New Titles Per Year: 15
- Price to Consumer Per Unit: 45.00
- Net Revenue after Shipping Per Unit: 24.75

As can be seen on the "Multi-Product Promotion Matrix" (Exhibit 6-3), the intention is to include "offers" in the hardware packages for both the DVDôke and "Games." Someone buying the hardware will certainly want the software. Without it, the hardware is nothing more than a hi-tech doorstopper. Furthermore, most retailers show little interest in carrying the software. They find the number of titles expensive and difficult to stock and the margins too low to make it interesting for them to take the risk.

The marketing issues for the two different types of software are identical:

▶ The "target" market is limited to everyone who has the hardware and should be identifiable both through the database of people to whom the hardware has been sold[4] and through a limited advertising expenditure in specialized magazines to reach hardware owners who purchased their units at retail and where no data was collected.

▶ An offer direct to hardware users providing new software on a regular basis (either through a catalog, club, or some other sequence) responds to a positive customer need as they would have difficulty finding the software at the rare retail outlet prepared to stock it.

▶ The hardware product packages provide an ideal and minimum cost "medium" to start the marketing process.

Let's look at the DVDôke software issue as an example.

One of the prime motivators for DVDôke fans is to be able to "perform" the latest songs—sing along against a music video background—as well as the "classics." Having easy access to these new "releases" is of great importance. Good content is key. If the content of the software doesn't meet the hardware owner's expectations, the customer feels doubly disappointed: he has made an investment in the hardware (perhaps but not always usable with alternative software), and he has nothing to use it for. He's expensively dressed up with nowhere to go.

Good Content Is the Most Important Churn Reducer

Content is king no matter what the nature of the product or service and good content is the greatest inhibitor of "churn." If the customers like the product or the service, the likelihood is that they will continue to wish to receive it. If they value it, they will be willing to pay a fair price for it.

A publication that doesn't deliver relevant and exciting content to its readers finds its circulation heading south no matter what promotional activities it undertakes. An "Association" that doesn't properly serve its members' needs and expectations quickly finds itself without associates. The best-promoted restaurant with poor food and service finds its tables empty.

All this seems obvious when we stand back and look at the issue. But all too often, marketing people let their focus waver: they are looking so closely at all the marketing issues that they sometimes forget the central reason why the customer purchases in the first place, *want* or *need* of the product or service. Thus, *when we see a pattern of rising attrition or churn, the first place to look for the cause and the remedy is in the product content.*

A "Club" structure with regular communications and promotions sent directly to DVDôke hardware owners appeared to offer

Exhibit 6-10 Determining Economic Viability

ITEM	DATA	COMMENT
First Unit Price	No Charge	Used as a "Premium."
Regular Unit Price	37.50	
Average Order Value Per Club Cycle	56.25	Assumption is that each purchase will be for 1.5 units at 37.50 each.
Distribution or Postage Charge-back	6.00	Assumption is that each "shipment" will have a 6.00 distribution (Postage and Handling) charge to the customer regardless of the number of units shipped. Actual cost of shipping is 4.50.
Number of Club "Cycles" Per Year	4	A "judgment" choice that needs to be tested against other possible cycles.
Maximum Number of Years	3	Subject to attrition that "nets" the number of purchases per member to 3.4 over the life of the membership.
Cycle Promotion Cost Per Member	1.00	This assumes a combination of postage and electronic delivery.
Percentage of Total Members Purchasing in Each Cycle	40%	Assumption is that product will be sufficiently attractive.
Percentage of Members who Return the Shipment Each Cycle	5%	Certain people will try and decide they don't want certain titles.
Bad Pay	2%	Because there will be no subsequent shipment until the previous one is paid and because 50% of members are assumed to pay by credit card, bad pay is low.
Fulfillment & Distribution	Initial = 12.80 Subsequent = 6.25	Distribution cost of all but first "premium" pack will be almost recouped through 6.00 charge back.
Profit/Contribution Objective	15%	

the best solution. What do we have to know to determine its economic viability?

The general economics of "Clubs" and other marketing systems are reviewed in considerable detail in Chapter 5. However, for the purpose of this example we are assuming a "negative option" club[5]— the member gets shipped and is charged for the "selection" for his type of music (there are four different types) *unless he indicates he doesn't* wish to receive it. The offer used (and the economics that condition it) is "One Free When You Purchase Your First DVDôke Disc."

Looking at the *Planning Summary—Club* (top part of Exhibit

Exhibit 6-11 Planning Summary: ACPO

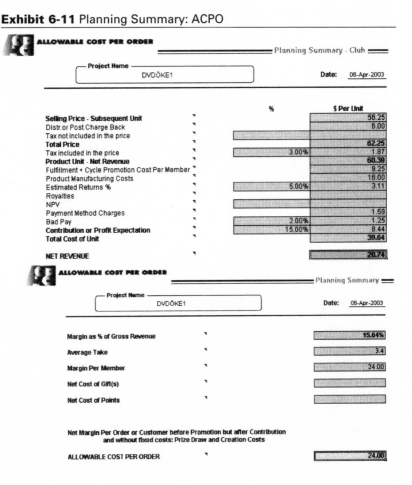

Exhibit 6-12 Per Thousand Promotion Evaluation

Media:	Cost of Media Per '000	Expected % Response	Number of Responses	Cost Per Response	Profit or (Loss) Against Allowable *	No. Responses Per '000: Necessary to Breakeven	% Response Necessary to Breakeven
ACPO (Member, Subscriber, etc...)	24.00						
Direct Mail	1,000.00	3.50%	35.00	28.57	(4.57)	41.67	4.17%
Press Advertisements	200.00	0.50%	5.00	40.00	(16.00)	8.33	0.83%
Press Inserts	250.00	1.00%	10.00	25.00	(1.00)	10.42	1.04%
Package Inserts	50.00	20.00%	200.00	0.25	23.75	2.08	0.21%
E-mail	20.00	5.00%	50.00	0.40	23.60	0.83	0.08%
Input Other 1			-	-	-	-	
Input Other 2			-	-	-	-	
Input Other 3			-	-	-	-	
Input Other 4			-	-	-	-	

*The "Profit or (Loss) Against Allowable" and the subsequent breakeven calculations do not factor in the percentage of profit or contribution taken into the costs. Adding this back will change the breakeven numbers

6-11) using the ACPO Model ® software[6], we can see all the revenue and cost assumptions that have been used in the modeling. In the final *Planning Summary* (bottom part of illustration), all the previous information has been combined to determine that the allowable cost of recruiting a member to the club is 24.00. The obvious question that arises is *whether this is enough?*

The recipe for evaluating promotional alternatives combines a large dose of number crunching with an equal measure of guesswork. We can examine all types of media studies and make all manner of calculations.

Measuring the *pulse* of the reader or viewer is an imprecise science at best and appears to gives the lie to the whole concept of accountability. It all comes back to the media content and the alignment the reader or viewer feels for this content. If you are passionately interested in home decoration or Formula 1 motor racing, the chances are greater that you will respond to offers made in the environment of these passions than you might in an environment in which you don't feel the same level of excitement and comfort.

Response—historic and projected—should condition all our media decisions. One of the characteristics of DM is that we are only peripherally interested in "readership" and circulation or viewer figures. In the last analysis what we are looking for is to *divide the cost of media by a measurable number of responses and come out with a cost-per-order (or subscriber or club member) lower than the amount we can afford.* After all, that's what we mean when we use the term "accountable."

Making Planning Calculations Should Be Easy

When you know how much you can afford for recruitment or to make a sale, templates, such Exhibit 6-12 (Template: Per Thousand Promotion Evaluation), can help.

This template is designed to provide a simple tool to evaluate the relative risk and potential reward from the use of comparative media and the order of magnitude of the results you need to justify specific promotional activity. It asks only for the existing ACPO and the cost per thousand and expected percentage response rates for the range of media you intend to use. It then calculates the number or responses, the cost per response, whether there is a surplus or deficit when compared to the "allowable" and finally the number and percentage of responses needed to breakeven.

What we see in this example is that "Press Advertisements," "Press Inserts," and "Direct Mail" are all in the red—with these expected percentage response rates they will all lose money against the allowable. "Press Inserts" have the smallest shortfall against the allowable of only 1.00 *before considering the add-back of the contribution factor*.

Of all the media, only the use of "Package Inserts" and "email" leave sufficient margin between the "allowable" and the estimated "actual" to assure success. The "Expected Response" of 20% for hardware package inserts and 5% for emails far exceeds the "Response % Necessary to Breakeven" of .21% and .08% leaving substantial room for maneuver.

Yet package inserts and email alone are unlikely to provide sufficient volume, and while theoretically everyone who has a DVDôke hardware unit will have received the initial promotion in the hardware package, many may have ignored it. The marketer must decide between two promotional options:

1. Use direct mail or better, email where the names and addresses (and in the case of email, email addresses) of the hardware owners gained through warranty cards or some other form of registration are available and/or

2. Use direct response inserts in "enthusiast" magazines and appropriate web sites.

The use of the three media together all provide opportunities to get business economically, even if the use of enthusiast magazine inserts might slightly diminish the anticipated profit/ contribution.

Content Is King: Consumers Will Subscribe and Pay for Superior Content

We live in a society in which services occupy a growing proportion of the economy. Increasingly delivered electronically, either on the Internet or through some other means such as "cable" or satellite, these services play an increasingly important part in our lives. Marketers vie for our custom in using and paying for these services. Subscription or "pay" television is a good example.

In most developed and developing markets around the world, TV market penetration comes close to 100%, higher than almost any other service except electricity. The ubiquitous TV screen is a central feature of even the poorest homes. While much TV content is "sponsored" by advertisers or paid for by taxes or national licenses, such as the charge made to all TV owners in the UK that supports the British Broadcasting Corporation's often outstanding output, more and more TV viewers are opting for higher levels of content through private cable or satellite services.

In its simplest form, consumers pay for these services on a normal subscription basis, a fixed monthly or annual rate for a range of program content (including films, sporting and other entertainment events, children's programs, even pornography) not available on "open" channels. The revenue from these subscriptions is received by the cable or satellite operator and divided among the many content providers who normally make up the offering. The economic model is relatively close to that of any normal subscription but with some significant differences.

The biggest difference is the cost of the hardware needed to capture the cable or satellite signal and the costs of installation. A secondary but important consideration is how to "tier" the content and how to market the different tiers and "premium" services.

The marketing decisions are almost always driven by a consideration of these factors:

▶ In a highly competitive environment, should the hardware (set-top-decoder for cable; dish and decoder for satellite) plus installation be:

- Charged as an *up-front* charge even though this creates a significant barrier to purchase because of the high investment?

- "Bundled" into the price of a subscription and, if so, for what minimum term to assure the high cost of the hardware and installation are recouped?

- Provided on some other basis?

▶ Is it likely to be more efficient selling:

- A full service including all the channels for a fixed price plus special "on demand" pay-per-view prices?

- A low-priced "basic" package that includes a minimum selection of content on the assumption that once the customer is happy with the channels and used to paying the basic price, he can be up-sold to a more expensive package with more content?

- A range of different programming options that allows the consumer to make a preliminary choice and change the package when desired?

Cable and satellite companies have tested almost every conceivable combination of options, and they continue experimenting as their market penetration goes deeper into the prospect base and meets economic resistance. What's more, the hardware and installation and the programming issues often conflict with one another in the economic planning.

The marketer's instinct is almost always to make the richest offer at the lowest possible introductory price to attract the most attention in the marketplace. In this case, following that instinct would have the effect of offering "Free" hardware and installation and an introductory programming package. The key question is whether it is reasonable to assume that a subscriber will remain long enough to justify the initial investment. The follow-on question is whether the marketer wouldn't be better off aiming for a smaller but more affluent market where he could be assured of an early return on his investment.

This is a classic example of the hardware/software conundrum and harks back to the razor and the razor blades, the camera and the film. Without the decoder and the installation, the service cannot be offered. These have the highest "cash" value and their cash costs need to be funded. Putting aside the enormous capital investment in the technological infrastructure, the marketer must determine the optimum way of recouping his investment in the hardware and installation and his additional up-front cost of acquiring the subscriber.

The task for the marketer is to assess different offers and then to test and validate those with the most economic and promotional potential. To aid in doing that it is essential to assess the key variables and to evaluate them.

All too often companies, especially large product companies, neglect to examine these issues, mostly through a lack of understanding. Many years ago, the President of COMSAT, the American satellite communications agency, asked me to look at a direct-to-home satellite broadcasting initiative in which his company had already made a massive investment. After some months of working through the issues, it became apparent that the company's technological focus had overwhelmed the needed consumer market focus. There was a large item in the budget for "marketing," but no one in the management had properly examined either the cost of obtaining a subscriber to the service or the offers that would be necessary.

When we looked closely at the issues, it became apparent that the plan was fatally flawed and had to be aborted at a very substantial write-off. Had management started from a view up from the consumer rather than down from the satellite, millions and millions of dollars could have been saved.[7]

To Test or Not to Test: Always Test and Compare

Exhibit 6-13 shows a "base case" and three arbitrary alternatives that focus on possible subscription price alternatives and "offers" for a subscription TV service or similar product that combines hard and software. To properly make an assessment of their relative merits, we need to evaluate the pricing options[8] for both the service and the hardware and installation.

Using these and/or other variables, we can model the comparative values as seen in Exhibit 6–14 (Template: Comparative Options) and derive all the essential data to understand the economics of the offers.

Based on this model, which uses the same "Estimated Acquisition Cost" for each of the sensitivities, the highest "Profit as % of Total Revenue" is Alternative 2. But that answer is certainly too simplistic: the *actual acquisition cost* will materially impact the final profit and this will be determined by testing the offers shown in the previous matrix or others.

Exhibit 6-13 Evaluating Pricing Options

CHARACTERISTICS	BASE CASE	ALTERNATIVE 1	ALTERNATIVE 2	ALTERNATIVE 3
First Year Monthly Subscription	50.00	25.00	50.00	50.00
Subsequent Years' Monthly Subscription	50.00	50.00	75.00	100.00
Net Years of Subscription after Attrition	4.5	4.5	4.5	4.5
Hardware & Installation Offer	250.00	250.00	350.00	0
Hardware & Installation Cost	350.00	350.00	350.00	350.00

What's different about these offers?

▷ The *Base Case* allows the new service subscriber to have the first year's subscription at a monthly rate equal to what he will pay in subsequent years but to save 100.00 off the 350.00 cost of the Hardware and Installation.

▷ *Alternative 1* offers the first year subscription at only 25.00 per month, half the normal rate payable in the subsequent years and again discounts the Hardware and Installation charge by 100.00.

▷ *Alternative 2* offers the first year subscription at 50.00 per month and increases this to 75.00 per month in subsequent years and makes no discount on the Hardware and Installation charge of 350.00.

▷ *Alternative 3* is the top end offer. It offers the first year at 50.00 per month increasing to 100.00 per month but provides the Hardware and Installation without a charge.

When we "guesstimate" the likely acquisition costs of each of the alternative offers based on their possible appeal, Alternatives 1 and 3 are likely to be the most appealing to the consumer, Alternative 2,

Exhibit 6-14 Comparative Service Options

Items	Base Case	Alternative 1	Alternative 2	Alternative 3
Revenue:				
First Year Monthly Service	50.00	25.00	50.00	50.00
First Year Service	600.00	300.00	600.00	600.00
Additional Year's Monthly Service	50.00	50.00	75.00	100.00
Additional Year's Service	600.00	600.00	900.00	1,200.00
No. of Years of Service (After Yr. 1)	5.0	5.0	5.0	5.0
Net Years of Service After Attrition	4.5	4.5	4.5	4.5
TOTAL No. of Months of Service After Attrition	54.0	54.0	54.0	54.0
TOTAL Revenue	2,700.00	2,400.00	3,780.00	4,800.00
Costs:				
Monthly Cost of Providing Service (50.00%)	25.00	25.00	37.50	50.00
Annual Cost of Providing Service	300.00	300.00	460.00	600.00
TOTAL Life Cost of Providing Service	1,350.00	1,350.00	2,025.00	2,700.00
Cost of Bad Debt (% times 3 Month's Cost) 2.00%	1.50	1.50	2.25	2.25
Profit/Contribution 12.00%	324.00	288.00	450.00	576.00
Fulfillment:				
Initial Order Handling	8.00	8.00	8.00	8.00
Initial Year Per Month	8.00	8.00	8.00	8.00
Subsequent Years Per Month	6.00	6.00	6.00	6.00
TOTAL Fulfillment 3.00%				
TOTAL Cost of Money Collection 3.00%	81.00	72.00	112.50	144.00
TOTAL Cost of (Sales & TVA) Tax Included in Price	81.00	72.00	112.50	144.00
TOTAL Cost for Life of Service				
TOTAL Net Revenue before Acquisition Costs				
Monthly Net Revenue Before Acquisition Cost	9.36	9.08	12.81	16.24
Hardware and Installation Offer				
Revenue:				
Charge to Customer for Hardware & Installation	100.00	250.00	350.00	350.00
Cost to Provide Hardware & Installation	350.00	350.00	350.00	(350.00)
Net Hardware & Installation Cost to Marketer	(250.00)	(100.00)	-	(350.00)
Allowable Acquisition Cost	296.00	172.00	691.75	527.00
Estimated Acquisition Cost	250.00	250.00	250.00	250.00
No. Months Net Revenue Necessary to Recoup Investment in Acquisition, Hardware & Installation	53.3	69.4	19.5	36.9
Length of Time Needed to Recoup Acquisition and Hardware/Installation Cost is Shorter or Longer than Estimated Length of Service Usage by Months	16.7	4.3	34.5	23.3
Net Profit on Service	330.50	210.50	891.75	865.00
Profit as % of TOTAL Revenue	12.24%	8.77%	23.78%	17.77%

Sensitivities	Base Case	Alternative 1	Alternative 2	Alternative 3
Estimated Acquisition Cost	100.00	150.00	250.00	150.00
No. Months Net Revenue Necessary to Recoup Investment in Acquisition, Hardware & Installation	37.3	49.3	19.5	40.8
Length of Time Needed to Recoup Acquisition and Hardware/Installation Cost is Shorter or Longer than Estimated Length of Service Usage by Months	18.7	45.3	34.5	24.9
Net Profit on Service	480.50	310.50	891.75	865.00
Profit as % of TOTAL Revenue	17.80%	12.94%	23.78%	18.23%

Exhibit 6-15 Cost Sensitivities

Sensitivities	Base Case	Alternative 1	Alternative 2	Alternative 3
Estimated Acquisition Cost	100.00	150.00	250.00	150.00
No. Months Net Revenue Necessary to Recoup Investment in Acquisition, Hardware & Installation	37.3	49.5	19.5	30.8
Length of Time Needed to Recoup Acquisition and Hardware/Installation Cost is Shorter or Longer than Estimated Length of Service Usage by Months	16.7	4.5	34.5	23.2
Net Profit on Service	480.50	310.50	891.75	953.00
Profit as % of TOTAL Revenue	17.80%	12.94%	23.78%	19.85

the least. If that appeal translates to a lower acquisition cost for these alternatives (remember the example of the highest interest rate for the UK bank), then the profit percentage numbers will change dramatically as demonstrated below.

While Alternative 2 (in Exhibit 6-15) still shows the largest percentage of profit, the percentages for Alternatives 1 and 3 have increased reflecting the lower acquisition costs.

Which Offer to Go With?

This obviously depends on a number of factors including the importance of total net revenue and volume of subscribers as well as percentage of profit. Which comes first: the offer construction or the economics? It totally depends on the situation and the personalities. *The idea for a great offer needs to be analyzed for its economic implications just as the theoretical economic analysis of any offer is meaningless if the offer will not generate the response.* Only by doing this type of thorough analysis is it possible to develop strategies from either starting point and produce a meaningful test matrix.

Clubs May Be Exclusive: Their Economics Are Not

When we assess the economics of Associations and Clubs that recruit new members and charge dues for membership, we see a somewhat different version of the same paradigm.

Imagine for the purposes of this example, a Marketing Society whose membership includes companies large and small as well as individuals from all the different marketing disciplines. The Society provides a range of services for its members and depends principally upon the members' dues and secondarily on sponsorship and participation in special events to fund its costs and deliver a surplus.

While in its early days, recruitment was not an issue as the leading marketing companies joined the Society with little persuasion; with maturity it became necessary to actively recruit additional members. And recruitment became more difficult as different categories of members wanted to push the Society in opposing directions and expected the Society to provide services that raised its costs and threatened to make some member categories uneconomic. "Churn"—members resigning from the Society—was becoming a big problem and even raising concerns about the future of the Society.

It is often said by doctors that the worst patients are doctors and by lawyers that their worst clients are other lawyers. Marketing people making marketing decisions follow a similar pattern.

The Marketing Committee of the Society was long on ideas about how to market memberships but short on the willingness to really step back and look at the Society's membership recruitment procedures and the overall economics of recruitment. It was not until someone suggested that if a "membership" was thought of as no more or less than a magazine "subscription" it might illuminate the problem.

This analogy focused attention on the reasons members joined the Society in the first place and after a certain period decided not to continue. This in turn made the Committee consider whether or not the recruitment procedure, and the membership offering, was consistent with what the new member received as benefits once he became a member. Was the expectation created during the recruitment process fulfilled during the first months of membership, they asked? And after the honeymoon of the first few months was over, did the membership benefits justify the expectations and the dues?

To get to the heart of the matter, a preliminary analysis was made of the different membership categories. These categories were defined based on the number of member company employees as shown in Exhibit 6-16.

Using this basic segmentation, the next thing that was analyzed was the distribution of income by category.

As can be seen in Exhibit 6-17, Category "C"—the largest com-

Exhibit 6-16 Comparative Analysis of Membership Categories

CATEGORY	NUMBER OF MEMBER COMPANY EMPLOYEES	ANNUAL DUES & OTHER REVENUES[9]	NUMBER OF SOCIETY MEMBERS IN CATEGORY	COMMENTS
CATEGORY "A"	1–50	2,642	2,264	Largest category of members includes individual members
CATEGORY "B"	51–500	6,436	638	Medium sized firms
CATEGORY "C"	501 +	14,436	272	Large product marketing companies

panies—was the smallest in terms of number of members (7%) but amounted to more than 25% of the income. The 72% of the membership represented by the smallest companies and individuals, Category "A," represented only 45% of the income and only Category "B" had a good balance between number of companies, 20%, and income, 29%.

Through these relatively obvious and simple steps, a clearer picture of the membership issues begins to emerge, and it is possible to make another essential calculation—the relative "churn" or "attrition rate"—by category (Exhibit 6-18).

This churn analysis determined whether there appeared to be any significant category differences.

While the actual churn was less than the Society had feared, it was still greater than it could have been and the analysis provided the specific information to understand and attack the problem if indeed there was one. To determine in economic terms[10] whether or not there really was a problem, it was necessary to understand:

1. The relative profitability of each membership category over its lifetime (after compensating for attrition).

2. The relationship between the actual and allowable costs of recruitment.

Exhibit 6-17 Distribution of Membership and Income by Category

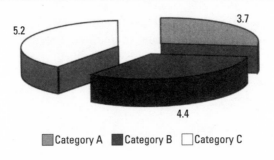

Exhibit 6-19 shows the result of that work.

As we can see, Category "C" is the most profitable, not surprising when we consider that its dues are the highest and its attrition the lowest. Category "A" is the least profitable on an individual member basis.

Exhibit 6–20 describes the economics of the recruitment process. Note that the *actual cost of recruiting a member is a constant 387.00*, substantially less for each category than the "allowable." This finding pointed to a recruitment procedure that made no distinction between the various categories of members. It also signified that there was considerable leverage—the difference between the actual

Exhibit 6-18 Attrition Rate by Category

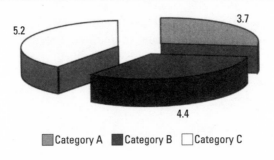

Exhibit 6-19 Lifetime Revenue, Expenses and Profits by Categories

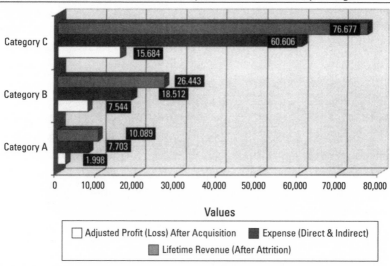

Exhibit 6-20 Actual and Allowable Costs Per Member

and the allowable recruitment cost—for using different recruitment strategies appropriate to each category rather than a standard procedure. And this made it possible to design new, segmented recruitment "offers" that could better align new member's expectations with reality.

The analysis also highlighted the fact that the Society could afford to spend considerably more than the allowable to recruit the

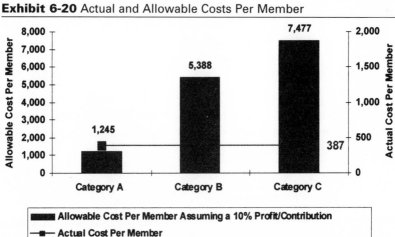

right members for each category. This meant that by changing the recruitment "mix" more new and profitable members could be recruited in each category. The expanded membership size had a profound effect on the amortization of fixed costs, thereby raising the amount of money available to fund better services or build reserves.

One further note on this case is worth considering. The Marketing Committee had something of a fixation on the idea that they could run out of potential new members—thus to their natural fear of "churn" was added another concern. What they came to realize was that just because a target group had been promoted once or twice didn't mean it could not be promoted with success over and over again, in fact, until it stopped producing new members at a cost below the allowable.[11]

Financial Service Products: Complex Products Needing a Unique Perspective

Financial services are like Lego. You take a pile of basic pieces—whether the financial services provider is lending you money (loans, mortgages, credit cards, etc.) or you are depositing money (savings, investments, pensions, insurance)—and the economic planning issues vary very little. You combine the pieces into infinite and exciting combinations, and these are the financial service "products" that are offered to the public. They can be reconstructed in minutes and new variations appear regularly.

While many financial service products are relatively simple from a marketing standpoint, many are sufficiently complex to warrant looking at them separately from nonfinancial services.

Credit Cards

Many years ago when Diners' Club was making one of its major efforts to directly compete with the larger, stronger American Express card, the company ran an extremely innovative and much talked-about advertising campaign in the U.S. The president of the Diners' Club, said the copy, wanted to *buy* your "used" American Express card.

At that time, both Diners' and American Express charged $15.00 per year for the card, and both companies were signing up thousands of new establishments who would accept their plastic. Diners' had more establishments, but Amex had more cardholders and was the substantial market leader. The Amex card also had considerable prestige attached to it. Diners' was eager to eat some of Amex's lunch rather than live on crumbs from their table.

Diners' strategy was to convince you to sign up for one of their cards on the theory that as it was accepted at more establishments than its competitor, once you started to use it you would find it was a "better" card than Amex's and continue using it. (Both companies then published a directory of establishments that accepted their cards so knowing which card had more was simply a matter of counting pages of very small type.[12]) The aggressive copy was an exciting way of personalizing the proposition, but there was solid economic thinking behind the initiative. The offer worked like this:

▶ The consumer would pay Diners' $15.00 and receive a card with a one year expiration.

▶ The consumer would give Diners' their Amex Card Number and Expiration Date.

▶ Diners' would then send a check to the consumer for the value of the unexpired portion of his/her Amex card. For example, if there were six months left before expiration, the check would be for $7.50, half the annual fee.

▶ The consumer would then have both cards and could decide which was better.

There was both marketing and economic strategy at work here. On the marketing side, Diners' figured that by advertising this offer in up-scale newspapers and magazines, they could:

▶ Economically reach their prime target audience of current affluent credit cardholders at a relatively low cost per thousand.

▶ Since the mailing list of Amex cardholders was obviously unavailable, they couldn't use direct mail.

▶ Amex's credit checking procedures were far more rigorous than Diners' were. As a significant side benefit, by simply checking the Amex card numbers to be sure they were still cardholders in good standing, the need for the normal expensive credit checking was eliminated at a substantial saving. And since all "live" Amex cardholders that applied would more than qualify to be Diners' members, the high cost of rejection would also disappear.

▶ By having the expiration dates of the Amex cardholders, Diners' was in a position to reinforce their offer just ahead of the date that Amex cardholders were going to receive a $15.00 debit for another year of use.

▶ Readers of the newspapers and magazines who were not Amex cardholders would increase their awareness of Diners' and see the company as an exciting David taking on an established Goliath. And hopefully, they would decide to join Diners', an option that was secondary but by no means lost in the promotion.

Here are the estimated economics. Starting from a known "allowable" of $50.00 for a new member, Diners' made a provision for the normal $7.00 cost of credit checking and a rejection percentage of as high as 50 percent (which doubled this cost per accepted cardholder). Even adding the payment of $7.50, the six-month portion of the Amex cardholders' membership fee, Diners' came out ahead by $13.48 per new member, as shown in Exhibit 6-21. And when the new Diners' members additionally recruited from the same advertising spend were added in, the campaign was highly profitable.

It took Amex a while to respond, but when they did, they once again took the high ground. They made two dramatic moves that saved them substantial money and made it too expensive for Diners' to continue the campaign:

▶ Amex stopped publishing their directory and sending it to all their members for a tremendous cost saving. Now Diners' could no longer make a *supportable claim* that it had more establishments, as there was no longer a way of counting them.

Exhibit 6-21 Economics of the Diners' Club/Amex Battle

$

Economics before Campaign:

	$
Established 'Allowable' for a New Diners' Cardholder Excluding Credit Checking	50.00
Normal Cost of Credit Checking each Applicant	7.00
Percentage of Applicants Normally Accepted	50%
Adjusted Cost of Credit Checking after Rejection	14.00
Total Allowable Cost	**64.00**

Campaign Economics:

	$
Established 'Allowable' for a New Diners' Cardholder Excluding Credit Checking	50.00
Cost of Credit Checking each Amex Applicant	0.50
Percentage of Applicants Accepted	97%
Adjusted Cost of Credit Checking after Rejection	0.52
Average Cost of Refund to Amex Cardholders (six months)	7.50
Total Cost	**50.52**
Savings to Diners' Club on New Member Acquisition	**13.48**

▶ Amex also *raised* its annual membership fee, both increasing its revenue and making it too expensive for Diners' to offer to refund the unused portion.

Giving Credit Where Credit Is Due

Credit card companies are frequently assessing how much they can afford to spend to acquire new cardholders based on a series of criteria.[13] As credit card debt has continued to rise, *managing the credit risk has become a principal economic issue,* and most banks and other financial institutions offering credit cards only promote to prospects who have passed through a rigorous credit screen.

Competition also plays an important part in this determination and managers are all too frequently willing to promote and promote without worrying about the "allowable" simply to prevent their competitors from attracting their cardholders or prospects.

Many nonfinancial businesses now offer their own special credit cards co-branded with one of the leading names (i.e., the American Airlines Visa card). These co-branded cards take advantage of the low-cost access to a customer base of the "co-brander" and are usually administered by the credit card companies. The assumption is that both sides win. This is sometimes, but not always, true as evidenced by a recent disaster in the magazine field.

The publisher of one of the world's leading weekly news magazines was seduced into believing that offering the magazine's subscribers and prospects a new credit card carrying the magazine logo would add substantial value to its current subscriber loyalty and new subscription acquisition efforts. Management's euphoria even extended to approving advertising copy and layout concept boards showing headwaiters at top restaurants fawning over customers displaying the card.

Had the publisher undertaken even the most rudimentary research and testing he would have discovered that the very subscribers he most wanted to keep—those who had renewed their subscriptions year after year—had more than enough credit cards sharing the space in their wallets. Since the only benefit differentiator between the co-branded card and a normal one was the questionably believable presumption that having the card would give the cardholder added prestige, the very people the publisher most wanted to impress had no interest in the card, even though there was no fee during the initial year.

The people who were excited by having the card were people who didn't have any cards and the door-to-door subscription salesmen offering the card with new subscriptions were signing up new subscribers at unprecedented rates. Unfortunately the bulk of these new subscribers had insufficient financial resources to pass the credit check imposed by the partner bank before issuing the cards, and more than 85 percent were rejected. The hapless salesmen then had to go back to their formerly happy customers to tell them they wouldn't be getting their credit cards after all. Almost all immediately cancelled their subscriptions, and many angrily threw the salesman out of their homes. Fortunately the national promotional campaign was cancelled before launch.

Had the publisher looked carefully at the economics of this venture and calculated the potential cost in money and image of rejecting current and potential subscribers, many millions would have been saved and a disaster averted.

Credit screening, however, is just one of the criteria used in developing a model for the offerings of credit cards. To better understand the dynamics of credit card marketing it is important to look at all the revenue sources and costs that are the foundation stones for credit card economics. The template (Exhibit 6-22, Credit Card Economics) captures these as well as providing an input—the Credit Risk Profile—that drives the percentage of bad debt that should be assumed as a cost even after the initial credit screening.[14]

Revenue is derived by credit card companies from a number of sources:

▶ Any annual charge made for the card.

Due to the competitive environment for cards, many companies no longer charge an annual fee. (For the purposes of this simulation, there is a charge of 25.00 per year which adds 83.33 to the 40 month life of the card.)

▶ Average commission on Sales.

The commission the card provider charges the establishment where the card is used. This is designated as "Average Commission on Sales" in the model. As commissions vary among retailers and other outlets that accept the card, it is necessary to use a weighted "average" percentage commission reflecting the "mix" of commissions the company will receive.

▶ Average Annual Interest on Outstanding Balances.

Credit card companies make a substantial portion—as much as 60%—of their revenues from *the difference between the interest earned on outstanding credit balances and the amount that the credit card issuer must pay the bank or the money market for the money.* While interest rates tend to vary, credit card companies use averages for their marketing calculations.

To properly estimate credit card revenue it is necessary to know how long the card is likely to be in active use. You also need to know the average monthly expenditures that will be billed through the card and critically, the percentage of the annual purchases—the

Exhibit 6-22 Credit Card Economics and Reactivation

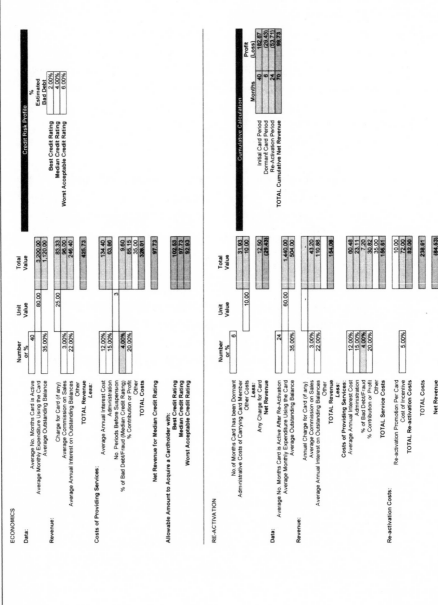

ECONOMICS

	Number or %	Unit Value	Total Value
Data:			
Average No. Months Card is Active	40		
Average Monthly Expenditure Using the Card		80.00	3,200.00
Average Outstanding Balance	35.00%		1,120.00
Revenue:			
Charge for Card (if any)		25.00	83.33
Average Commission on Sales	3.00%		96.00
Average Annual Interest on Outstanding Balances	22.00%		246.40
Other			
TOTAL Revenue			425.73
Less:			
Costs of Providing Services:			
Average Annual Interest Cost	12.00%		134.40
Administration	15.00%		63.96
No. Periods Before Suspension		3	
% of Bad Debt/Fraud (Median Credit Rating)	4.00%		9.60
% Contribution or Profit	20.00%		85.15
Other			35.00
TOTAL Costs			328.01
Net Revenue for Median Credit Rating			97.73

Allowable Amount to Acquire a Cardholder with:	
Best Credit Rating	102.63
Median Credit Rating	97.73
Worst Acceptable Credit Rating	92.93

Credit Risk Profile

	% Estimated Bad Debt
Best Credit Rating	2.00%
Median Credit Rating	4.00%
Worst Acceptable Credit Rating	6.00%

RE-ACTIVATION

	Number or %	Unit Value	Total Value
Data:			
No. of Months Card has been Dormant	6		
Administrative Costs of Carrying Card Member		10.00	31.93
Other Costs			10.00
Less:			
Any Charge for Card			
Net Revenue			(29.43)
Data:			
Average No. Months Card is Active After Re-Activation	24		
Average Monthly Expenditure Using the Card		60.00	1,440.00
Average Outstanding Balance	35.00%		504.00
Revenue:			
Annual Charge for Card (if any)		-	
Average Commission on Sales	3.00%		43.20
Average Annual Interest on Outstanding Balances	22.00%		110.88
Other			
TOTAL Revenue			154.08
Less:			
Costs of Providing Services:			
Average Annual Interest Cost	12.00%		60.48
Administration	15.00%		23.11
% of Bad Debt/Fraud	4.00%		7.20
% Contribution or Profit	20.00%		30.82
Other			35.00
TOTAL Service Costs			156.61
Re-activation Costs:			
Re-activation Promotion Per Card			10.00
Cost of Incentive	5.00%		72.00
TOTAL Re-activation Costs			82.00
TOTAL Costs			238.61
Net Revenue			(64.53)

Cumulative Calculation

	Months	Profit (Loss)
Initial Card Period	40	182.87
Dormant Card Period	6	(29.43)
Re-Activation Period	24	(53.71)
TOTAL Cumulative Net Revenue	70	99.73

average outstanding balance—which will *not be paid at the end of the month and on which interest will be charged.* It is good practice to be conservative in estimating the number of months and the average outstanding balance percentage.

Costs for providing the credit card services include the "Average Annual Interest Cost" noted above—the annual rate the credit card issuer pays to raise the money it "lends" to the credit card users. Then there is the cost of administering the card, a percentage amount for bad debt and fraud[15] and finally, the "Percentage Contribution or Profit" objective. What's left is what the company can afford to pay for cardholders with different risk profiles.

For banks and other credit card issuers, heavy users with good credit, especially those who don't pay off their balances at the end of each month and essentially "borrow" money from the issuer, are like the prettiest girls at the Prom. Everyone is asking them for the next dance.

Unused Credit Cards Share Space in Wallet, Not Share of Wallet

This creates a substantial competitive problem for the credit card companies. It's one thing to have a lot of cards in circulation. But even if the card company charges for the card, it makes its money from its commissions on use and from the spread between the interest it pays for money and the greater interest it charges card-users who do not pay up at the end of each month. If the cards are sitting idly in purses and wallets, the company has the costs of maintaining the account, sending out statements and the like.

Reactivation of cards—getting cardholders not using their cards to start using them again—becomes a major marketing issue and impacts the total economics of the card business. It is exactly this issue that caused American Express to drop its historic "green" card in the U.S.: Cardholders had reduced their use of the card because competitive cards made it more attractive to use theirs instead. And what made the competitive cards more attractive was a combination of incentives for use and lower interest rates on outstanding balances.

Said the *Wall Street Journal* article at the time of the American Express announcement:

> American Express has decided to replace the original green
> card . . . with newer-fangled charge cards that allow holders
> to earn merchandise points and frequent-flyer miles for
> every dollar charged . . . The move reflects a growing reality
> in the industry . . . People increasingly won't use their
> charge cards unless they're rewarded with points and miles
> for each purchase.

What the credit card issuers want is the maximum "share of wallet"
in its truest sense. The economic question becomes how much of
an incentive can the card company afford to re-activate a card and
how much card usage will the incentive generate?

In the "Credit Card Economics" model (Exhibit 6-22) we looked
at earlier, the Net Revenue available for marketing for the cardholder with a "median" credit rating was 97.73. That assumed an
"Average Monthly Expenditure Using the Card" of 80.00 for 40
months and an "Average Outstanding Balance"—the amount left un-
paid at the end of each month—of 35 percent. It also assumed that
the "Percentage Contribution or Profit" was 20 percent of the total
revenue or 85.15.

Let's say that after the 40 months the cardholder receives a sexier offer from a competitor and starts to use that card, leaving the
former card in his wallet or worse, in a desk drawer. On the assumption that all of the 97.73 available for marketing to the median
credit rating prospect was used and the issuer had put his contribution of 85.15 into his profit account, what happens next?

The average monthly expenditure now drops to 0.00 as does the
contribution or profit as this is based on card usage. The six-month
dormant period, even with the proportionate card charge (probably
not available as a necessary expense to meet competition) has a loss
of 29.43.

Cumulatively over the first 40 profitable months and the next 6
unprofitable months the issuer still has a cardholder who has recouped his recruitment and administrative costs and contributed
the first 40 month profit of 182.87 less the "dormant" six-month loss
of 29.43 for a total of 153.44 to the bottom line.

The conundrum for the marketer—the 153.44 question so to
speak is: Should he cancel the card and write-off the cardholder as

not worth keeping or reinvest some of his hard-earned 153.44 in re-activation with all its new dimensions?

Exhibit 6-23 (an extension of Exhibit 6-22, the "Credit Card Economics" template) makes some additional assumptions (as one always must for any economic planning purposes):

▶ The continued "life" of this card will only be another 24 months.

▶ There will be no annual charge for the card.

▶ The average expenditure will drop to 60.00 per month.

▶ It will cost 10.00 per card member in promotion to reactivate the card.

▶ An incentive such as airline miles will have to be offered, and this will cost 1 percent of revenue.

As can be seen in Exhibit 6-23, the Net Revenue[16] is an additional loss of 26.93 less an add-back of the 20 percent contribution or profit amount of 30.82 for a net loss of 26.75. Thus when the initial card period profit and previous profits are combined with the reactivation exercise the cumulative still delivers a profit of 157.33 (Exhibit 6-24).

An optimist would make the assumption that now that the card-holder has been rescued, his performance will improve and more profits will flow in. A more conservative (and pessimistic) marketer might do one more calculation. He might ask: How much would the numbers have to change negatively for the reactivation to have been not worth the effort?

Surprisingly, he would discover that even if after all the reacti-vation promotion the cardholder still didn't spend anything using the card, the 70 months would have shown a minimal profit of 108.44, not exactly a fortune but not a disaster either.

If the cardholder had been replaced with a new one at the same acquisition cost as the first, (62.53) would this new cardholder have performed as well during the first 40 months? Also, had the issuer been more alert to the competitive challenges, could the subsequent loss have been prevented? It's impossible to know, and while we can model probable scenarios, the dynamic of marketing means that in

Exhibit 6-23 Reactivation

Template CREDIT CARD ECONOMICS & RE-ACTIVATION

ECONOMICS

	Number or %	Unit Value	Total Value
Data:			
Average No. Months Card is Active	40		
Average Monthly Expenditure Using the Card		80.00	3,200.00
Average Outstanding Balance	35.00%		1,120.00
Revenue:			
Charge for Card (if any)		25.00	83.33
Average Commission on Sales	3.00%		98.00
Average Annual Interest on Outstanding Balances	22.00%		246.40
Other			
TOTAL Revenue			428.73
Less:			
Costs of Providing Services:			
Average Annual Interest Cost	12.00%		134.40
Administration	15.00%		83.86
No Periods Before Suspension		3	
% of Bad Debt/Fraud (Median Credit Rating)	4.00%		9.60
% Contribution or Profit	20.00%		85.15
Other			35.00
TOTAL Costs			328.01
Net Revenue for Median Credit Rating			97.73

Allowable Amount to Acquire a Cardholder with:

Best Credit Rating			102.53
Median Credit Rating			97.73
Worst Acceptable Credit Rating			92.93

Credit Risk Profile

	% Estimated Bad Debt
Best Credit Rating	2.00%
Median Credit Rating	4.00%
Worst Acceptable Credit Rating	6.00%

RE-ACTIVATION

	Number or %	Unit Value	Total Value
No of Months Card has been Dormant	6		
Administrative Costs of Carrying Card Member		10.00	31.93
Other Costs			10.00
Less:			
Any Charge for Re-Activation			12.50
Net Revenue			(29.43)
Data:			
Average No. Months Card is Active After Re-Activation	24		
Average Monthly Expenditure Using the Card		60.00	1,440.00
Average Outstanding Balance	35.00%		504.00
Revenue:			
Annual Charge for Card (if any)		-	
Average Commission on Sales	3.00%		43.20
Average Annual Interest on Outstanding Balances	22.00%		110.88
Other			
TOTAL Revenue			154.08
Less:			
Costs of Providing Services:			
Average Annual Interest Cost	12.00%		60.48
Administration	15.00%		23.11
% of Bad Debt/Fraud	4.00%		7.20
% Contribution or Profit	20.00%		30.82
Other			35.00
TOTAL Service Costs			156.61
Re-activation Costs:			
Re-activation Promotion Per Card			10.00
Cost of Incentive	1.00%		14.40
TOTAL Re-activation Costs			24.40
TOTAL Costs			181.01
Net Revenue			(26.93)

Cumulative Calculation

	Months	Profit (Loss)
Initial Card Period	40	182.87
Dormant Card Period	6	(29.43)
Re-Activation Period	24	3.89
TOTAL Cumulative Net Revenue	70	157.33

Exhibit 6-24 Cumulative Calculation

Cumulative Calculation		
	Months	Profit (Loss)
Initial Card Period	40	182.87
Dormant Card Period	6	(29.43)
Re-Activation Period	24	3.89
TOTAL Cumulative Net Revenue	70	157.33

the end, instinctive judgment calls backed by as much data as possible are the best you can hope for.

Unique Aspects of Selling Insurance

One of the greatest direct-response lead-gathering insurance ads had the unforgettable headline: "You Are Probably Worth More Dead Than Alive: We Have a Plan to Change That." The proposition was one of the first equity-linked insurance plans providing the insured with a combination of a mutual fund and insurance. Leads flooded in.

Marketing planning for insurance policies is often based on what are sometimes called "life changes"—those moments when we get married, have children, move, buy a new car, and so forth. Being "dead" is certainly a significant "life change" but not one much liked by insurers, especially "life" companies who have to pay out when this event occurs.

The use of direct marketing methodologies is well established within the insurance community, and many companies offer policies to the public on what amounts to a "trial" basis with a low first monthly or even yearly premiums. The sales process is based on extensive "up" and "cross" selling from the original policy. In planning this marketing, it is always necessary to distinguish between the original "promotional" price and the "regular" price.

A major international insurance company offering household and automobile coverage found that the most important factors in acquiring new clients and selling their policies were:

▶ For household coverage:

- Size of the household (number of rooms and type of dwelling for household insurance) and the expiration date of the current policy.

▶ For automobile coverage:

- The type and make of the prospect's car and the expiration date of the current policy.

With this knowledge, gleaned from responses from consumers who completed an extensive general marketing questionnaire, they were able to make specific and pre-priced offers based on this knowledge. And by knowing the expiration date of the current policies, they were able to time individual promotions just in advance of the annual renewal date when the policyholder would have to pay his existing insurance company a new premium. Often these offers had a low "front-end" premium as an incentive and the premium rose over time.[17]

So successful was the use of this data that the marketing cost of acquiring a new policyholder for the company was reduced to one-fourth of what it had traditionally been paying to sell the same policies.

Keeping the Insurance in Force: Where the Profit Is

As a rule, insurance policies are paid for either monthly or annually and while most have no fixed "term"—the length of time they will be in force—and are renewed automatically, the policy holder has the option to cancel either:

▶ Through ceasing to pay the premiums or,

▶ Giving notice of the wish to cancel.

Let's look at an insurance policy paid monthly. It doesn't much matter whether it is for automotive or household insurance or one of the far more complicated "life" and pension products. *Thinking of it as a "subscription" with an open-ended term should provide an accountable planning reference.*

The key variables for economic planning purposes for insurance that differ from other marketing forms are:

▶ The maximum number of months the insurance will be paid and in force. This is an estimate based on past experience and does not yet take into account attrition.

▶ The estimated attrition:

- This will be an estimate of the past attrition experienced by the insurance company for the particular type of policy. Policyholders of motor and household insurance are more likely to be attracted by competitive offers and have shorter lifetime values than "life" policyholders who often have a build-up of cash values in their policies.

▶ The "cost" (in lost revenue) of a low introductory offers.

▶ The "cost" of providing the service including all operating costs (other than underwriting and general administration) pertaining to the policy.

▶ The cost of "underwriting"—providing the insurance coverage. This is the cost of providing the insurance as calculated on the basis of the degree of actuarial risk and many other factors. All insurance companies will have expert underwriters who calculate the percentage needed to cover the risk of a specific type of policy.

Exhibit 6-25[18] shows a promotional plan to run free standing inserts in three magazines designated Magazines "A", "B" and "C." This plan shows two magazines, "A" and "B," producing orders at substantially less than the allowable and Magazine "C" coming in at a cost higher than the allowable. It would be a judgment call for the marketer whether he was prepared to use Magazine "C" even at the high cost per new policyholder. Certainly, the average cost per new policyholder of the three magazines together, 76.29 would argue in favor of going ahead even if this one publication was estimated to be more expensive than the allowable.

There is a caution, however. The vertical line on the graph in the illustration indicates that the expected response percentages (0.8690 percent) exceed the response percentages normal for magazine inserts (the shaded area between 0.3 percent and 0.7 percent). The marketer must therefore ask himself what good reasons he has to believe that he will achieve these percentages and if the reasons are not good enough, to scale back his estimates and think again.

As noted previously, many policies are offered to the public on

Exhibit 6-25 Alternative Magazine Promotional Plans

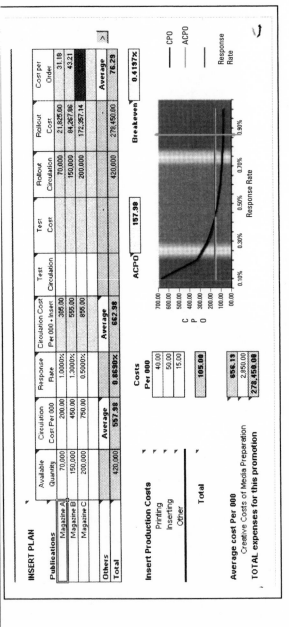

INSERT PLAN

Publications	Available Quantity	Circulation Cost Per 000	Response Rate	Circulation Cost Per 000 + Insert	Test Circulation	Test Cost	Rollout Circulation	Rollout Cost	Cost per Order
Magazine A	70,000	200.00	1.0000%	305.00			70,000	21,825.00	31.18
Magazine B	150,000	450.00	1.3000%	555.00			150,000	84,267.86	43.21
Magazine C	200,000	750.00	0.5000%	855.00			200,000	172,357.14	76.29
Others									
		Average		**Average**					**Average**
Total	420,000	557.98	0.8690%	662.98			420,000	278,450.00	76.29

ACPO 157.98   **Breakeven** 0.4197%

Insert Production Costs

	Costs Per 000
Printing	40.00
Inserting	50.00
Other	15.00
Total	**105.00**

Average cost Per 000 656.19
Creative Costs of Media Preparation 2,850.00
TOTAL expenses for this promotion 278,450.00

CPO —
ACPO —
Response Rate

CPO values: 700.00, 600.00, 500.00, 400.00, 300.00, 200.00, 100.00, 00.00

Response Rate axis: 0.10%, 0.30%, 0.50%, 0.70%, 0.90%

Response Rate

what amounts to a "trial" basis with a low first monthly or even yearly premium. That's why it is always necessary to distinguish between the original offer price and any new price and to deal with the different prices accordingly. It is also necessary to estimate the percentage of people taking the trial offer who will accept the higher price after the trial and the costs of promoting to them to achieve the "conversion."

Like magazine subscriptions, insurance policies that need a conversion or renewal sequence[19]—a series of promotional activities to achieve a conversion or renewal after a trial offer or a specific term (i.e., the first year)—have the additional cost of the renewal process and this can be significant. Obviously, the percentage of people who renew is a critical factor in assessing the potential profitability.

Don't Sell Only One Policy: Sell as Many as Possible

Since most insurance companies offer a broad range of policies, it is important for them to carefully decide which should be offered in traditional sales channels and which might be better (or also) offered through direct marketing.

One insurance company approached the issue by looking at each type of policy and building a total marketing model for all the different types of policies. Their approach was extremely careful and detailed because their overall objective was the construction of a model that could be used over and over again.

The accompanying overview of their "Model Development Sequence" (Exhibit 6-26) is instructive not only for the planning of insurance marketing but almost all other forms of marketing as well. Starting from the particular (the basic policy data) and continuing to combine the various sections of the model, they built a series of interactive spreadsheets. This allowed them to plan all aspects of their marketing on a "micro" basis and then aggregate all the data into a comprehensive "macro" P&L.

Knowing what they could afford to pay for each policyholder— the difference between the estimated lifetime policy revenue less all the underwriting and administrative costs plus the profit target— the marketing people began planning their efforts. Because they had considerable media (both lists and print media) available to

Exhibit 6-26 Insurance Model Development Sequence

STEP 1: BASIC POLICY DATA

STEP 2: INSURANCE KEY DATA

STEP 3: DIRECT MAIL AND PRESS DATA

STEP 4: MARKETING SUMMARY

STEP 5: CAMPAIGN SUMMARY

STEP 6: PROFIT & LOSS
SUMMARY

them, they decided to test thoroughly and then follow-through with rollouts of the most successful efforts.

Detailed matrixes were constructed to capture all the necessary costs of both direct mail and the use of press inserts, flyers, and other media.

The matrix Exhibit 6-27 shows only two of the eight list segments tested and was developed to clearly assign costs where they belonged. Note that each segment has a promotional code that will stay in the model throughout the campaign allowing tracking that is the keystone of accountability.

This matrix served as a basic tool for the insurance company in developing all its direct mail costs and making critical marketing decisions. The same template was used for all the different types of policy offerings as the basic mailing elements were not related to the product and specifics for each type of policy could easily be added or subtracted. The boxed information provides the common aspects of all order handling.

The same form of matrix was used for press media. As can be seen in Exhibit 6-28, it captured all the necessary information for the planning of the press inserts, "stuffers" for the insurance com-

Exhibit 6-27 List Segment Cost Analysis

Marketing Cost Input -1-
Direct Mail:

Product Test Code	LTA Segment 1 LTA1	LTA Segment 2 LTA2
Mailings:	Cost Per (000)	Cost Per (000)
Letter	18.00	18.00
Brochure	30.00	30.00
Order Card	8.00	8.00
Outer Envelope	9.00	9.00
BRE	5.00	5.00
Postage	150.00	150.00
Other 1	0.00	0.00
Other 2	0.00	0.00
Total	220.00	220.00
Lists	70.00	70.00
Deduplication	12.00	12.00
Mailsort	8.00	8.00
Total	90.00	90.00
Lettershop	12.00	12.00
Other 1	0.00	0.00
Other 2	0.00	0.00
Total	12.00	12.00
Total All Elements	322.00	322.00
Total Mailing Size	12,500	12,500
Total Cost	4,025	4,025
Estimated Net Response % *	0.45%	0.45%
Number of Responses	56	56
Cost Per Response	71.56	71.56
Note: * Conversion Percentage	90.00%	

Order Handling:	Cost Per Unit Currency
Incoming Telephone	0.00
Incoming Postage	0.30
Handling	2.25
Mail/Phone	2.55
Total DM & Order Handling Cost	133.008

pany's other statement mailings, and off-the-page response advertisements that were planned for newspapers and magazines.

The direct mail, press marketing and fulfillment cost data fed the "Promotion Matrix"—the "Marketing Summary" that followed.

Exhibit 6-28 Print Promotion Analysis

Print Media

Product	Code	Test	Media Type/Name	Media Type	No. Insertions	Circulation Per Insertion	Unit Media Cost Per (000)	Unit Insert Per (000)	Total Media & Insert	Cost Per Thousand
LTA	LTAPI1	One Step	Consumer (Inc. Nat. Press)	Insert	2	1,000,000	30.00	30.00	120,000	60.00
LTA	LTAST1	One Step	Statement Stuffers	Insert	1	500,000	0.00	30.00	15,000	30.00
LTA	LTAAD1	One Step	Press & Magazines	Ads	10	50,000	35.00	0.00	17,500	35.00

Product	Code	Test	Media Type/Name	Media Type	Est. Gross Response	Conversion %	Est. Net Response*	Total Number Responses	Cost Per Response
LTA	LTAPI1	One Step	Consumer (Inc. Nat. Press)	Insert	0.050%	75.00%	0.038%	750	160.00
LTA	LTAST1	One Step	Statement Stuffers	Insert	0.100%	75.00%	0.075%	375	40.00
LTA	LTAAD1	One Step	Press & Magazines	Ads	0.050%	75.00%	0.038%	188	93.33

Its objective was to compare *estimated* and *allowable* marketing costs and determine the percentage response levels necessary to "breakeven."

Following the examples provided in this chapter and using the accompanying templates will hopefully make the planning of complex product and service offerings more manageable. The secret is to keep the focus on the delicate balance between the need to acquire customers with the sexiest possible offers and the rigorous demands of disciplined economic planning.

Notes

[1] UK regulators have recently begun investigating the practice of offering extended warranties, concerned with possible abuses and over-charging by the offering companies.

[2] While not a primary concern, direct marketing makes it easier for the manufacturer to inventory components separately and in one place and to package and assemble them to meet the individual choices of the customers whereas retailers are unlikely to want to carry this "variable" inventory. They want the customer to buy what's "in the box".

[3] DVDokê is the video version of Kereokê where there is a well-produced video for visual environment, which, along with the pre-recorded instrumental tracks creates a total background for the singer.

[4] In theory, a complete database should exist of all hardware owners either compiled from "warranty" and registration cards or compiled at the point-of-sale. In practice, this is seldom the case. Manufacturers tend not to hold the warranty and registration information on a database (if they keep the warranty registrations at all) and retailers are reluctant to share the data with the manufacturers.

[5] The issues concerned with "Positive" and "Negative" option promotional efforts are discussed in Chapter 5.

[6] The ACPO Model is a software package created by the author for the purpose of planning DM & CRM actions. For more information and trial, visit *www.acpomodel.com*.

7 The COMSAT initiative pre-dated Direct TV by a number of years.

8 These sensitivities to the base case are obviously optional. Any possible offers can be modeled in the same way.

9 Dues and "Other Revenues" (participation fees, etc.) have been "weighted" to eliminate discrepancies.

10 The essence of the issue was more than economic. While the economics were important, what was critical in developing the new strategies was to assess and then reconfigure the range of services wanted and needed by each member category (and many sub-categories) and to assure that these were tested and offered appropriately.

11 Marketers always ask the question of how many times you can promote the same target group. The answer is simple: you can keep promoting until the cost per response exceeds the allowable.

12 An earlier part of the campaign had the President of Diners' Club offering a "friendly wager" to the President of American Express. "I'll pay you a dollar for every establishment that accepts the American Express card if you'll pay me a dollar for every one that accepts Diners' Club. That's the easiest way I know to make $75,000." It was reported that the then President of American Express, James Robinson, became increasingly annoyed when friends at dinner parties asked him if he had accepted the wager.

13 In the summer of 2003, Citigroup purchased the credit card business of catalog retailer Sears for more than $3 billion. The portfolio is the largest private-label card in the U.S. and is reported to have 25 million accounts and $18.4 billion in receivables. This values each account at $120.00.

14 Each financial institution has its own systems for calculating credit risk and these are used to decide whether to accept or reject an application for a credit card. These have not been addressed here. But despite banks' best efforts to avoid bad debt before it happens by rejecting applicants deemed unsuitable for credit, bad debt and fraud add additional costs and these have to be calculated in determining how much can be spent to acquire each new cardholder.

15 The template provides three inputs under the "Credit Risk Profile". These deliver a separate "allowable" for the best, median and worst acceptable credit ratings. The "Percentage of Bad Debt/Fraud"

input always references the median credit risk from the "Credit Risk Profile" classifications.

[16] These figures apply only to the customer with the Median Risk Profile. However, the template allows identical calculations for each of the risk profiles.

[17] "Term" insurance, which does not build up any "cash" values but simply covers the risk is most often marketed this way. The economic assumption is that the policyholder, once he has the insurance, will not wish to give it up and will pay the increased premiums.

[18] The illustration is taken from a run of the ACPO Model®.

[19] The terms "conversion" and "renewal" have as many definitions within insurance and other financial service companies as they do within publishing companies that offer magazine subscriptions. Normally (but not always), a "conversion" is someone who has had a trial offer and accepts the service as a regular policyholder (subscriber). He "converts" from trial to full service. A "renewal" is normally (but not always), a person who "renews" his policy after a specific term or, in some cases, the expression is used to mean someone who has completed a year of policyholding or subscription and agreed to continue for a second or subsequent year.

▶▶▶ 7

Using Incentives to Stimulate and Enhance Sales and for CRM

There is a magic moment when we are on the cusp between the contemplation of a purchase and actually putting our money on the table or in an envelope and making it. One of the things that will often nudge us into the purchase is an incentive—some form of enticement to help overcome the always-present purchase barrier.

Industry experience teaches that customers respond positively to incentives, and the whole CRM discipline is built on both "fiscal" incentives (rewards) and emotional incentives (recognition as a special customer).

The incentive may be something that comes "free" with the purchase, extra quantity in the bottle, an interest-free loan, a cash rebate or other discount, a chance to win millions in a sweepstake or a trip around the world. Or it may be some form of special recognition, even membership on a special "valued customer consumer panel."[1] Whatever the type of incentive, the key objectives are to encourage us to *buy now* or to *give us a good reason not to become an attrition casualty*. The incentive as part of the offer can make the difference between making a sale and having your promotion ignored[2] and between keeping or losing a valued customer.

The following news announcement appeared in a *DM News/E Marketing Daily* email. It is illustrative of one of the types of incentives used by marketers.

> Best Buy Stores announced yesterday the national rollout of Reward Zone, a loyalty program to recognize its best customers. Available in all of Best Buy's 550 U.S. loca-

tions, Reward Zone is open to any shopper 13 or older. After paying a $9.99 annual fee, members get a Reward Zone membership card that credits them with 100 points for each dollar spent. Every time a member's balance reaches 12,500 points, a $5 award certificate redeemable for any Best Buy purchase over $10 is issued.

Incentives or Bribes: A Two-Edged Sword

What we do when we make an investment to acquire a new customer or in CRM activities to retain that customer and enhance the amount he spends with us is effectively to "purchase" the customer and his continued loyalty.

It is important to recognize that "purchased" customers or loyalty are subject to the same rules as customers who come in without incentives. They must be offered what they perceive they want and not simply "bribed" by large incentives to buy something they don't really want.

The use of incentives such as million dollar sweepstakes—most often associated with multiple magazine subscriptions (as illustrated in Exhibit 7–1)—that promise the sweepstakes' winners giant sums of money may temporarily increase subscription circulation, but they also fight with the product's (to say nothing of the industry's) integrity.[3]

The opposite is true when the premium is directly relevant to the product as could be seen in the "Competitive Interest Rate Example" in Chapter 1. *If the bribe is large enough, you can get almost anyone to buy something to get the incentive even if they have no interest in the product.* To make the next purchase, the customer will want a repeat of the bribe or an even bigger one. It's an addictive process.[4] Don't forget: *It is not the number of responses you get but the quality that determines your profit.*

Incentives should be used to hasten action to purchase not as a substitute for sincere interest in the product. Relationships built on incentives—like marriages for money—do not have the same dynamic as those constructed on deeper foundations. Better to make sure that the reason the customer is buying from you or staying

Exhibit 7-1 Sample Sweepstakes Promotion

with you is because he wants and values the product or service you are offering rather than because he just hopes to win something.

We make an investment in acquiring and keeping customers and our intent should always be to determine the appropriate "spend" for each acquisition or CRM activity. This can be reasonably complex for products and services where there are a significant number of product and promotional variables. The costs of the premiums we either give away "free" or charge for on some basis are an integral part of the acquisition or CRM investment and must be carefully figured into the revenue and cost equations.

The *perceived value* of an incentive to the consumer often has little to do with its cost to the marketer: A "free" seat given by an airline with plenty of empty seats to give away may have only a marginal cost to the carrier, but a high perceived value to the recipient.

Incentives Come in All Forms and Sizes

There are unnumbered types of incentives, but they almost always fall into one of five categories:

▶ Free Premiums:

"Free" premiums include gifts of all kinds that are either contingent upon a purchase or given simply for a willingness to receive more information with no obligation to purchase. A "Free" CD when you purchase three other CDs would be one example; the first year's use of a credit card without a fee would be another. "Free credit" (with no interest charge) or "rebates" when buying an automobile or major appliance would also qualify as a free premium.[5] A company selling holiday homes in the Bahamas flew a planeload of English prospects from London to Grand Bahamas Island for a weekend. The only obligation on the part of the prospects was to visit the property and hear a sales presentation. Despite its high per-person cost, it proved extremely cost-effective. In the case of free premiums the entire cost of both the premium and the associated shipping, etc. is almost always borne by the marketer.

▶ Self-liquidating Premiums:

These are premiums for which the marketer makes a charge in the expectation of receiving enough money to pay for (or even exceed) the actual cost to him of what he is "giving away". Offering a designer watch with a retail value of $100.00 for only $10.00 would qualify in this category.

"Self-liquidating" premiums are not always fully self-liquidating even if this generic expression is used to define them. Sometimes the marketer asks the purchaser to make a nominal payment[6] that doesn't in fact cover his whole cost and he has to absorb the difference between the actual cost to him of the premium and its delivery and the amount he receives.

▶ Premiums as Revenue Generating Products:

"Self-liquidating" premiums are intended to recoup all or at least some of their cost. But premiums can also be profit-makers. This is possible because of the often-significant difference between the cost of the premium to the marketer and the perceived commercial value to the consumer. As an example, assume that the marketer has been able to acquire the product he plans to use as a premium at a "close-out" or other very low cost. He may decide that the perceived value of the premium will be such that he can charge more than his actual cost and the consumer will still see the premium as a substantial bargain.

▶ Sweepstakes and Prizes:

The chance (however small) of winning a big prize always has a strong appeal.[7] And while the value of the prize may be extremely high (see Exhibit 7–1) the cost per person spread over a large group of customers and prospects may be relatively low.

Sweepstakes and prize draws can be very effective not only in capturing immediate consumer interest but in maintaining that interest by adding "chances to win" with additional purchases. This amortizes the cost of the prizes over a larger number of customers and purchases without increasing the fixed cost of the prizes.

▶ Miles and Loyalty Bonus Points:

Collecting "green stamps" or the equivalents as incentives to win prizes has always been a popular promotional device. The introduction of bonus "miles" for frequent airline flyers[8] raised the level of incentive collection to new heights and created a whole new class of "currencies" invented and given value by marketers. These have become a favored incentive both because of their flexibility, high perceived value and relatively low cost. Some credit cards such as American Express now give points based on each purchase and Internet sites give points for visits. Some marketers even use points as prizes in sweepstakes. Some marketers like Best Buy Stores make a charge for joining the program.

Reward and/or Recognition

Not so long ago, at the beginning of a long holiday weekend, I was waiting in an endless line at an airport for a seat on a "no reservation" shuttle flight. I watched with envy as a business colleague came into the airport, went to a special desk, and was immediately given a seat on the next departing flight. I later learned that he had arrived at his home before I even took off. Thanks to the "gold" card the airline had awarded him in recognition of his frequent travel with them, he got preferential treatment and priority seating plus the use of a comfortable lounge while waiting for his flight. He was recognized as a good customer and treated accordingly.

It cost the airline very little to give him that *recognition* in addition to its usual incentive rewards: Gold or platinum colored plastic cards don't cost more than any other color. Standing in that line, I would have happily exchanged all the bonus miles the airline was giving me for that same recognition and the saving of two and one half hours of waiting.

In thinking about *rewards*, marketers must also consider the perceived value of *recognition* and where appropriate build that recognition into their incentive programs, especially with their best customers. One Paris department store located in an area with notoriously few places to park recognized its best customers by *guaranteeing* them a parking space any time in the store's underground garage. Sales to those best customers grew by more than 17 percent directly as a result. The cost to the department store was nothing more than the communication and some modest barriers in their parking area.

As indicated earlier, a leading magazine found that its renewal rate from subscribers *who had their copies hand delivered* to them each week was more than ten percentage points higher than with those subscribers who received the copies in the post. These are perfect examples of how customer recognition and service reduced attrition and increased profits.

With so many potential incentive combinations, the economics of incentives can seem more complicated than they actually are. What do we have to know to build a model that calculates the real costs?[9]

Each of the three forms of incentive has its own economic parameters and can be analyzed on its own. However, it is advisable to consider using a comprehensive model to assess the total incentive costs where a single incentive form or combined forms are being employed. The "Incentives" Template allows the user to calculate individually each of these forms or collectively with any combina-

Exhibit 7-2 The Economics of Different Incentives

FORM OF INCENTIVE	KEY CHARACTERISTICS	COMMENT
FREE GIFTS, SELF-LIQUIDATORS, OR PROFIT MAKING INCENTIVES	• Description and cost of the Initial Gift (including shipping) • No. of **Initial** Gifts per Person (normally only 1) • Shipment number with which gift is sent • Customer payment for the gift (if any) • Description and cost of the **Subsequent** Gift(s) (including shipping) • Number of Subsequent Gifts per Person • Shipment number(s) with which gift(s) are sent • Customer payment(s) for the gift(s) (if any)	The simplest type of incentive whether freely given away, self-liquidating, or producing a surplus. Costs and any revenue must be assessed. So too does the point of shipment as all gifts given after shipment No. 1 are likely to have lower quantities than the initial gift if given at the beginning of a purchasing sequence. To determine the number of gifts that will be needed for a promotional program, the "Incentives" Template needs to link to the "Attrition" Template.
SWEEPSTAKES OR PRIZE DRAWS	• Description and cost of each "Top" prize(s) • Nos. that will be awarded • Description and cost of each of the other prize(s) • Nos. that will be awarded • No. of prospects in the promotion eligible to win a prize if open to prospects • No. of customers in the promotion eligible to win a prize	One of the beauties of sweepstakes and prize draws is that the cost of the prizes is a ***constant***, and the larger the pool of entrants, the lower the cost per customer of the actual prizes. There is usually a hierarchy of prizes ranging from the "top" prize down to as many lower value prizes as the organizers determine.

(Continued)

Exhibit7-2 The Economics of Different Incentives (Continued)

FORM OF INCENTIVE	KEY CHARACTERISTICS	COMMENT
FREE OR PAID FOR POINTS	• Actual cost to marketer per point (even if marginal) • Number of "Points" awarded for each currency unit of purchase or some other criterion (i.e., Bonus Miles model) • **Alternatively or additionally**, number of points awarded for each **regular** and/or **specific** transaction • Estimated value of per person consumer sales during the life of the program • Manner in which points will be awarded (for regular, specific transactions, etc.) • Percentage of points awarded but never redeemed, either because purchasing thresholds were not reached or through inadvertence	The "points" of bonus miles system allows the marketer to create a currency and give it value. He can give each point a value equivalent to a unit of currency. One marketer might chose to award one point for every dollar while another might say you get ten points for every dollar. What matters is the consumer perception of the value. Points can be created (as airlines and hotels have done) or purchased from companies who develop the point programs and find benefits for point redeemers. Each point has a cost and this must be factored into the total economics. Points can also be used as signals for "recognition" benefits: more than "X" points gets you a gold or platinum card. Non-redemption cuts the total cost of point systems and while companies offering points have a contingent, liability for redeeming all the points outstanding until their expiry dates, once the expiry has been reached, liability can be reduced accordingly.

tion, its objective is always the same—*to be able to assess how much the response to a marketing initiative must increase in order to pay for the incentives used to stimulate this increase.*

While the whole of the template may be greater than the sum of its parts, let's start with a look at each individual incentive form.

Free Gifts, Self-Liquidators, and Profitable Premiums

These are the most common incentive form and the easiest to calculate.

This methodology is as relevant to traditional sales promotion marketing as to direct marketing. As long as we can get a good fix on the cost per thousand of the promotion, the number of people to whom it will be directed and the number who are likely to take advantage of the offer, we can determine how much uplift we need to justify the promotion.

In Exhibit 7-3 we see a theoretical program in which a single initial gift and then two subsequent gifts are offered:

▶ An "initial" gift will be given with the first (or only) shipment ("Shipment Number") of a product or service. It has a cost to the marketer (including delivery) of 5.00. The marketer will charge the customer 1.00 for packing and shipping of the gift.

▶ There will be two subsequent gifts per customer, contingent on continued purchases and delivered with shipments number 5 and 10. Because the "Attrition" template is not linked, it will be necessary for the user to adjust the numbers for the subsequent premiums. For the purposes of conservative planning however, the costs of these two subsequent premiums have been assumed as an expense against all customers.[10] Each subsequent gift has a cost of 3.00 and each will ask the customer for 1.00 in shipping and handling.

Giving "subsequent" incentives during a long-term sales program is often both economically wise from a profit point of view and from a CRM perspective as well. Like the carrot in front of the donkey, holding those prizes out ahead of the consumer stimulates continuing purchase activity.

▶ It is assumed that 100,000 communications will be sent (the mailing or emailing campaign) at a per-thousand cost of 1,000.00 and that a 2 percent response can be safely predicted.[11]

What we see in Exhibit 7-3 is that without the incentives, the CPO is 50.00. Adding in the cost of the incentives less the distribution charge-backs adds 8.00 to the CPO, bringing it to 58.00.

The "Sensitivities" table has been set at 10 percent, plus and minus the target of a 2 percent response, to indicate what happens if the response is higher or lower (and costs more or less) than forecast. The bottom line "Additional % Response Needed to Justify Incentive" tells us that to economically justify the use of this incentive program, we need an additional .38 percent response over the target (or varying percentages if we exceed or fall short of the target). If we are not confident—as a result of testing or previous experience—that we can achieve this lift, then we ought to abandon the incentive or find some other that will justify its expense.

Sweepstakes and Prize Drawings

As discussed earlier, sweepstakes and prize draws are a popular form of incentive and particularly suited to large-scale promotional efforts where the marketer wishes to get the highest level of response even if the ultimate number of converted customers, those who end up buying something, is only a relatively small percentage of the total respondents participating in the sweepstakes. Often (and depending upon local legislation)[12] the consumer can be part of the contest and/or receive the premium, *whether or not he makes a purchase.* In economic terms, the entire cost of the sweepstakes must be amortized against *the customers* who result from the effort. Normally, promoters attract consumers by some variation of the headline, "You may already have won. . . . " Since nearly everyone has a gambling streak and wants to win something for nothing, these sweepstakes often bring in large numbers of respondents. But as indicated earlier, it is not the size (*quantity* of responses) that matters; it's the *quality* (those who become and continue to be customers) that matters.

Prize draws tend to be more low-key and depending on the local regulations often have a simple "quiz" attached.[13] The quiz is almost

Exhibit 7-3 Economics of a Gift Incentive

Initial Gift [Describe]	Product Description
Cost (Including Shipping) of Initial Gift	5.00
No. of Gifts Per Customer	1
Shipment Number	1
If there is a charge for the Initial Gift, How Much?	1.00
TOTAL Cost of Initial Gift	**4.00**

Subsequent Gift(s) [Describe]	Product Description
Cost (Including Shipping) of Subsequent Gift(s)	3.00
No. of Subsequent Gifts Per Customer	2
Shipment Number(s)	5 & 10
If there is a charge for the Subsequent Gift(s), How Much for each?	1.00
TOTAL Cost of Subsequent Gift(s)	**4.00**

TOTAL Cost of Gift(s) Per Customer	**8.00**

Forecast Number of Communications to be Sent	100,000
Forecast Communications Cost Per '000	1,000.00
Forecast Response %	2.00%
Cost Per Order/Customer, etc. Without Incentive	**50.00**
Cost Per Order/Customer, etc. With Incentive	**58.00**

Sensitivities (+ or -) To CPO As Result of Incentive

			Target		
Degree of Sensitivity	10.00%				
CPO *without* Incentive	40.00	45.00	50.00	55.00	60.00
CPO *with* Incentive	48.00	53.00	58.00	63.00	68.00
Response % without Incentive	2.60%	2.22%	2.00%	1.82%	1.67%
New Response % Needed to Justify Incentive	3.13%	2.70%	2.38%	2.13%	1.92%
Additional % Response Needed to Justify Incentive	0.63%	0.48%	0.38%	0.31%	0.25%

always related to the product being sold and entices the reader to look more closely at the offer.

Exhibit 7-4—the "Sweepstakes or Prize Draw" section of the Incentives template—requires the following information:

▶ A specific definition of all the prizes and their costs.

- Usually, sweepstakes and prize draws have a hierarchy of prizes from a "Top" prize through to some smaller prizes.[14] The template provides appropriate inputs.

▶ The forecast communications costs per thousand.

▶ The forecast number of people to whom the promotion will be made and the cost per thousand of reaching them.

▶ The forecast response percentages:

Exhibit 7-4 Economics of a Sweepstakes or Prize Drawing

Top Prize [Describe]	Product Description
Quantity of Top Prize(s)	2
Cost of Each Top Prize	50,000.00
TOTAL Cost of Top Prize(s)	100,000.00
Next Prize [Describe]	Product Description
Quantity of Next Prize(s)	5
Cost of Each Next Prize	5,000.00
TOTAL Cost of Next Prize(s)	25,000.00
Next Prize [Describe]	Product Description
Quantity of Next Prize(s)	25
Cost of Each Next Prize	50.00
TOTAL Cost of Next Prize(s)	1,250.00
TOTAL Cost of Prize(s)	126,250.00
Forecast Communications Cost Per '000	1,000.00
Forecast No. of Prospect Communications to be Sent	500,000
Forecast Response %	20.00%
Cost Per Response	5.00
No. of Respondents for Sweepstakes or Prize Draw	100,000	20.00%
TOTAL Cost of Prize(s) Per Respondant	1.26
% Who Become Customers	10.00%
Number who become Customers	10,000	2.00%
TOTAL Cost of All Prize(s) Allocated Only to Customers	12.63
TOTAL Response Cost (Incl. Sweepstakes costs) Allocated Only to Customers	62.63

Sensitivities (+ or -) for Cost of Response & Sweepstakes at Different Response Rates				
Expected % of Promotion Response *If No Sweepstakes*	2.00%			
Degree of Sensitivity	10.00%			
				Target
Expected % of Response without Sweepstakes Incentive	1.60%	1.80%	2.00%	2.20%	2.40%
Cost Per Order without Sweepstakes Incentive	62.50	55.56	50.00	45.45	41.67
Expected % of Customers with Sweepstakes Incentive	1.60%	1.80%	2.00%	2.20%	2.40%
Cost Per Order (Incl. Sweepstakes costs) Allocated Only to Customers	78.28	69.58	62.63	56.93	52.19

- For those people who just "play" in the sweepstakes and,

- For those who become customers and those who are awarded *extra opportunities* to enter as a result of their measured purchase activity.

▶ It is also necessary to know or estimate the expected percentage response from a similar promotion *without this incentive.*

Again, the purpose is to plan the sweepstakes or prize draw initiative and calculate both the cost per order with and without the sweepstake as well as necessary increases in customers to justify the costs of the sweepstakes. Sensitivities have been developed plus and minus of the "Target" starting from the expected percentage response and CPO if there were no sweepstakes.

In Exhibit 7-4, we see that the sweepstakes in its planned configuration *would not* produce a sufficiently increased return to justify its expense. Other than the prize costs, which total 126,250, the other key driver is the "% Who Become Customers" line. The keen observer will notice the "2.00**%**" to the right of the "Number who become Customers" line. What the model is telling us (see Exhibits 7-4 and 7-5) is that if after the sweepstakes only 2.0 percent of the total prospect universe become customers, *we would have achieved that without the sweepstakes.* Therefore it is only an expensive wheel spinner exercise.

However, as we contemplate a higher percentage of the universe that become customers (from 10 percent in Exhibit 7-5 to 15 percent in Exhibit 7-6), the sensitivities show us how the CPO for those customers decreases substantially and the sweepstakes looks like it will pay for itself.[15] Using the theoretical data in the model,

Exhibit 7-5 Cost Sensitivities

Sensitivities (+ or -) for Cost of Response & Sweepstakes at Different Response Rates				
Expected % of Promotion Response *If No Sweepstakes*		2.00%		
Degree of Sensitivity		10.00%		
Expected % of Response			Target	
without Sweepstakes Incentive	1.60%	1.80%	2.00%	2.20%	2.40%
Cost Per Order **without Sweepstakes Incentive**	52.50	55.56	50.00	48.45	41.67
Expected % of Customers **with Sweepstakes Incentive**	1.60%	1.80%	2.00%	2.20%	2.40%
Cost Per Order (Incl. Sweepstakes costs) ***Allocated Only* to Customers**	78.28	69.58	62.53	56.93	52.19

Exhibit 7-6 Cost Sensitivities

Sensitivities (+ or -) for Cost of Response & Sweepstakes at Different Response Rates					
Expected % of Promotion Response *If No Sweepstakes*	2.00%				
Degree of Sensitivity	10.00%				
Expected % of Response without Sweepstakes Incentive	1.60%	1.80%	**Target** 2.00%	2.20%	2.40%
Cost Per Order without Sweepstakes Incentive	62.50	55.56	60.00	48.45	41.67
Expected % of Customers with Sweepstakes Incentive	2.40%	2.70%	3.00%	3.30%	3.60%
Cost Per Order (Incl.Sweepstakes costs) *Allocated Only* to Customers	52.19	48.38	41.75	37.95	34.79

simply raising the percentage of people who become customers by five percentage points makes the project worthwhile.

Obviously, each marketer's objectives and data will be unique. Some will wish to simply enhance the total response; others will wish to use the technique, as Reader's Digest does, to build their prospect database. Still others will wish to make sure that their loyal customers will get additional chances to win the prizes and will stay around to collect them.

Whether or not to use sweepstakes and prize draws will depend to a great extent on the total marketing objectives and the individual parameters of the marketing initiative.

Points and Bonus Miles: The "In" Incentive

No one can dispute the basic logic of rewarding purchasers proportionate to their total purchase activity. Companies have always given their large customers *quantity discounts* and other incentives to increase their purchasing and to keep them loyal. If the myriad points and miles programs have become ubiquitous and appear to cancel one another out through over-use, until recently, the customers don't seem to have noticed. They keep collecting their bonus points or miles or any of the other new forms of currency.

Points are either "created" (as is the case with airlines, hotel chains, etc.) or purchased from a third party issuer at a negotiated rate per point. This rate is considerably less than the perceived value to the person who receives the point. It takes a certain number of points to achieve a benefit whether it is a free flight or a discount on merchandise. Sometimes points are awarded on the basis of the total amount of the spend (i.e., a certain number of points for each $X spent), sometimes for each transaction, sometimes as surprise "bonus" gifts. The uses are limited only by the marketer's imagination and by the cost.

The collector of the points is little interested in how much the issuer has paid for the points being given away: he is interested only in what the points will do for him. He wants to know how many he needs to take the family on a holiday or to get some desired item from a catalog. This essential difference between the real cost of the points and their perceived value is one of the things that give them their promotional power.

The objective of these programs is enhanced loyalty. If they don't accomplish that, they are never worth their cost—in fact, they can have a negative effect.

Consumers have become keenly aware of "points" programs that do not deliver sufficient benefits to justify the effort of dealing with them. An article in London's popular tabloid *The Evening Standard*[16] under the headline "Consumer backlash threatens store cards" highlighted this:

> The value of "gimmicky" store loyalty cards is being called into question amid signs of a growing consumer backlash. . . . Shoppers regard the tiny savings offered by loyalty cards such as Tesco Clubcard or Nectar as not worth switching stores for, according to new research.

Using Nectar, a multistore card program run in conjunction with the popular credit card, Barclaycard, as an example, the article shows that it would take an expenditure of £20,000 to save £50.00, valuing each point at 0.25 pence. It is hardly surprising that research showed "that only eight percent of shoppers would change stores to take advantage of a loyalty card compared with 58 percent who would move for lower prices.

In building an economic model of a "points" program, here are questions you will have to answer:

▶ Is there any payment to become a member of the program?[17]

While most programs encourage membership without any

kind of entry fee, some do make a charge and this must be considered in any analysis of the economics.

▶ How many points will be awarded for each currency unit if the plan is to award points on the basis of total spend?

It is almost always up to the marketer to decide how many points he will give and for what reasons. A good place to start is defining how many points will be given for each currency unit.[18]

▶ The estimated total value of sales to this customer.

▶ The profit or contribution expectation expressed as a percentage of total sales.

▶ How many points will be awarded for each "regular" transaction?

▶ How many points will be awarded for "Specific Bonus transactions"?

One of the flexible advantages of points is that they can be awarded (like "merit" bonuses) at the discretion of management. Thus, in planning the economics it is necessary to allocate sufficient points for this use if it is contemplated.

▶ How many regular and "special" transactions are contemplated?

If points are being awarded on a "per transaction" basis or for certain "special" transactions, these need to be quantified.

▶ What is the actual cost per point to the marketer?

As noted above, the points must be created or purchased and even where the reward is excess inventory (unused airline seats or hotel rooms) a cost—even a nominal one— must be attached.

Different issuers of points charge for them in different ways. The most common is that the company desirous of giving points purchases a specific number from a provider and then uses them for the promotion. Sometimes undistributed points can be returned but points given away and "unredeemed" by recipients usually cannot be returned to the issuing company.

▶ What percentage of the points that will be given to the customers will never be redeemed?

While points may be given away, many are never redeemed either because the recipient doesn't have enough for some specific award or "gives up" collecting points or for a number of other reasons. If purchased from a vendor (say an airline or 'incentive' company) these points can often be reused after they are no longer valid for the first person to whom they were awarded. However, it is good to remember that for many people, the unused points in their account are an incentive to make additional purchases so the points can be used. Marketers often give points even when the customer is using a reward. This way, the customer will always have the further purchase incentive of some unused point in his account.

There is a further related issue here. As mentioned in the incentive matrix (Exhibit 7-2), the points distributed should have a specific date beyond which they are no longer valid. Once this date has passed, the liability inherent in having granted the points is eliminated. The input of an assumed percentage for points *never used* allows you to better calculate the *real cost* of offering the points.

Once these parameters have been established, it is relatively easy to calculate the cost of points for almost any promotional program[19] and how much they must enhance your sales to be worth their cost.

In Exhibit 7-7 we see an example of an incentive "points" program that awards a single point for each unit of currency spent as well as awarding ten points for each regular transaction and an additional ten points for each of two "special" transactions. The number of points issued but not redeemed ("% Never Used") is 30% and the total value of sales to customers is 300.00. The cost to the marketer of each point is .10.

This is a rich program, probably too rich and in need of scaling

Exhibit 7-7 Economics of Points Incentives

	Regular Transaction	Specific Transaction 1	Specific Transaction 2
No. of Points Awarded Per Currency Unit	1		
Estimated TOTAL Value of Sales Per Customer	300.00		
Profit or Contribution Expectation %	15.00%		
TOTAL Points	**300.00**		
No. of Points Awarded Per Regular Transaction	10		
No. of Points Awarded Per Specific Transaction 1		10	
No. of Points Awarded Per Specific Transaction 2			10
Cost Per Point	0.10	0.10	0.10

How will Points Be Awarded?	Currency Unit	Regular Transaction	Specific Transaction 1	Specific Transaction 2
Transactions Per Customer		1.00	1.00	1.00
% Never Used	30.00%	30.00%	30.00%	30.00%
Net Points (after % Never Used)	210	7	7	7
Costs	21.00	0.70	0.70	0.70

TOTAL Cost of Points Per Customer	23.10

Sensitivities (+ or -) Additional Sales Revenue Necessary to Justify Points Program

		Regular Transaction	Target	Specific Transaction 1	Specific Transaction 2
Degree of Sensitivity	10.00%				
Estimated TOTAL Value of Sales Per Customer	240.00	270.00	300.00	330.00	360.00
Estimated Profit or Contribution Per Customer	36.00	40.50	45.00	49.50	54.00
TOTAL Incentive Program Cost Per Customer	18.50	21.00	23.10	25.20	27.00
Necessary TOTAL Value Increase to Justify Points Program Costs	128.00	140.00	154.00	168.00	183.00
Necessary % TOTAL Value Increase in Revenue	52.60%	51.85%	51.33%	50.91%	50.65%

Exhibit 7-8 Cost Sensitivities: Points Program

Sensitivities (+ or -) Additional Sales Revenue Necessary to Justify Points Program						
Degree of Sensitivity	10.00%					
Estimated TOTAL Value of Sales Per Customer	240.00	270.00	300.00	330.00	360.00	
			Target			
Estimated Profit or Contribution Per Customer	36.00	40.50	45.00	49.50	54.00	
TOTAL Incentive Program Cost Per Customer	3.78	3.99	4.20	4.41	4.62	
Necessary TOTAL Value Increase to Justify Points Program Costs	25.20	26.60	28.00	29.40	30.80	
Necessary % TOTAL Value Increase in Revenue	10.50%	9.85%	9.33%	8.91%	8.56%	

down. To justify the program the value of sales would have to climb by 154.00–from 300.00 to 454.00 or 51 percent. This is asking quite a lot and the promoter would be wise to revisit the program with other less expensive parameters.

By reducing the points given for each unit of currency from 1.00 to 0.10, and leaving everything else the same, the picture improves dramatically as we see in Exhibit 7-8.

Instead of a cost of 23.10 per customer, the cost drops to 4.20 and the uplift to justify the points promotion comes down from 51 percent to 9.33 percent. Admittedly, this is a giant step down in extra value to the customer but it need not be perceived that way. The points benefits illustrated in Exhibit 7-7 might have been stated as "one point for each dollar (or other currency unit) you spend." The same statement could be made of the example in Exhibit 7-8 simply by creating ten times as many points, each with one-tenth the redemption value of the Exhibit 7-7 case. The "flexibility" opportunity rests totally with the marketer.

The complete Incentives Template allows any or all of the incentives to be calculated and delivers a "Net Total Incentive Cost Per Customer" (Exhibit 7-9)[20] at the bottom—a summary of all the incentive costs of the program less any payments for being part of the program.

An incentive is a powerful driver of action but like any stimulant, too much is too much. Great care needs to be exercised in the use of incentives and they must never compete with the product itself. If they do, the customer will become conditioned to the premium and develop little natural loyalty to the product. Used creatively however and within acceptable economic limits, incentives can add spice to a bland offering or make the essential difference between capturing and losing the prospect's attention.

Exhibit 7-9 Program Using All Incentive Types

Incentive Program Cost Per Customer	22.72
Less:	
Program Joining Fee (If Any)	
Net TOTAL Incentive Cost Per Customer	22.72

Notes

[1] Tests have indicated that the simple idea of asking prospects their opinions on relevant subjects significantly increases response. People like to be recognized and to have their opinions solicited. They feel important and that contributes to their positive feeling about the product being offered.

[2] "The proposition you make to customers—more often referred to as *offers*—can mean the difference between success and failure. Depending on the offer, differences in response of 25, 50, 100 percent, and more are commonplace." Bob Stone, "Importance of the Offer," *Successful Direct Marketing Methods*. Lincolnwood, Illinois: NTC Business Books, 1988, Page 59.

[3] In particular, sweepstakes have been and are used by multiple magazine subscription sellers such as Publishers' Clearing House (PCH) and American Family Publishers as well as by *Reader's Digest*. Sweepstakes have recently come under attack by regulatory agencies in some countries because it is perceived that they confuse the customer into believing that he must buy something to participate. The aggressive promotional techniques have convinced many people that they have "won" a major prize when in fact they have not. As a result, sweepstakes activity has received some very bad publicity and needs careful consideration if they are to be used.

[4] Dieter Zetsche, Chief Executive of Chrysler, "has likened [automobile incentive] rebates to heroin," reported the *New York Times* (August 27, 2003) in an article on the auto industry's increasing spend on incentives.

[5] The same *New York Times* article (August 27, 2003) reported that "car companies spent an average US $2,668" per car on incentives during the previous month. Whether a little more or a little less, the order of magnitude for these incentives is a substantial part of the total marketing cost.

[6] The nominal payment may be as small as "the cost of packing and shipping" or substantially more.

[7] "Sweepstakes make the most sense when applied to a comparatively high ticket or high-mark-up sale" write Rapp & Collins in *MaxiMarketing* (Page 166).

[8] Some products and services are highly time-sensitive. An empty

airline seat has no value after the airplane door has closed. An empty hotel room is worthless unless someone is paying to use it. By making access to this unused capacity available as a currency themselves or through other marketers, the owners of the capacity can give it a value.

9 Because its purpose is to help the planning of incentive promotions and their economics, it should be noted that the "Template: Incentives" does not provide for the cost of conversion from respondent to buyer (as might be the case for sweepstakes) as there are so many variables here that it would prove unmanageable. Where additional "conversion" costs will be incurred, these can be calculated using one of the other templates.

10 If there is only a single sale and a single premium with no subsequent sales or incentives, the "Subsequent Gift(s)" section can be left blank and the effect is to eliminate the additional costs.

11 The choice of medium for the communications campaign is not relative to the model. One need only input the cost-per-thousand you would have to pay to reach the audience and the estimated response percentage.

12 It is important to become familiar with local rules and adhere strictly to them. The Reader's Digest sweepstakes for example allow buyers and non-buyers equal participation.

13 Prize draw rules in some countries make it mandatory to ask the participant in a prize draw to answer some questions or otherwise use their "intelligence" rather than simply having a chance to win.

14 An innovative UK marketing company took advantage of the popularity of the National Lottery and instead of creating its own prize list, took the much less expensive route of piggy-backing onto the National Lottery's prizes. They offered ten "Top" prizes under the headline: "50 chances to win millions of pounds" plus a number of smaller prizes. The winners were each given checks for fifty pounds, the amount needed to enter the National Lottery fifty times at one pound per time. The results were very good and produced a lift of five percent over the best previous incentive. However, the National Lottery organizers complained that the company was using their "property" and trademark and forbid future uses without a substantial payment to them.

[15] It is worth noting that in addition to acquiring new customers, the sweepstakes effort also acquired a substantial number of what could well be described as "qualified prospects". It can be assumed that a good percentage of them will be "willing" and "ready" to become customers with repeated promotion although all the sweepstakes costs have been allocated against those who become customers right away.

[16] 6th January 2004 by Jonathan Prynn, Consumer Affairs Editor, Pg. 15.

[17] Issuers of points have discovered that the best time to get customers into the program is right at the beginning of the relationship, satisfying our natural desire for instant gratification. That's why applications for membership, usually found at the store or on the hotel or the airline counter contain a temporary membership card with a unique identification number that lets the applicant start collecting points immediately and receive his permanent membership card (containing the same identification number) later.

[18] There are a number of theories on whether recipients of points want big numbers of points or whether they focus on how much benefit they can enjoy for how many points. There is also the competitive issue of other marketers using points, which then have a perceived value. All users should carefully consider this issue.

[19] If you plan to use points as prizes in sweepstakes or prize draws, you should calculate the number of points you will give away for each prize and determine their total cost and use the "sweepstakes" section of the template. This is just the same as you would if you were giving away a car and knew how much that car would cost you.

[20] The numbers shown in this summary do **not** reflect the examples shown previously. However, in using the template the summary will produce the sum of all the incentives.

▶▶▶8

Testing and Archiving:
The Foundation Stones for
Marketing Improvement

ccountability is the ability to measure your marketing actions. But to enhance them, you need to test and test and never stop testing. To get maximum benefit from what you learn from these tests, you need to carefully archive the results as the foundations for your next actions.

Although the testing and archiving methodologies explained in this chapter derive from direct marketing disciplines where the results are most accurately measurable, the principles apply to all the disciplines in the Marketing Continuum. Image advertisers, sales promoters and direct marketers all have the same objective: They want to minimize risk and know, in advance and as accurately as possible, if their marketing efforts are going to meet accountable criteria.

In this chapter we examine testing priorities—what's really important to test–and different types of testing procedures, and examine how best to read both the initial results and whether these can be relied upon for final marketing decision-making. We also look at the need for archiving of results and suggest how this can best be accomplished.

Testing: The Key to Success

Careful testing can make the difference between success (profit) and failure (loss). It can provide insight that can be used to improve all your marketing before you waste promotional monies. It can often tell you what *not* to do as well as what *to* do.[1] Speaking to the 2003 US Direct Marketing Association Annual Conference, John

Marinello, President of Marinello Advertising said: "Deciding who you are going to test to and what you are going to test, those are the key elements that make successful testing."

Nothing beats the reality of offering the product or service to consumers in real time, so to speak, and counting the orders and their cost.

There is a natural hesitancy on the part of many marketers throughout the continuum, especially those not schooled to the direct marketing disciplines to rely on traditional market research methodologies such as focus panels or just to "go for it" when planning a campaign.

How much accuracy you can achieve in testing is to a great extent governed by the degree of feedback you receive. A flight of TV commercials announcing a new and better computer, digital camera, or washing powder can be researched using standard interview methods to measure heightened awareness of the brand and product, and retail sales can be carefully tracked to measure the uplift in sales. Sales promotion efforts can be measured by increased store traffic and sales, even by the redemption levels of "coupons" used as part of the promotion or similar devices. These metrics provide a baseline for campaign expansion and future efforts.

Without a good feedback mechanism however, it is difficult to make "live" tests and read them with accuracy.[2] In theory, sales promoters could use different media and different creative approaches to drive potential customers to a specific retail outlet using "split runs" in the same medium or different media with parallel characteristics. The problem is in transforming the theory into practice and building a measurement technique that identifies which customers come from which promotion and using this data for an assessment of which approach or medium worked best. Giving people redeemable "coded" coupons that are delivered for a benefit at the retail outlet works best. Also, matched outlets or geographic areas are often used for a form of "split" testing. It's not perfect, but it is better than flying blind.

Market research can be extremely helpful in narrowing the focus of any marketing effort and carefully organized focus panels made up of likely prospects can add valuable insight on what *not to do* in the promotional initiative. The panels will often help you discover things in your product or advertising that turn people off. But, unfortunately, research will never tell you for sure whether consumers will rush out and buy.

Testing, using an offer proposition that the potential customer can act on and that allows the precise measurement of these actions, is basic to direct marketing. It tests *what the prospect does, not what he may do.* Another advantage of testing that uses direct mail or email is that tests can be conducted discreetly and out of sight of competitors. Only the individuals who receive the test promotions know about them, and, therefore, offers, prices, and incentives can be tested and the tests rolled out before the competitor becomes aware of your strategy.

Following the same reverse tennis seeding methodology as illustrated in the "Media Testing Table" in Chapter 9 (Exhibit 9-19) for the other key elements of a promotional program can be useful.

Direct marketing testing orthodoxy demands that you *always start with your "control"*[3]—the initiative that you know delivers an acceptable cost per response and the best result achieved so far. This becomes the benchmark for all improvements. If you don't have a control, then you must start with the promotion that you believe has the best chance of success and verify that it will produce orders at less than your allowable before going any further.

If possible, test only one thing at a time: media, offer, price, or creative. Otherwise, even if you get a positive response you won't know why. And, in analyzing the results, be careful to *exclude* any unique costs attributable only to the tests. As discussed in Chapter 5, if included in analyzing the results of tests, fixed costs that would normally be amortized over large quantities will badly distort test results and may make you think you have a loser when in fact you have a winner.

Tests of offers, copy, and the like should only be made in media for which you have a profitable baseline result. Make sure that the quantities you use are statistically viable. You have to garner a sufficient number of responses to give the tests validity.[4] When testing media make sure that the test segments have a large enough rollout potential to make them worth testing. And don't rollout any major "breakthrough" until you have re-tested it for validity. Testing is not the place to throw caution to the winds.

If you are using your control and testing in direct mail or email, always allocate the largest test quantities to the control. This way, you will derive some profitable income from the tests even if the other test segments do not perform as well as the test.

Test major modifications first but don't be afraid to also test "crazy" ideas. "Crazy " ideas may lead to breakthroughs and may not be as crazy as you think.

Finally, keep tests as simple as possible. Testing is a long and laborious process (although email testing is much cheaper and faster than direct mail) and needs a dedication that is often wanting when management wants results, now.

Eugene Raitt, of the insurance giant AIG and a dedicated accountable marketer, developed an important course for direct marketers in Japan. In his module on testing he wrote simply "testing is the key to successful direct marketing." He went on to assign a logical hierarchy (Exhibit 8-1) for the testing methodology. It is an excellent place to begin looking at effective testing.

As can be seen in Exhibit 8-1, Gene Raitt's diagram breaks the component parts of the testing hierarchy into its "Strategic," "Tactical," and "Subtactical" components. While the terminology used with the diagram is somewhat different from the list below, the thrust of what needs to be tested is essentially the same.

Exhibit 8-1 Testing Hierarchy

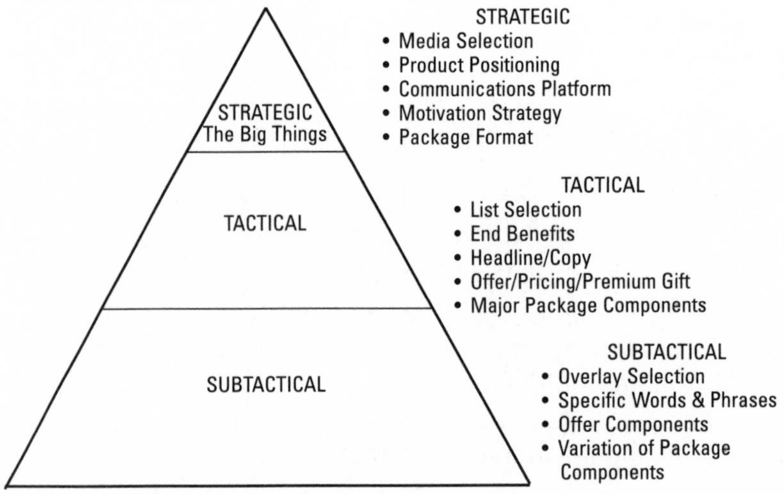
STRATEGIC
The Big Things
TACTICAL
SUBTACTICAL
STRATEGIC
• Media Selection
• Product Positioning
• Communications Platform
• Motivation Strategy
• Package Format
TACTICAL
• List Selection
• End Benefits
• Headline/Copy
• Offer/Pricing/Premium Gift
• Major Package Components
SUBTACTICAL
• Overlay Selection
• Specific Words & Phrases
• Offer Components
• Variation of Package Components

Here is a checklist of the hierarchy of testing—the order of importance of tests:

▶ The Media:

- The *product* and its *positioning*

    Media and product positioning are the first priority. We need to know that the product is right for the market, and the best media to present it to the target audience. We also need to have clearly in our minds the motivations that will induce purchase and to communicate these to the prospect.

▶ The Offer:

- Price

- Premium

- Commitment

- Term

    What is the offer we are going to make? What are the prices and the premium(s)? If the offer has a commitment and a term, what is the best mix?

▶ Creative Executions:

- Copy

- Layout

    We need to know what headlines and copy points have the best pulling power and how the total "package"—the way we are going to present the material—will affect response.

There are many ways to undertake tests, and each plays a valuable role in the total testing methodology. Some, such as "Survey" and "Dry" tests, *inform product development even before campaign media is selected*. However, to be valid, these tests like the marketing initiatives that will follow them must be directed at the right target groups. The other types of tests listed below come later in the testing process and each has a specific purpose.

▶ Survey tests (sometimes called "concept" tests):

Tests in which the potential consumer is asked (usually for a small premium) to indicate which of a number of products he would buy. The advantage of using this technique, pioneered and perfected by *The Reader's Digest,* is that for a relatively small expenditure, it can narrow a field of potential product ideas to those most likely to get consumer acceptance.

▶ Dry tests:

Tests in which you make an offer but do not send the product and apologize (usually with a gift). Where allowed by law, this is an effective way of transforming "survey" testing into a specific test of whether people will actually purchase the product before having to make a final product production investment.

▶ Element tests:

Tests in which the offer and various elements of the offer and the product are presented and the prospect is asked to purchase (whether or not the product is "ready"). This technique, combined with dry testing, can isolate the positives and negatives in a promotional approach.

▶ Split runs:

Tests that are run in publications (or in direct and email) in which the prospect universe is "split" a number of ways and results are compared. Split runs are the most effective testing technique for making actual offer and creative comparisons because the relative cost per order of the different segments inform the total marketing program.

▶ Test campaigns:

The final set of tests to determine the viability of the program. These are often incorporated into split runs.

The ultimate purpose of these tests is to provide a comparative cost per order and to assure that it is lower than the allowable even if

"Survey" tests fall outside that dictum. For a "sequenced" product, it is wise to manage the test responders for a sufficient length of time to make sure that the estimated net sales value of each person over time is on target.

To properly analyze test results you must:

▶ Make a direct economic comparison of each variant.

▶ When you are testing both offers and lists or media, combine the results and assess if they are projectable.

▶ Always "back-test" new results to assure viability.

▶ Always archive test details and results.

That said, there is more to evaluating test results than simply comparing CPOs. What we want to know is which test cells or segments are most profitable and will meet our economic objectives.

The Highest Response Percentage Is *Not* *Always* the Most Profitable Segment

Our initial reaction to any test is that the winner is the segment that returns the greatest number of responses. Certainly, in image advertising, the advertiser would be wise to use that message and execution that has the highest positive recall. All things being equal, the sales promotion that produces the most sales should be rolled out, and the lead generation promotion that generates the highest number of leads is often deemed the best.

However, more often than not, all things are not equal. As discussed in Chapter 7, the use of different incentives can have a profound influence on the *quality* of sales derived from a sales promotion campaign. If the incentive is too rich, the customer may be more interested in the incentive than the product that is being promoted and actually purchase less of the product than he might with a smaller incentive. In the case of a lead generation program it may be better to have fewer leads with a higher conversion rate than more leads with a lower one. The criteria for making these decisions and the reading of the test results will totally depend on the marketing objectives.

In Exhibit 8-2, we can see a range of an eight-part split run of

Exhibit 8-2 Eight-Way Offer Test for a Music Club

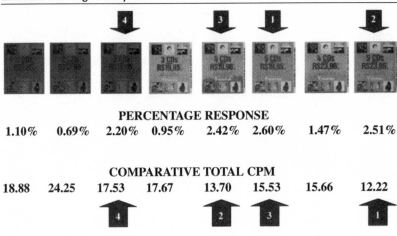

PERCENTAGE RESPONSE

1.10%   0.69%   2.20%   0.95%   2.42%   2.60%   1.47%   2.51%

COMPARATIVE TOTAL CPM

18.88   24.25   17.53   17.67   13.70   15.53   15.66   12.22

magazine inserts for a music club in Brazil along with the comparative results. Although the insert offering five CDs for 19.95 was the winner in terms of *percentage response*, after factoring in the revenue generated by the offer (19.95 in this case) less the cost of the additional CDs, the winner in terms of *cost per member* (CPM) was five CDs for 23.95 followed closely by four CDs for 19.96.

But that still leaves the overall economic questions unanswered. Having decided which test segment to rollout on the basis only of the percentage response would have materially diminished profits. What we need to know is *which offer is likely to be the most profitable and which will produce the greatest volume of profitable business?*

Making these additional calculations is essential. In the absence of hard data from previous experience, they demand that we make assumptions on the future purchasing performance of responders acquired with different offers.[5]

Using this data we can build a basic comparison model that will inform our rollout decisions as seen in the Template: Testing (Exhibit 8-3). For the purpose of this example, we have made the assumption that the lifecycle of each member will be 18 months and that the monthly value (contribution or profit) of each member will be 2.00.[6] We know the cost per thousand of the promotion (600) and the cost of each incentive unit.[7]

What we see in the template graph (Exhibit 8-4) is the hierarchy

Exhibit 8-3 Testing

Marketing Cost Per '000	600.00
Cost of Each Unit of Incentive	2.00

	% Response	Number of Members Per '000	Offer Revenue Per Member	Cost of Incentive	Cost Per Response	Lifetime Value Per Response	Cost Per '000 Promoted	Gross Value Over Life	Net Benefit Per Customer	Net Value Per '000 Promoted
5 CDs for 19.95	2.80%	28.0	19.95	10.00	11.48	36.00	321.40	1,008.00	24.52	686.60
5 CDs for 23.95	2.71%	27.1	23.95	10.00	8.19	36.00	221.96	975.60	27.81	753.68
4 CDs for 19.96	2.27%	22.7	19.96	8.00	14.47	36.00	328.51	817.20	21.53	488.69
3 CDs for 14.95	2.20%	22.0	14.95	6.00	18.32	36.00	403.10	792.00	17.68	388.90
[Describe Test Segment]										
[Describe Test Segment]										
[Describe Test Segment]										
[Describe Test Segment]										
[Describe Test Segment]										
[Describe Test Segment]										
[Describe Test Segment]										
[Describe Test Segment]										
[Describe Test Segment]										
[Describe Test Segment]										
[Describe Test Segment]										
[Describe Test Segment]										
[Describe Test Segment]										

	Net Value Per '000	% Response	CPO
5 CDs for 19.95	686.60	2.80%	11.48
5 CDs for 23.95	753.68	2.71%	8.19
4 CDs for 19.96	488.69	2.27%	14.47
3 CDs for 14.95	388.90	2.20%	18.32

Exhibit 8-4 Comparative Test Results

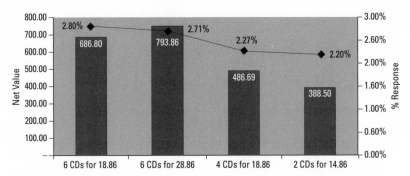

COMPARATIVE TEST RESULTS

of both the percentage response and "Net Value per 000 Promoted." The 5 CDs for 23.95 offer is the "winner," delivering the greatest profit, which is, in the last analysis, the name of the game.

The one caveat is that the 5 CDs for 19.95 offer produced the largest quantity of members for the promotional investment and, while less profitable per thousand people promoted, might in the long run help amortize fixed costs over a larger membership base and be a serious candidate for rollout.

Reading Test Results Takes a Combination of History and Judgment

Whatever the promotional activity, reading and correctly interpreting the test results is essential. Whether the test is a simple comparison of headlines with all other elements unchanged or a complicated price and offer test as described above for the Music Club, the first criterion is always the percentage response and the cost per response. This needs to be compared to:

▶ The "control" if one exists and/or

▶ The allowable cost per response.

If the control is the proven benchmark and the allowable cost per response has been carefully calculated, the comparison against these two metrics should point clearly to whether a rollout of the test is likely to produce a better final result or not.

For more complicated products or services that rely on a sequence of purchases or the probable lifetime value (LTV) of the customer, assumptions and judgments need to be made. Those entered in the "Lifetime Value Per Response" column of the "Template: Testing" (Exhibit 8-3) will normally be based upon history—responders to a similar offer (albeit at a different price, etc.) have consistently produced LTVs within a certain range. Therefore, taking the low end of the historical results as the baseline for further modeling should provide the basis for making decisions about rollouts. In the last analysis, a certain amount of guesswork and crystal ball gazing will almost always be necessary.

The Sooner You Can Predict Final Test Results, The Sooner You Are Ready to Rollout

Results from tests and campaigns can trickle in for months or sometimes years, even if there is a stated cut-off date in the promotion. Obviously, we cannot wait forever to make an evaluation of the success or failure of the test. That's why marketers in all marketing disciplines have developed response histories that they can use to predict the flow of responses over time and estimate the final result without waiting until it arrives.

Movie companies watch test screenings and the first weekend of exhibition box-office figures to project revenues and profits and adjust promotion strategy and budgets accordingly. Manufacturers often release new products in a selected group of stores in which they know what to expect to determine whether product sales meet that expectation and fashion their marketing accordingly. All good marketers build "histories" as guides to help them predict the future. Because direct marketers tend to have more specific data on response, those that archive it well have faster turn-around times and can "rollout" programs with a high degree of confidence.

In the 1960s, book club marketers in the US used the Book Review section of the Sunday edition of the *New York Times* as a bellweather for their advertising. Experience had taught them that by doubling the number of orders received by the end of the working day on the Thursday following the Sunday appearance of their ads, they would be able to predict the final number of responses plus or minus about 5 percent—accurate enough for rollout purposes.[8]

Today, depending on the advertising medium used, we receive responses electronically or by telephone (very quickly) or by "snail mail" through the postal system. Developing histories of response patterns can inform projections with considerable accuracy.

Two factors condition when responses will come in and how fast:

1. The date and time[9] that the promotion is "dropped"—dispatched using whatever media.

   Direct mail is often dropped on a staggered basis perhaps 25 percent of the total each couple of days. Flights of broadcast commercials may run throughout a week or month. In reading and projecting test results, knowing the distribution pattern is essential.

2. The date and time that first responses are received.

   This proves that the promotional material is in the hands of the prospect and is the time to start recording responses. (Of course we never know for direct mail and email when the communications are delivered, but we can estimate it with a high degree of confidence.) Exhibit 8-5 is taken from the ACPO Model and shows how the data is entered.

The next step is capturing the data for all responses against the appropriate codes (A1, B2, etc.). Without this, you will never be able to recreate the data. If these responses have been properly recorded and archived, they provide the basis for projecting future uses of the same media. Exhibit 8-6 provides an example of the methodology for recording responses that can be adapted to any media.

What's important is to link this to the promotion data in Exhibit 8-5 and to capture not only the daily totals by code and cumulative count, but also the percentage of response and percentage of budget that has been reached (sometimes called the percentage of "completion"). This is helpful not only for measuring how the campaign is going but also for projecting future response.

Building your own templates for promotional management is a challenge. Since the characteristics of any promotional initiatives

Exhibit 8-5 Campaign: Data Entry Sample

ALLOWABLE COST PER ORDER — Campaign Management

Project Name: ACPOSAMPLE-CLUB

Date: 02-Jan-2001

What is the First Date ? 02-Jan-2001 (•) Week ( ) Day ( ) Hour

What is the Medium ? Mail

( ) Test (•) Rollout

Code	Media	Available Circulation	Amount Used	Circulation Week 8-Jan	Week 15-Jan	Week 22-Jan	Week 29-Jan
A1	List A	120,000					
B1	List B	300,000					
C1	List C	445,000	500,000	250,000	250,000		
D1	List D	795,000					
E1	List E	200,000	200,000	200,000			
F1	List F	98,000	90,000		90,000		
G1	List G	250,000					
			Total Week	450,000	340,000		
			Total Cumulative	450,000	790,000	790,000	790,000

vary widely, it is advisable to fashion your own system rather than rely on standard templates.

In addition to its important immediate and archival value in a campaign management system, this data can be the basis for using the Template "Projecting Test or Rollout Results Based on Past History" (Exhibit 8-7).

Exhibit 8-6 Campaign: Sample Recording Methodology

ALLOWABLE COST PER ORDER — Campaign Management

Project Name: ACPOSAMPLE-CLUB

Date: 02-Jan-2001

RESPONSE

Media: Mail

Rollout

Code	Media	Amount Used	Total Budgeted Response	Resp. 8-Jan 1	Resp. 15-Jan 2	Resp. 22-Jan 3	Resp. 29-Jan 4	Resp. 5-Feb 5	Resp. 12-Feb 6	Resp. 19-Feb 7	Resp. 26-Feb 8	Resp. 5-Mar 9	Resp. 12-Mar 10	Summary Totals	% of Resp.	% of Budget
A1	List A															
B1	List B															
C1	List C	500,000	8800	5,244	2,908	2,156	854	214	67	58	22	1		11,524	2.30%	129.48%
D1	List D															
E1	List E	200,000	4000	3,154	1,841	455	201	15						5,666	2.83%	141.65%
F1	List F	90,000	1960		1,121	413	87	66						1,687	1.87%	86.07%
G1	List G															
	Total	790,000	14,760	8,398	[illegible]	3,024	1,142	295	67	58	22	1		18,877	2.39%	127.83%
	Total Cumulative			8,398	14,268	17,292	18,434	18,729	18,796	18,854	18,876	18,877	18,877			

Exhibit 8-7 Projection of Test Rollout Based on Past History

Medium: | Newsmagazine |

Previous Usage
[Input Date]

					Time Unit					
	1	2	3	4	5	6	7	8	9	10
% TOTAL Response	5.3%	24.3%	32.5%	18.3%	9.9%	4.5%	2.1%	1.0%	0.8%	0.9%
Cum. % Resp.	5.3%	29.6%	62.1%	80.4%	90.3%	94.8%	96.9%	97.9%	98.7%	99.6%

Previous Usage
[Input Date]

					Time Unit					
	1	2	3	4	5	6	7	8	9	10
% TOTAL Response	2.0%	9.0%	41.0%	21.5%	14.6%	7.5%	0.3%	0.2%	0.6%	0.3%
Cum. % Resp.	2.0%	11.0%	52.0%	73.5%	88.1%	95.6%	95.9%	96.1%	96.7%	97.0%
Average	3.7%	20.3%	57.1%	77.0%	89.2%	95.2%	96.4%	97.0%	97.7%	98.3%

New Promotion:

	1	2	3	4	5	6	7	8	9	10
Response		900	11,411	6,784	-	-	-	-	-	-
Cum. Resp.		900	12,311	19,095	-	-	-	-	-	-

	1	2	3	4	5	6	7	8	9	10
Likely FINAL Result		4,433	21,578	24,815	-	-	-	-	-	-

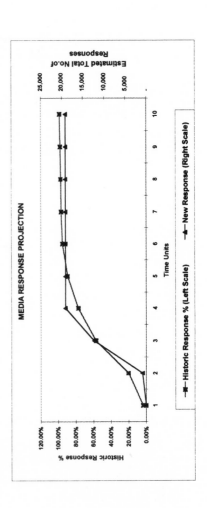

MEDIA RESPONSE PROJECTION

Historic Response % (Left Scale)   Estimated Total No. of Responses (Right Scale)

— Historic Response % (Left Scale)   — New Response (Right Scale)

Each medium has a response pattern that will, with minor variations, repeat itself each time it is used although the actual numbers will change as the "cream" customers are skimmed off the top.[10] Nonetheless, if experience has proven that you will have "N" percent of the response from a medium after "X" time units, it should be easy to plot the response to a test (or rollout) against this history and then be able to project the final result without waiting for the late results to come in.

What do you have to do to make use of this tool?

The first thing is to capture the results from each test or previous use of this medium as illustrated in the bottom section of Exhibit 8-6. Knowing the final results of the previous usage(s) of a specific medium, it is an easy matter to calculate the percentage of the total response received from this medium in each time unit.

To use the Template (Exhibit 8-7) first enter a description of the "Medium" and the date(s) of its most recent usage (or better, two usages) where you are asked for "Input Date." Then, on the line(s) titled "% Total Response," enter the percentage of the total response received in each "time unit" (hours, days, weeks, months, etc.).[11] Obviously, two previous uses are better than only one but you have to use what you have.

Having completed this, you have a reliable baseline for projecting future "Final Results" for this medium, built on your past experience.

Now when you use the medium again, for a test or a full-scale promotional campaign, you need only enter the response received in each time unit and the template will calculate and graphically display the likely "Final Result."

As seen in the example given in Exhibit 8-7, an average of 77 percent of the response (averaging previous response and the latest promotion) should have arrived by the end of Time Unit 4 (even though none arrived in Time Unit 1), and that reliably projects to plus or minus 24,815 orders in total. It isn't exact, but it is sufficiently accurate for the marketer to use the projection as the basis for quickly formulating new plans or rollouts without waiting until the last orders have been received.

Archiving Is Critical: It Paves the Way to a Successful Future

The number of times that marketing executives have asked for "last year's results" and been given a page of numbers that they cannot relate to actual promotional initiatives is legion. Actual mailing pieces and ads disappear from files and trying to match up source and promotion codes without visual references to specific promotional initiatives is often impossible. Reliance on personal memory is dangerous, especially when executives change jobs and companies as regularly as they do.

One of the most valuable assets of any company that wishes to make its marketing accountable is a well constructed and accurate archive of previous promotional initiatives—what has been tested, what has been rolled out and why. Yet this is something that exists in very few companies.

With today's scanners and other tools, it is relatively easy to archive all relevant promotional materials and to keep this archive up to date so that it is a simple matter to revisit previous promotions and see exactly how they performed. Exhibit 8-8 is the archive for a Music Club insert giving all the essential data for a Newsmagazine promotion. The executive who asks about this side of the split insert campaign can find everything he or she can use.

On one page we have offer, the media code, a description of the medium, the format, the test or rollout circulation, the unit cost per thousand, the % response achieved for each net of incentives cost (if a negative number) or contribution and finally the net cost per response. We also have all the important details in the summary, a scanned illustration of the promotion piece itself, and a description of the key characteristics of the offer. We have everything we need to evaluate the offer and perhaps to use it as the basis for new tests.

Building an archive of this type to your needs is relatively simple and should be a basic tool for any company undertaking accountable marketing and desirous of preserving "learnings" and making use of them.

The importance of testing and archiving cannot be overstated. The direct marketing discipline is built on it, and while we can measure what we do to achieve accountability, the testing discipline

Exhibit 8-8 Archiving

Description:	Media Code	Medium	Format	Test Circulation Used	Rollout Circulation Used	Unit Circ. Cost Per '000	% Response	Number of Responses	Cost Per Response	Net Incentive Cost	Net Cost Per Response
Music Club: 5 CDs for 23.95	INS1	Newsmagazine	4 Pg. Insert		1,200,000	500.00	2.51%	30,120	19.92	7.70	12.22
Name of Test or Rollout								-	-		-
Name of Test or Rollout								-	-		-
Name of Test or Rollout								-	-		-
Name of Test or Rollout								-	-		-
Name of Test or Rollout								-	-		-
Name of Test or Rollout								-	-		-
Name of Test or Rollout								-	-		-
Name of Test or Rollout								-	-		-
Name of Test or Rollout								-	-		-
Name of Test or Rollout								-	-		-
Name of Test or Rollout								-	-		-
Name of Test or Rollout								-	-		-
Name of Test or Rollout								-	-		-
Name of Test or Rollout								-	-		-
Name of Test or Rollout								-	-		-
Name of Test or Rollout								-	-		-
TOTALS				-	1,200,000			30,120			

Summary:

Circulation Quantity	1,200,000
TOTAL Cost of Promotion	368,076
Allowable Cost Per Response	50.33
Breakeven % Response	0.61%
TOTAL Number of Responses for Breakeven	7,313
Actual Response %	2.51%
Actual TOTAL Number of Responses	30,120

Key Offer Characteristics

Type of Test:

1. Five CDS for 19.95
2. Agree to buy 6 as member
3. One Free for every 3 purchases
4. Other

Place Scanned Sample of Promotion Below

5 CDs R$19.95* MusicClub

provides the opportunity to find constant improvements. With successful testing and subsequently archiving of results the majority of the marketing risk can be eliminated.

Notes

[1] An excellent overview of testing methodology appears in Bob Stone/Rob Jacobs, *Successful Direct Marketing Methods*, pp. 477–86.

[2] Getting retailers to co-operate in tracking the responses from sales promotion is notoriously difficult. They seldom see this as part of their function and even the best laid plans often go awry in their execution.

[3] The expression "control" is used to signify that promotion that has worked best for you in the recent past and on which you have reliable data. Since you know how that promotion *should* perform it acts as a control—a measure of how the other promotion segments perform in a head-to-head test.

[4] "Some direct marketers live by probability tables that tell the mailer what the sample size must be at various response levels within a specified error limit, such as 5 or 10 percent . . . Probability tables can't be relied on too heavily because it is impossible to construct a truly scientific sample, yet such tables, within limits, can be helpful." See Stone/Jacobs, *Successful Direct Marketing Methods*, pp. 477–80.

[5] As discussed in detail in Chapter 7, too large an incentive will produce low-cost orders from people more interested in the incentive than the product itself and the purchasing performance of these customers is likely to be inferior to that of people who were attracted primarily by the product offering.

[6] If we know that members acquired from different incentive offers have different purchasing characteristics, the figures input in the model under the "Lifetime Value Per Response" heading should reflect this knowledge.

[7] Where the incentive is a multiple of a single "unit" (in this case a single disc) this is comparatively easy. Where the incentive is more complicated, it may be necessary to calculate the cost of the

incentive for each test segment and input it directly under the "Cost of Incentive" heading.

[8] The only time the author experienced an exception to this rule was when there was an unusually heavy snowfall on the Saturday preceding the distribution of the Sunday paper. No results came in until the middle of the week and there was no predictable pattern. The exceptions tend to prove the rule but unusual events—great political or social disturbances such as the 9/11 attack in the US—do influence both the flow and number of results and sometimes require re-testing even at a high cost.

[9] Before the Internet and email, the "time" of dispatch didn't come into the equation. All that has changed and if we send emails at 10:00 AM we can expect responses in minutes or hours.

[10] A caveat here and an important reason for keeping the data as recent as possible is that media audiences change over time and with these changes come changes in response trends.

[11] Since the final responses can appear at any time, don't worry about hitting 100 percent. You can cut off anywhere after about 70 percent without problem.

▶▶▶ 9

Promotional Planning and Control

E very day, everywhere we look we see promotions. They shout their messages at us from billboards, on television, pop-up on our computer screens or are received as email messages or as ads and inserts in publications. They come through our front doors as direct mail, we hear them on the radio as we drive, they brazenly arrive by telephone at odd hours and there is almost no place to hide from them.[1]

Since, as consumers, we can't stop these messages, our next best defense is just to "turn-off," ignoring them as if they weren't there at all. It's what some psychologists call the "wallpaper effect": It's there but we just don't take any notice of it.

To the marketer and advertiser who have spent large sums to get our attention and have us notice and respond to their messages, that's extremely bad news. And it is one of the prime reasons an increasing number of marketers throughout the continuum are looking for accountability in their advertising spend. As Stan Rapp and Tom Collins wrote so perceptively in 1987:

> The proliferation of media choices and the escalation of media costs have increased the need for accountability in advertising expenditure. Until recently conventional wisdom for general advertising dictated that media be evaluated by the advertising cost per impression and readership studies . . . In the increasingly fierce competition for customers, the winners will be those who make their advertising expenditures more accountable.[2]

The 175% Solution

All marketers, and especially direct and data-driven marketers, know that the hierarchy of importance of elements in a marketing campaign looks something like Exhibit 9-1.

Exhibit 9-1 Elements of a Marketing Campaign

MARKETING ELEMENT	DEGREE OF IMPORTANCE
Media Reaching the Right Target	100%
Offer Exciting the Prospect and Giving Him a Reason to Buy Now [3]	50%
Creative Execution Expressing the Offer in a Clear, Relevant, and Exciting Fashion	25%

As archers know, if you are not aiming at the target, it doesn't matter how straight your arrows or the strength of your bow. If the medium chosen isn't going to reach your real prospects, you cannot reasonably expect that sales will follow. If you are on target, while one offer may be better than another, you should find some takers. Despite the wholly disproportionate concentration of attention given the creative execution of the advertising, if you are not talking to the right people and offering them a product or service they want at a price they see as acceptable, even the most compelling articulation will be lost. How many times can you remember a wonderful ad but not the product name or brand?

In Chapter 3 (Exhibit 3-4) we saw that all the target audience should be "able" to buy the product, some will be "willing" to buy it and an even smaller segment will be "ready." Obviously, in choosing the most appropriate media we need to keep this very much in mind because it goes hand-in-hand with the "able," "willing," and "ready" paradigm. The media choice must be of people demographically *able* to purchase and potentially interested in the product. The right media environment and offer should provide people who are *willing* to buy. The right offer, creatively articulated and

Exhibit 9-2 Steps in the Promotion and Sale Process

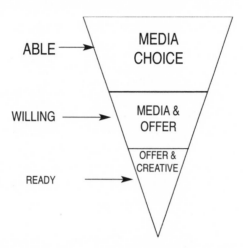

presented, should attract those people *ready* to purchase and move them to the act of purchasing, as illustrated in Exhibit 9-2.

Cost Per "Contact" Conditions Cost Per Order

When we buy media for image advertising, sales promotion or direct response, we are buying a means of reaching a target audience. Almost all media is sold on the basis of two factors:

1. The cost (usually expressed as a cost-per thousand) of making "contact" with an individual reader, viewer or listener.

2. The environment in which the advertising message appears.

This sounds simple, but it is not always. Since media normally charge for the number of people reached, they obviously wish to maximize this number: the more people, the more money. But there are two kinds of cost per contact, and they need serious consideration if we are to avoid costly errors.[4]

The first is the *actual cost for the advertising unit divided by the audited circulation or viewing figures*. While publications trumpet the number of "readers" of each copy, providing statistics to show that each copy is read by, say, 4.5 people, it is strongly recommended that these blandishments be ignored. If true, this multiple readership will be reflected in the response figures. The second is the existence of the target group situated within the medium. The more general the medium: The harder this is to determine. Even if it is a specialist medium directed at tennis enthusiasts, for example, the number of prospects for a new tennis racket offer will never be 100 percent of the circulation.

Comparing cost per contact (or cost per thousand) is a good first step in assessing the comparative value of one medium to another, and this is standard procedure for all media planners and buyers. It creates a useful benchmark for planning.

Image advertisers think in terms of reach (the number of targeted people reached by the advertising message) and frequency (the number of times these people are likely to see or hear the message). They are buying "share of mind" and hoping that with the brand image and the product in mind, the consumer will be moved to purchase the product. The problem is that even with sophisticated measurement techniques and research, it is almost impossible for the advertiser to know how much the advertising impacted sales unless there is a measurable response device.

For the direct marketer who lives or dies on the basis of the measurable and accountable response, *the ultimate bottom line is always whether or not the medium will generate a sufficient number of orders at a cost per order at or lower than he can afford.* For these marketers *accountability is key,* and if everything else isn't irrelevant, it is certainly secondary.

The Prospect Is Almost Always Multidimensional

A provocative and perceptive article, "Pigeonholing Limits Prospect Universes, or Who Says That Baseball Fans Don't Go to the Ballet?"[5] by Holly Eaton, National Account Manager for American List Counsel, Inc., adds an interesting dimension to the choice of media, albeit talking specifically about direct mail list choices. She argues persuasively for breadth rather than too narrow a list (media) choice:

> We all assume various roles of parent, child, sibling, spouse, co-worker, friend, sports fan, hobbyist, patron of the arts, volunteer, etc. While we may find ourselves only on a cultural

arts list, in reality, every direct mail buyer is actually a multi-faceted responder to many categories. Take a look at my "contradictory" profile: I frequently buy baby items, but I have no children; I make multiple purchases from both low-end household goods catalogs as well as upscale jewelry and gift catalogs; I buy sports-related merchandise, and attend theatre and opera; I subscribe to magazines targeted to younger women as well as those targeted to older women with families; I donate to a variety of charitable organizations; I place orders by mail, phone, fax, and online. All this, and I am only one person!

If this sounds like you or someone you know, then you realize there are more consumers of multiple types of products and services than "one-dimensional" single-category buyers.

All media are not equal in producing response to promotions. They have:

▶ Different demographic and psychographic profiles.

▶ Different costs per thousand or per contact.

▶ Different constituents—viewers, readers, etc.—who may have come from different sources for different reasons. Some may be serious, some may have subscribed to receive some incentive or even just participate in a sales promotion.

Exhibit 9-3 compares the characteristics, costs and likely response from key media used primarily for response advertising.

While Driving on the Highway, Stop and Eat Where Lots of Trucks Are Parked

There is really only one way to *know* whether a particular medium is optimum for a given promotion and should be at or near the top of your media priority list. That's through previous experience confirmed by rigorous testing. This follows the old rule about deciding which highway restaurant to stop at on a journey: If there are a lot of trucks parked at the establishment, the likelihood is that the food will be good and the prices reasonable. The Teamsters have put the

Exhibit 9-3 Typical Characteristics, Costs, and Response Rates of Key Media

MEDIUM	CHARACTERISTICS	NORMAL RESPONSE RANGE	COST
DIRECT MAIL	• Highly targeted • Allows high degree of segmentation • Gives maximum opportunity to present a comprehensive message • Complex management and logistics • Is discreet: can be tested much more subtly than most other media	.75% to 3.0%	Depends on complexity of package but US $900.00 per thousand is normal.
PRESS & PRESS INSERTS	• Offers wide range of targets and wide reach with large circulation • Is much easier to manage than direct mail • Allows fast expansion of media providing appropriate titles exist • Can be tested using "split runs" or inserts • Provides a good environment for the product if the right title	.075% to .3% for Run of Page (ROP) ads .15% to .75% for inserts	Usually in a range of US $90.00 to 120.00 per thousand for full page, less for smaller units. Inserts add approximately US $25 to US $50 per thousand to cost including cost of printing.
OUTBOUND TELEMARKETING	• Highly targeted although at high cost per contact • Level of effectiveness highly dependent upon the quality of telephone scripts, tele-sales personnel, and telephone number lists • Intrusive and often resented by recipients of unwanted calls [6]	Can run as high as 20% to 40% for completed calls	Cost of outbound calls is a product of cost of telesales agents and call charges. US $3.00 or more per minute is normal.

Exhibit 9-3 Typical Characteristics, Costs, and Response Rates of Key Media (Continued)

MEDIUM	CHARACTERISTICS	NORMAL RESPONSE RANGE	COST
BROADCAST: TV & RADIO	• The largest reach for the lowest cost per thousand • Ability to target is poor • Difficult to tell a complicated story except using two minute or longer "Infomercials" • Difficult to test except by regions • Best for getting people to "raise their hands" by calling toll-free number or going to web site.	As a rule, produces between .0075% to .02% of audience depending on offer	Costs vary widely depending on length of commercial, time of day, and program adjacency. Usual range is US $9.00 to 12.00 per thousand viewers.
EMAIL	• Very low cost medium with excellent targeting possible if up-to-date email lists available • Because of increasing SPAM problem, increased consumer resistance to opening unsolicited emails	Response rates can vary from virtually nothing to as high as 20%	Negligible cost per thousand depending on creative and sending costs.
INTERNET	• Banners, pop-ups, and other imaginative formats are effective as means of getting people to click on web sites that provide more information in depth • Targeting depends upon placement in "content" sites and varies widely • While some available programs eliminate these ads, they are still very popular with some marketers	Responses depend upon where the advertising units appear and search engine placement	Costs are widely variable in amount and form. Some sites charge per thousand viewers, some by number of "clicks", some by a percentage of sales or a combination of these.

(Continued)

Exhibit 9-3 Typical Characteristics, Costs, and Response Rates of Key Media (Continued)

MEDIUM	CHARACTERISTICS	NORMAL RESPONSE RANGE	COST
PACKAGE INSERTS	• Response marketing materials included in product packages offer a wide range of targeting opportunities • Low distribution costs make this a low-cost per thousand medium • Slow and hard to predict response flow is dependent on product shipments carrying promotion for direct consumer shipments and even longer for products sold at retail • Marketing materials are frequently lost with packaging materials	Responses come in slowly and are unlikely to exceed .5% except where very closely related to product	Costs vary widely and are dependent upon carrier's desire to carry the insert.
TAKE-ONES	• Found on hotel and other service counters and in taxi cabs, etc., targeting is only as good as the match of the product offered in the take-one and where the take-one material is displayed • Used frequently by airline "mileage" clubs and credit card companies • Extremely difficult to track and control • High wastage	Responses tend to be very low (.1% to .5%) except where there is direct relationship between take-one environment and take-one offer	Costs tend to be relatively low for materials but highly variable for placement.

eatery to the test, and it has obviously passed; they have come back for another helping—that's an endorsement not to be ignored.

It is also a worthwhile general media lesson. When considering new media, one of the first things to do is check to see:

▶ If advertisements for similar products (especially ads that demand a "response") have used the medium *and been repeated.*

▶ If there have been other "response" ads on a continuing basis.

What we are looking for first when we compare one medium against another is quite simply *the optimum measurable efficiency expressed as the most number of sales for the lowest cost per sale.*

Perhaps it is an oversimplification, but success or failure in choosing media can be precisely measured and accountability determined by dividing the cost of the marketing by the number of orders received.[7] This equation delivers the cost of each order (CPO), policyholder, subscriber or club member. It is obvious that the lower the cost per thousand of reaching the target audience, the greater the likelihood of achieving a low CPO. But just choosing the lowest cost per thousand medium may mean ignoring other media that would produce excellent orders at equally low or even lower costs.

While there is a natural tendency to become obsessed with "costs" we need to overcome this. It's not the cost of the media, but the cost of each response that drives success and profitability. And while cost and response are critical there are other important considerations that condition our media planning as well:

▶ Will the medium produce a sufficient number of responses to make it worthwhile? Even a 100 percent response from a medium with only 100 readers or listeners is hardly going to grow your business.

▶ Will the medium provide the advertiser with sufficient flexibility to test as well as rollout campaigns? Will it be able to offer split run tests, a choice of positions or timings, freefall and bound-in inserts and other tools?

▶ Is the medium appropriate to the complexity of your marketing message? If you have a complicated message, you need a medium that will allow you to deliver that message. As a rule, broadcast media are best for delivering simple messages with phone-in response mechanisms; print and direct mail lend themselves to more complicated messages.

▶ Is the medium willing to "bet" on its success by accepting revenue based upon the number of orders or a percentage of the total revenue generated by the advertising *at least until the medium has been proven effective?* Many media owners will provide time or space on a negotiated "PI" (Per Inquiry) or "PO" (Per Order) basis. If you know your ACPO, you will know what you can afford to pay for an order. Obviously you will wish to pay less but the ACPO provides you with the maximum "PI" or "PO" amount.[8]

Rigorous Analysis and Experience Required

Choosing the right medium or media combination for any marketing initiative is an exercise in comparisons and the juggling of priorities and opportunities. Readership or viewer studies can be helpful, but they can produce distortions. First and foremost, you want media that will deliver "quality" customers, orders, or responses at the lowest cost per order in an appropriate environment for your message and brand. Next you want volume and extendibility: If your tests prove positive you want to be able to expand your reach

Exhibit 9-4 "I Love Messing with Data."

to gain the maximum market. Finally, you want facilities to test and to experiment with various media formats and various response devices. In the last analysis, *any medium that allows you to target your potential market and that will generate a response at a CPO lower than your ACPO should be considered.*

In *MaxiMarketing*, Stan Rapp and Tom Collins put it this way:

> Before you do anything else, you need to find out who and where your best prospects are and what are the most efficient ways to reach them. A market research firm can help you develop the profile of your best prospects. So can psychographic classification systems like VALS. So can the actions of your prospects and customers, through the kinds of appeals they respond to and the information they can provide on questionnaires.[9]

Each media type (broadcast, Internet, direct mail, publications, outbound telephone, etc.) and each specific medium have different economic parameters, and these must be carefully weighed when choosing among them. While a lot of hard work is necessary, planning and executing promotions is almost as much fun as seeing that your economic assessments were correct and that you are going to reap the profits you anticipated.

The place to start for all media planning is past experience. If there are media that have worked for you in the relatively recent past, like the restaurants on the highway with lots of parked trucks, they should certainly be central to your media plan.[10]

What must drive the decision about which medium or combination of media to use will be:

▶ *Availability of media* (including lists) to best reach your target market with the minimum amount of wastage.

▶ *Complexity of the marketing message* and media most appropriate to the message.

▶ *Estimated cost per thousand* of reaching the target market.

▶ *Estimated response rates* from each medium.

Let's look at each of the principal characteristics of the most used media and examine their economics.

Direct Mail

Direct mail is addressed mail sent through the postal system or an alternative delivery system. After outbound telemarketing, it has the highest cost per thousand (including the list, the mailing package, and the postage, etc.), but, properly targeted, it normally delivers the highest percentage response of any mass medium. It offers the marketer an excellent vehicle to tell the complete story of the product or service and to detail and repeat the consumer benefits—the key selling points. The reader looks at direct mail without the distraction of other ads. The medium allows the inclusion of all kinds of devices (stamps, "peel-offs" small premiums or gifts, etc.) to enhance response.

Like all promotional initiatives, the planning process starts from knowing what you can afford to spend to get an order, a subscriber, a member, etc.—the Allowable Cost Per Order. While some marketers may wish to build a planning model of their own, a template for planning direct mail has been provided (Exhibit 9-5).

This template is made up of two related sections:

1. The costs (stated as cost per thousand) of the mailing piece and its distribution (Exhibit 9-6). This includes the letter, the response device, the addressing and the postage or other distribution costs etc. There is also ample room in the "Other" categories for including the per thousand costs of modeling etc. Since the creative and other one-time costs of preparing the mailing are an important cost element, there is a special input to allow the capture of these costs as a total that comes after providing a summary of the "Total Mailing Package" costs. This section *does not include the lists* to be used (although it does include a derived summary total of the weighted average of the list costs). Finally one can see the "Breakeven Response %" needed to produce the mandated profit.

2. The second section is devoted to the lists to be used in the mailing. There is room for 20 different lists (although in this example we have only used three), and their names or other designation can be input in the boxes that are titled "Lists."[11] What we need to know for each list to be used are the following:

Exhibit 9-5 Direct Mail Planning

Allowable Cost Per Order: 60.00

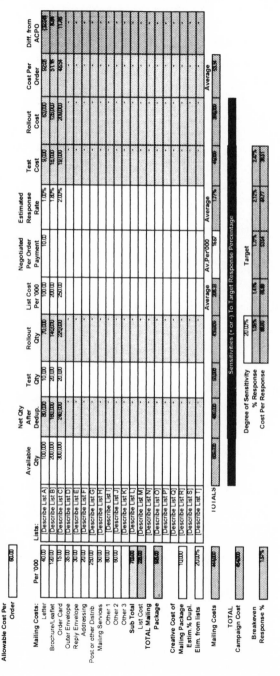

Mailing Costs:	Per '000
Letter	40.00
Brochure/Leaflet	120.00
Order Card	15.00
Outer Envelope	35.00
Reply Envelope	30.00
Addressing	20.00
Post or other Distrib	250.00
Mailing Services	50.00
Other 1	80.00
Other 2	60.00
Other 3	
Sub Total	**780.00**
List Cost	216.00
TOTAL Mailing Package	**944.00**
Creative Cost of Mailing Package	10.00
Estim. % Dupl. Elim. from lists	20.00%

TOTAL Campaign Cost

Breakeven Response % : 1.57%

Lists:	Available Qty	Net Qty After Dedup.	Test Qty	Rollout Qty	List Cost Per '000	Negotiated Per Order Payment	Estimated Response Rate	Test Cost	Rollout Cost	Cost Per Order	Diff. from ACPO
[Describe List A]	100,000	80,000	10,000	70,000	100.00	10.00	1.00%	9,000	63,000	92.86	-32.86
[Describe List B]	200,000	160,000	20,000	140,000	20.00		1.80%	18,000	126,000	51.98	8.02
[Describe List C]	300,000	240,000	20,000	220,000	250.00		2.00%	19,000	209,000	48.54	11.46
[Describe List D]											
[Describe List E]											
[Describe List F]											
[Describe List G]											
[Describe List H]											
[Describe List I]											
[Describe List J]											
[Describe List K]											
[Describe List L]											
[Describe List M]											
[Describe List N]											
[Describe List O]											
[Describe List P]											
[Describe List Q]											
[Describe List R]											
[Describe List S]											
[Describe List T]											
TOTALS	600,000	480,000	50,000	430,000				46,000	398,000		
					Average 20.63	Av. Per '000 1.65?	Average 1.77%	2.47%		Average 53.?	

Sensitivities (+ or -) To Target Response Percentage:

Degree of Sensitivity	20.00%		Target
% Response	1.26%		1.51%
Cost Per Response	66.00		44.77

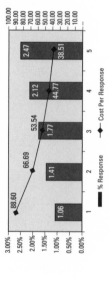

Sensitivities of Direct Mail Planning

	1	2	3	4	5
% Response	3.00%	2.50%	2.00%	1.50%	1.00%
Cost Per Response	88.60	66.69	53.54	44.77	38.51
	1.06	1.41	1.77	2.12	2.47

— % Response   ◆ Cost Per Response

Exhibit 9-6 Production and Distribution Costs

Estimated % of Duplication Eliminated from Lists	20.00%

Mailing Costs:	Per '000
Letter	40.00
Brochure/Leaflet	120.00
Order Card	15.00
Outer Envelope	35.00
Reply Envelope	30.00
Addressing	20.00
Post.or other Distrib.	250.00
Mailing Services	50.00
Other 1	80.00
Other 2	60.00
Other 3	
Sub Total	700.00
List Cost	225.00
TOTAL Mailing Package	925.00
Creative Cost of Mailing Package	10,000
Mailing Costs	444,000
TOTAL Campaign Cost	454,000
Breakeven Response %	1.57%

- The total available quantity of names and the quantity of these names that will be used for any tests. The rollout quantity that is computed by the template is the "Available Quantity" less the "Test Quantity."

- The "per thousand" cost of each list to be considered for use. These are likely to differ, as some lists—especially those rented from third party suppliers—will have a greater cost than others.

- The estimated percentage response rate for each list to be used.

Smart Mailers Pay Only for Net Names

When a number of different lists of names are rented from external sources, it is likely that there will be duplicates among them—the same name will appear on different lists—and these duplicates will need to be eliminated. Mailers normally pay only for "Net Names," those names that do not already exist in the mailer's own marketing database or on already rented outside files. Determining the exact parameters for dealing with "Net Names" is a matter of negotiation. What is important for planning purposes is to make a determination of the percentage of duplicate names that will be eliminated and that percentage (or an estimate of it) should be used to develop the economic model. As can be seen in Exhibit 9-6 there is an input box "Estimated Percentage of Duplication Eliminated from Lists" that allows the template user to input that percentage and adjusts the totals (but not the individual list quantities) accordingly.[12]

As can be seen in Exhibit 9-7, the template delivers key planning information that informs the total mailing program. The data includes:

▶ The test and rollout quantities and costs.

▶ The cost per order for each list.

▶ The difference between the actual CPO and the ACPO, shown in brackets when the CPO exceeds the ACPO.

▶ The totals or the weighted averages for all the columns and the "Breakeven Response Percentage" needed to have the mailing program produce an average response to match the ACPO.[13]

▶ The total mailing cost and the total campaign, which is the mailing cost plus the creative or other fixed cost.

The final section (Exhibit 9-8) allows the user to run sensitivities on the previous results, simply inputting the degree of sensitivity desired. In the example we have used 20% sensitivity either side of the "Target" percentage. Here we can see what happens to the CPO if the average contemplated percentage response of 1.77 is not attained or it is exceeded. In this case, any significant shortfall from the target 1.77 percent response will increase the CPO from 53.54 to exceed the 60.00 ACPO and either eat contemplated profits or create actual losses.[14]

Exhibit 9-7 Management and Control Template: List Performance

Available Cost Per Order [60.00]

Lists:	Available Qty	Net Qty After Dedup.	Test Qty	Rollout Qty	List Cost Per '000	Negotiated Per Order Payment	Estimated Response Rate	Test Cost	Rollout Cost	Cost Per Order	Diff. from ACPO
[Describe List A]	100,000	84,000	10,000	70,000	100.00	10.00	1.00%	9,000	63,000	92.06	(32.06)
[Describe List B]	200,000	160,000	20,000	140,000	200.00		1.90%	18,000	126,000	51.16	8.84
[Describe List C]	300,000	240,000	20,000	220,000	250.00		2.00%	19,000	209,000	48.54	11.46
[Describe List D]											
[Describe List E]											
[Describe List F]											
[Describe List G]											
[Describe List H]											
[Describe List I]											
[Describe List J]											
[Describe List K]											
[Describe List L]											
[Describe List M]											
[Describe List N]											
[Describe List O]											
[Describe List P]											
[Describe List Q]											
[Describe List R]											
[Describe List S]											
[Describe List T]											
TOTALS	600,000	460,000	50,000	430,000	Average 228.33		Average 1.77%	46,000	398,000	Average 63.64	

Exhibit 9-8 Sensitivities to Target Response Rate

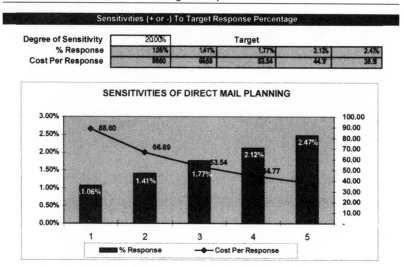

Sensitivities (+ or -) To Target Response Percentage					
Degree of Sensitivity	20.00%	**Target**			
% Response	1.06%	1.41%	1.77%	2.12%	2.47%
Cost Per Response	88.60	66.69	53.54	44.7	38.5

SENSITIVITIES OF DIRECT MAIL PLANNING

Print Advertising

Magazines and newspapers are frequently excellent media for reaching prospective customers. Where better to get a message to antique car owners than in a specialist magazine directed at them or to book buyers than in the literary supplements of leading newspapers? The numbers of titles is endless, and making a preliminary assessment of whether they are likely to be "responsive" is as easy as getting hold of some back issues and counting the number of couponed ads and/or bound or free-standing inserts. The publishers are happy to provide the potential advertiser with the demographics of their publications and the content, especially of the specialty titles, gives clear signals about the psychographics of the readership.

The US Direct Marketing Association reports that in 2002, more than US$28 billion was spent using newspapers and magazines for direct marketing. This is 36.6 percent of total newspaper spend and 55 percent of total magazine spend and taken together is the highest direct marketing spend for any media category except telephone and direct mail.

Print media and inserts are almost always less expensive per thousand than direct mail but can be just as effective in cost per order terms and can add substantially to the reach (number of people exposed to the advertising) of the promotion. Because the medium is by its nature less targeted than direct mail, it generally delivers a substantially lower percentage response as indicated in Exhibit 9-3.[15]

As can be seen in Exhibit 9-9, the key drivers in building a model to plan a print media campaign are:

1. The circulation of the publication.

2. The estimated response rate.

3. The total and per thousand cost of the media.

4. Any "Per Order" payments negotiated with the media owners.[16]

5. The costs for creative work and any other fixed expenses.

These drivers deliver the number of anticipated orders, the critical costs per thousand of each publication, the average cost per thousand, the CPO, and the comparison of the CPO with the ACPO, showing any publications whose CPOs exceed the ACPO in brackets. It also derives a "Breakeven Response Percentage" and the total cost of the campaign.

In this example, three publications have been used, but the template will take up to twenty and can be enlarged by the user to add more, remembering always to change the formulae for the totals accordingly.[17] Two publications produced costs per order lower and one higher than the ACPO. A full media schedule must produce an *average* cost per order lower than the ACPO with some room to spare. Remember that some publications will bring in higher and lower percentage responses than your estimates, and a comfortable cushion is advisable. A user-defined sensitivity table and graph at the bottom of the template show what happens to the CPO if the percentages are greater or less than the target.

Inserts

Up to now we have dealt almost exclusively with direct response ads that are printed on the pages of newspapers and magazines. However, another major press advertising form is the use of pre-printed, free-standing or bound-in inserts that get carried by these

Exhibit 9-9 Print Media Cost Calculator

Allowable Cost Per Order: 100.00

Publication Titles:	Ad Size/Type	Circulation Quantity	Estimated Response Rate	Media Cost	Negotiated Per Order Payment	Number of Responses	Cost Per Thousand	Cost Per Order	Difference from ACPO
Describe Publication A	Full Page	200,000	0.20%	23,500.00	10.00	400	137.50	82.54	17.46
Describe Publication B	Half Page	350,000	0.19%	26,250.00		665	75.00	53.98	46.01
Describe Publication C	Full Page	175,000	0.14%	21,000.00		245	120.00	105.42	(5.42)
Describe Publication D									
Describe Publication E									
Describe Publication F									
Describe Publication G									
Describe Publication H									
Describe Publication I									
Describe Publication J									
Describe Publication K									
Describe Publication L									
Describe Publication M									
Describe Publication N									
Describe Publication O									
Describe Publication P									
Describe Publication Q									
Describe Publication R									
Describe Publication S									
Describe Publication T									
TOTALS		725,000	Average 0.18%	70,750.00	Total Cost 4,000.00	1,310	Average 100.19	Average 72.33	

Negotiated Per Order Payment: -
Advertising Cost: 74,750.00
Creative and Other Fixed Costs: 20,000.00
TOTAL Campaign Cost: 94,750
Breakeven Response %: 0.13%

Sensitivities (+ or -) To Target Response Percentage

Degree of Sensitivity	20.00%		Target		
% Response	0.11%	0.14%	0.18%	0.22%	0.25%
Cost Per Response	118.51	89.65	72.33	60.78	52.54

SENSITIVITIES OF PRESS ADVERTISING PLANNING

■ % Response ◆ Cost Per Response

publications and offer an excellent direct response marketing medium.[18]

Inserts can come in as many varieties of sizes, shapes and numbers of pages as the marketer has imagination and money and the publication can handle either with machines or people.

This is especially true with respect to testing, which, while sometimes limited by a publication's production process, is virtually unlimited when inserts are the chosen medium. Because inserts are produced separately from the publications that carry them, the marketer can print and collate materials any way that suits his testing matrix. This means that, theoretically at least, there can be virtually any number of variations of offers, prices, copy, and creative treatments and response vehicles produced by the marketer and carried in the same publication, with the publication reader seeing only the one that falls out or is bound into his copy.

With the use of modern printing and binding machinery, it is possible to personalize subscriber copies with an impact akin to direct mail. The economics and key drivers for inserts (Exhibit 9-10) are very similar to normal press advertising. The only economic differences are:

▶ The cost charged by the publication for circulation.

▶ The costs of printing and inserting the inserts.

▶ Any "Negotiated Per Order Payment" costs agreed with the insert carrier. However, the template allows for both testing and rollouts and has a somewhat different format than that of off-the-page response advertising in press media.

We begin with defining the publication titles that will carry the inserts, the type of insert defined by the number of pages, and the total circulation quantities available.[19] Then we need to consider the media cost per thousand (the most usual way that inserts are priced by the media). As ever, we need to estimate the percentage response from each of the inserts. The template asks for the test circulations and generates a cost-per-thousand and total costs for both the tests and the rollouts.[20] The template also generates the number of estimated product sales, the CPO for each medium and whether or not these are less than or exceed the allowable.

Again in the example in Exhibit 9-10, we see that one of the three media used show a loss against the allowable. In addition to the media details, we need to estimate the cost of printing and inserting (although, as a rule, publications include the cost of inserting in their per thousand media price). In the template there is a box for this input. The template generates total test and rollout costs including the cost of creative and other fixed costs and delivers them as a "TOTAL Campaign Cost." It also outputs the percentage response needed for breakeven.

When we look at the sensitivities, we see the dynamic of the different response percentages and this can be an important guide to all our planning. In this example, even with a drop of 20% from the targeted response percentage, the cost per order would be less than the ACPO.

Package Inserts and Take-Ones

Package inserts and "take-ones" are low-cost media that can stand alone or add reach to a broader media plan. They have essentially the same characteristics as press media inserts and can be modelled using the same template.

When we open a package of merchandise (whether purchased direct or at a retail outlet) or even an invoice or other commercial communication, we often find inserts that promote line extensions of the product purchased or related merchandise. Good examples are an offer for an extended warranty on an appliance, an additional software offer found in a hardware package, or a credit-card fraud insurance offer in a credit card billing statement. Because the actual costs of printing and inserting the promotional material in the packages and the negotiated payment to the "carrier" are relatively low compared to other forms of promotional distribution, the marketer can live with a lower percentage return than most other media.

Obviously, *the relevance of the promotional message to the product package that carries it is critical* whether the promotion calls for a direct response or whether it is an image or sales promotion initiative. An offer of a range of cheeses that accompanies a fruit shipment may be successful where that same offer in a package containing a microwave oven is less likely to be. As with all media, the closer we can get to the target audience, the higher the response or impact we

Exhibit 9-10 Cost Calculator for Inserts

Allowable Cost Per Order ___10000___

Publication Titles:	Insert Size / Type	Available Quantity	Circul. Cost Per'000	Negot. Per Order Payment	Estm. Response Rate	Circulation Cost Per '000+ Insert	Test Circul.	Test Cost	Rollout Circulation	Rollout Cost	Rollout Number of Responses	Cost Per Order	Diff. from ACPO
[Describe Publication A]	4 Page	300000	40.00	10.00	0.3%	13000	25,000	4,125	275000	45,375	1,050	9956	404
[Describe Publication B]	4 Page	250000	50.00		0.25%	14000	25,000	3,540	225000	31,860	625	7936	2145
[Describe Publication C]	4 Page	200000	35.00		0.6%	12500	20.00	2,540	180000	28,850	369	6657	3873
[Describe Publication D]													
[Describe Publication E]													
[Describe Publication F]													
[Describe Publication G]													
[Describe Publication H]													
[Describe Publication I]													
[Describe Publication J]													
[Describe Publication K]													
[Describe Publication L]													
[Describe Publication M]													
[Describe Publication N]													
[Describe Publication O]													
[Describe Publication P]													
[Describe Publication Q]													
[Describe Publication R]													
[Describe Publication S]													
[Describe Publication T]													
TOTALS		750000	*Average* 41.33		*Average* 0.38%	*Average* 13,175	70,000	10,205	710,000	106,085	2,043	*Average* 72.56	

Sensitivities (+ or −) To Target Response Percentage

Degree of Sensitivity		Target		
% Response	20.00%	0.38%	0.26%	0.31%
Cost Per Response	117.52	89.42	72.56	61.33

Inserts

	Cost Per '000
Printing Cost	5000
Inserting Cost	3000
Other	1000
TOTAL Insert Cost	9000

Test Cost	10,205
Rollout Cost	106,085
Creative and other Fixed Costs	35000
TOTAL Campaign Cost	146,290
Breakeven Response %	0.59%

SENSITIVITIES OF INSERT PLANNING

can expect. Thus, the use of package inserts with the maximum relevance to the product carrying the insert stand the best chance of producing successful results.

One problem with this medium is that the distribution chain of many products is a long one, and the marketer will find it almost impossible to judge how many of the inserts are in the hands of consumers and how many remain in packages that have been prepared but have not been distributed direct or may be sitting in a warehouse somewhere or in the storage facility of a retail outlet.[21]

"Take-Ones" can be found on hotel and airline counters, in taxis, in stores, and in many other places where there is high consumer traffic of the kind desired by the marketer. They are often identical to inserts[22] or small versions—self-contained promotional pieces with a response vehicle as part of the unit.

Some form of "instant gratification" can greatly enhance the results from all media, especially take-ones. Airlines and other loyalty clubs have discovered that by pre-printing unique "membership numbers" on the take-ones, consumers can start collecting their miles or points immediately and response increases dramatically.

Take-ones are not a major medium and cannot be counted on to produce large volumes of orders. One of the difficulties with this medium is that because it is extremely difficult to control distribution, it is almost impossible to know the percentage response because the orders you have received at any given time may not reflect the total number of take-ones printed or even distributed. Nonetheless, many marketers create them as stand-alone promotions or more likely, as part of a multi-media campaign. They take the view that if the number of orders received brings in a cost-per-order lower than their allowable, it is not necessary to worry about whether or not the medium is "efficient" by any other criterion.

The economics of package inserts and take-ones mirror publication inserts. As noted above, the costs of the creation, printing and distribution and payment to the carrier tend to be low, and the logistics can often be handled by specialist companies at a negotiated cost.

The "Print Media, Package Inserts and Take-Ones" template (Exhibit 9-10) can be used to evaluate the economic options simply by entering the appropriate circulation and response data for publica-

Exhibit 9-11 Insert Costs Per Thousand

──────────────── **Inserts** ────────────────

	Cost Per '000
Printing Cost	5000
Inserting Cost	3000
Other	1000
TOTAL Insert Cost	9000

tion inserts and using the "Other" input box (Exhibit 9-11) to summarize all distribution and maintenance costs. In the "Circulation Cost Per Thousand" column of the original template, you can enter the carrier costs if they are negotiated on a per thousand basis in the "Other" input box, or, if the carrier is receiving an amount for each order received, you can input the weighted average of that amount in the box labeled "Negotiated Per Order Payment."

Telemarketing

The true one-to-one nature of telemarketing and the ability of a skilled telemarketing agent to interact with an existing customer or prospect is extremely powerful—so powerful and sometimes so irritating that as mentioned previously, legislation in some countries now prohibits unsolicited outbound calls. In 2001, before this prohibition came into effect in the U.S., 39 percent of the US $196.8 billion in total DM advertising spending was for telephone marketing, *the largest expenditure in any single medium* and an amount considerably greater than that spent for direct mail.

Back in 1976 when telephone-marketing pioneer Murray Roman wrote *Telephone Marketing*, the telephone's use as a marketing tool was less ubiquitous than it is today. Yet his description of the medium has, to the best of my knowledge, never been bettered:

> The telephone is an electronic tool that is available to every marketer for use as a rigidly controlled, sophisticated immediately measurable production-line base for sales and sales related operation that meets the requirements of the contemporary market.

Exhibit 9-12 Telemarketing List Costs

	Per Call
Average List Cost	0.18
Number of minutes Per Completed Call	3.00
Number of min. Per Non-Completed Call	1.50
Call Cost Per minute	1.20
% of Completed Calls	40.00%
Average Cost Per Call	2.70

Its unique person-to-person attributes, when carefully combined with manufacturing-type controls, provide for a productive and profitable marriage of uniform message presentation and alert reaction to the needs of an individual prospect . . . In no other form of promotional communication does the medium so profoundly influence the message.[23]

With the penetration of fixed-line telephones in almost all homes in the developed countries and rising rapidly in all countries throughout the world, the telephone is a powerful marketing medium. Used ethically and responsibly and only with "permission" granted by the recipient, it allows the marketer to customize his selling message to each individual customer or prospect and can play an important role not only in making primary sales but in servicing clients wants and needs.

Due to the one-to-one nature of telemarketing, it is a very expensive medium.

Not surprisingly, *the key driver for telemarketing activities, whether for direct sales or customer service, is the cost per call.*[24]

As we see in Exhibit 9-12, to derive the "Average Cost Per Call" we have to know the number of minutes used for the average completed and noncompleted calls and the call costs per minute. We also need to know the percentage of the total number of calls made that are completed and derive an average based upon these percentages.

Telemarketing is distinguished by the speed with which a campaign can be tested and adjusted and the relatively low cost of this testing and adjustment. That's the good news. The bad news is that the ability to roll out large campaigns without the use of pre-recorded messages, is limited by the number of skilled and trained

Exhibit 9-13 Telemarketing Cost Calculator

Allowable Cost Per Order 60.00

Lists:

	Available Quantity	Net Qty After Dedup	Test Qty	Rollout Qty	List Cost Per '000	Negotiated Per Order Payment	Estimated Response Rate	Test Cost	Rollout Cost	Cost Per Order	Diff. from ACPO
Describe List A	18,000	14,400	250	14,150	150.00	3.00	20.00%	825.65	46,731.81	17.30	42.70
Describe List B	16,500	13,200	100	13,100	200.00	5.00	13.00%	335.26	43,918.90	27.00	33.00
Describe List C	23,000	18,400	120	18,280	185.00		16.00%	324.31	49,403.30	17.87	42.13
Describe List D	14,000	11,200	100	11,100	200.00		21.00%	276.28	29,968.72	13.62	46.38
Describe List E											
Describe List F											
Describe List G											
Describe List H											
Describe List I											
Describe List J											
Describe List K											
Describe List L											
Describe List M											
Describe List N											
Describe List O											
Describe List P											
Describe List Q											
Describe List R											
Describe List S											
Describe List T											
TOTALS	71,500	57,200	570	56,630	Average 182.50		Average 17.29%	1,735.47	170,022.83	Average 18.28	

Estimated % of Duplication Eliminated from Lists 20.00%

Creative Costs of Script Preparation	
Training	3,000.00
	4,000.00
Other	2,000.00
TOTAL	9,000.00

	Per Call
Average List Cost	0.18
Number of minutes Per Completed Call	3.00
Number of min. Per Non-Completed Call	1.50
Call Cost Per minute	1.20
% of Completed Calls	40.00%
Average Cost Per Call	3.76

Telemarketing Costs	171,906
TOTAL Campaign Cost	180,906
Breakeven Response %	4.91%

Sensitivities (+ or -) To Target Response Percentage

	Target				
Degree of Sensitivity	20.00%				
% Response	10.36%	13.83%	17.26%	20.79%	24.21%
Cost Per Response	29.30	22.41	16.38	16.53	13.55

SENSITIVITIES OF TELEMARKETING

% Response: 10.36%, 13.83%, 17.29%, 20.75%, 24.21%
Cost Per Response: 29.30, 22.41, 18.28, 15.52, 13.55

— % Response   — Cost Per Response

Exhibit 9-14 Telemarketing Breakeven Estimates

Training	3,000.00
Creative Costs of Script Preparation	4,000.00
Other	2,000.00
TOTAL	9,000.00

	Per Call
Average List Cost	0.15
Number of minutes Per Completed Call	3.00
Number of min. Per Non-Completed Call	1.50
Call Cost Per minute	1.20
% of Completed Calls	40.00%
Average Cost Per Call	2.70

Telemarketing Costs	171,000
TOTAL Campaign Cost	180,000
Breakeven Response %	4.91%

telemarketing salespeople available and the number of calls they can make in a given time period. Unlike broadcast, press or even direct mail, it is impossible to quickly expand the media schedule simply by purchasing more media.

The model for planning telemarketing initiatives (Exhibit 9-13) closely resembles that for direct mail. We need to have lists of telephone numbers and the quantities of each. Because we can expect a high percentage of sales per thousand calls, we can use small test quantities. The rollout quantities reflect the elimination of duplication. We also need the list costs and an estimate of the response percentages of completed calls.

The model derives the test and rollout costs, the costs per order for the different telephone number lists used, and the difference between the actual CPO and the ACPO, highlighting any list segments that exceed the ACPO.

Finally, the model produces the total telemarketing costs and adds to these the fixed costs for telemarketing representatives, staff training, creative script preparation and other fixed costs (Exhibit 9-14).

Broadcast: Radio and Television

Broadcast media offer wide reach and a relatively low cost per thousand and are principally used by brand advertisers eager to reach a large audience with a strong and memorable message. Consistent with all media, marketers look for ways of effectively reaching the maximum number of prospects (measured in "gross rating points"[25]) at the lowest cost per thousand.

While television and radio broadcasts can enliven a product presentation with sound, movement or animation, the inherent time limitations of commercials demands that the viewer concentrate only on the key elements of the marketing proposition. The offer must be simply stated, and the call to action must make ordering as simple as possible: "800" or other "free" telephone numbers and Internet addresses are used for just this reason.

It may cost one million dollars for a thirty-second spot on the TV network presentation of a widely watched sporting event such as America's Super Bowl, but that amount is calculated as a product of the expected giant audience and what the TV network thinks it can get for this time slot. In fact, the actual price for the spot is derived from what amounts to an auction—the amount the highest "bidder" is prepared to pay. Because brand image advertisers cannot accurately measure the results of their advertising, it is easier for them to justify the use of this type of spot than an advertiser who has to judge the cost-per-order of each marketing action.

Sometimes TV or Radio is used to get the prospect to indicate an interest (but not make a purchase in the first instance). Not everyone who expresses an interest will end up purchasing the product. In these cases the marketer must make a provision for the cost of "conversion" from interest to order, discounting the percentage of response accordingly and calculating the costs of handling the responses as part of the fulfillment calculation.

"What is the value to your network of an un-sold thirty-second commercial slot at airtime?" a contentious direct marketer asked a TV media executive who was defending his network's high prices at a conference. "Obviously, nothing!" answered the annoyed executive. Like airline seats after the door has closed and the flight is ready to take-off, empty hotel rooms or rental cars sitting unused in the renter's parking area, broadcast time is a perishable commodity.

The price, therefore, is frequently negotiable and tends to be reduced as the "sell-by" date approaches. However, brand advertisers need to make their media buys coincide with a series carefully coordinated marketing events. An automobile manufacturer launching a new model needs its advertising to appear at the time of the launch; a retailer offering a major promotion has to secure the desired advertising time slots to drive customers into his outlets when the promotional merchandise is on display. Thus, they are not in a position to bargain except as a product of their volume of airtime purchases. Direct marketers are seldom bound by these restrictions, and their flexibility can mean exceptional savings over the "card rates."

Cable and satellite channels often offer better opportunities than the more popular broadcast channels. The programming is already segmented by interest, and therefore the target audience has a more concentrated profile and costs tend to be lower than for "open" channels. Much the same can be said of radio stations whose content is highly focused: classical music stations have a very different profile from those giving the latest sports results or "call-in" talk shows. Matching the product offer to the content is one of the keys to success.

It is always necessary to test "response" commercials thoroughly even if they have been run successfully in different markets. The first few times an offer is aired on a station may not pay for themselves, as there is traditionally a "build" for a commercial and then a fall-off. Frequency of running the commercials is necessary to obtain the maximum response but too much frequency is uneconomic. Getting it right is a constant process of trial and error. Establishing response patterns and then managing media purchases accordingly is essential but can only come with experience and tight control.[26]

Responses from TV and radio come in very quickly, sometimes even before the commercial is completed. Lost calls (due to too many calls for too few incoming telesales representatives) mean wasted money and annoyed callers, many of whom will give up and not call again. Planning of potential call flow is critical.

Like print advertising, a good way of determining the potential for any TV or radio channel is to see if other response advertisers are using it. Watch the channels you are considering using and ask the media representative or agency for samples of response commercials that have been successful on the channel.

Direct marketers tend to buy on a more aggressive basis and often seek "remnants," time that has not been sold as airtime approaches. These marketers allow the broadcaster to fill unsold time slots with their commercials at very preferential rates. The broadcaster gets "something" for the time rather than "nothing." These commercials tend to be run during non-prime time, late at night, together with re-runs of old movies, etc. But it doesn't matter just as long as the commercials produce an acceptable level of response measured by the CPO.

Even when buying pre-defined time slots, direct marketers tend to buy better than brand advertisers who spend far more with the broadcast media. The simple reason is that the media owners are aware that the direct marketers know just what they can afford to spend and won't pay a penny more.[27] If the commercials do not bring in the responses at or below the allowable, the marketer stops spending. If they do, he would be very unwise to stop until he either runs out of merchandise or the CPO rises to unacceptable levels.

In the late 1970s, the Wunderman agency developed an imaginative, if limited, measurement tool for television advertising for its Columbia Record Club client who was at the time running "brand" commercials supporting their print advertising. According to Wunderman, the client "didn't know if the commercials he was running to support his press advertising were successful, because it was difficult to measure the results accurately." In Lester Wunderman's book, *Being Direct*, he tells the story of devising a solution to that problem:

> What if we hid a secret "buried treasure" in the coupon of our print ads? And what if we showed on television where the treasure was hidden? . . . all we needed was to print a "gold box" on the ad. To the unknowing, it would look like a design element, just a yellow bar at the bottom of the coupon, until a television commercial revealed it to be a special "Gold Box." The commercial would state that anyone who found it could get an additional free record. Only viewers who saw the TV commercial would recognize the Gold Box as a special offer and write the number of an addi-

tional free record on it. We could safely print the yellow bar in all our ads because it would have no meaning or value except in those cities where we chose to test the commercial and measure the effect of television support. All we had to do was count the number of coupons with the Gold Box filled in, and we would then know exactly how many people who responded to our print ad had been motivated by the television commercial. We could test various levels of TV support in different cities and measure the value of the incremental TV responders.

It wasn't a perfect measure: people who saw the commercial and filled in the Gold Box to get their extra free record *might have purchased from the print advertising anyway*. But short of "pure" direct response advertising, it was the closest thing to an "accountable" technique for measuring TV that had been developed. Its success is attested in an internal Columbia Record Club memorandum quoted in the book, which said: "Notice that the overall cost per estimated application (non-TV supported) is $18.60, while the overall incremental application (due to TV support) is only $4.00."[28]

As noted previously, radio and TV can only tell simple stories in thirty seconds or one minute. The record club experience is a good case in point. It would have been almost impossible to show the wide range of music albums available on TV or describe them in a radio commercial and get the viewer or listener to pick the ones he wanted. By incentivizing the viewer or listener to find the Gold Box in the print advertising where the full product and its benefits could be displayed, the broadcast medium had a simple and compelling story to tell.

"Infomercials"—long spots that can run many minutes (usually in the middle of the night or on stations with excess advertising capacity)—can tell a complicated story and generate direct orders. From an economic perspective, they can be treated just like shorter commercials.

Planning for the use of TV and radio needs the following data:

▶ The TV or radio stations to be used.

▶ The length (in seconds) of the spots to be broadcast. (The

length of different spots does not bear directly on the economics except in so far as the cost of spots will be at least
partially determined by their length as will the likely response percentage.)

▶ The cost per spot.

▶ The estimated number of viewers/listeners per spot. This
will be a product of ratings as given by the broadcasters.

▶ The cost per thousand viewers/listeners.

▶ The number of spots to be run.

▶ The average estimated response rate from each commercial. Because the response rates will vary spot to spot, it is
recommended to use an average response rate.[29]

The template Broadcast Cost Calculator in Exhibit 9-15 provides the tools for the planning of a TV or radio advertising schedule. As can be seen, the model is a "test" campaign, in fact, a test
of each of the four stations used. The number of spots is relatively
low. What the marketer must do as part of his planning is to evaluate the "Potential Rollout Multiple"—a judgment of how many
times the initial or "test" flight of spots could be aired *if successful.*
The model then projects the total cost of the campaign (the sum of
the "test" and the rollout) including the one-time creative and
other fixed costs. It also calculates the sensitivities of different average response rate percentages.

What we see in this example is three stations producing CPOs
lower than the ACPO and one in the "red." We must remember that
these "test" commercial flights do not carry any of the 25,000 creative or other fixed costs. This cost is only amortized for the total
campaign and incorporated into the "target" and other sensitivities.
This shows us that at a response rate of .0150 percent,[30] the CPO exceeds the ACPO by 6.67, still a relatively safe response rate when
the "Profit or Contribution" is added back.

Broadcast media can be extremely powerful generators of both
sales and "leads,"[31] but the use of these media demand a special expertise and for the novice, professional expertise is highly recommended before embarking on large broadcast expenditures.

Exhibit 9-15 Broadcast Cost Calculator

Allowable Cost Per Order: 60.00

Broadcast Stations:	Length of Spots (Seconds)	Cost Per Spot	Estimated Number of Viewers/ Listeners Per Spot	Cost Per '000 Viewers/ Listeners	Number of Spots	Estimated Response Rate	Total Cost	Number of Responses for Breakeven	% of Responses for Breakeven	Cost Per Order	Difference from ACPO
[Describe Station A]	60	400.00	60,000	6.67	5	0.02%	2,000.00	33.33	0.01%	33.33	26.67
[Describe Station B]	60	475.00	105,000	4.52	7	0.02%	3,325.00	55.42	0.01%	28.27	31.73
[Describe Station C]	120	700.00	110,000	6.36	5	0.02%	3,500.00	58.33	0.01%	33.49	26.51
[Describe Station D]	120	600.00	60,000	10.00	4	0.02%	2,400.00	40.00	0.02%	66.67	(6.67)
[Describe Station E]				·			·	·	·	·	·
[Describe Station F]				·			·	·	·	·	·
[Describe Station G]				·			·	·	·	·	·
[Describe Station H]				·			·	·	·	·	·
[Describe Station I]				·			·	·	·	·	·
[Describe Station J]				·			·	·	·	·	·
[Describe Station K]				·			·	·	·	·	·
[Describe Station L]				·			·	·	·	·	·
[Describe Station M]				·			·	·	·	·	·
[Describe Station N]				·			·	·	·	·	·
[Describe Station O]				·			·	·	·	·	·
[Describe Station P]				·			·	·	·	·	·
[Describe Station Q]				·			·	·	·	·	·
[Describe Station R]				·			·	·	·	·	·
[Describe Station S]				·			·	·	·	·	·
[Describe Station T]				·			·	·	·	·	·
TOTALS			335,000	Average 6.15	21	Average 0.0%	11,225.00	10,725	Average 0.01%	Average 38.35	Average 38.35

TOTAL Reach (Est. Viewers * No. Spots): 8,325,000

Potential Rollout Multiple: 3.0

TOTAL Potential Rollout Reach: 8,475,000

Rollout Media Cost if Potential Implemented: 33,675

Test Media Cost: 11,225

Creative Costs & Other Fixed Costs: 25,000

TOTAL Test & Rollout Costs: 69,900

Breakeven %: 0.02%

Sensitivities (+ or -) To Target Response Percentage

Degree of Sensitivity		Target	
20.00%			
% Response	0.01%	0.01%	0.02%
Cost Per Order	68.67	64.84	59.28

(Inc. Creative & Other Fixed Costs)

SENSITIVITIES OF BROADCAST PLANNING

	1	2	3	4	5
% Response	0.01%	0.01%	0.02%	0.02%	0.02%
Cost Per Order	91.56	68.67	54.94	45.78	39.24

Legend: % Response, Cost Per Order

The Internet and E-Commerce

The Internet, in theory at least, is the perfect medium for direct and data-driven marketing, the "killer application" as one pundit described it during the gold rush days before the "technology" bubble burst and the undisciplined blizzard of SPAM cooled the receptivity of the market and starved the goose laying all those golden eggs.

It is still unique, offering marketers in all parts of the continuum a low-cost, highly targeted, and amazingly rapid way of reaching customers and prospects with segmented and attractive messages both for image and direct response purposes. While its share of total ad spend is growing rapidly, it remains relatively modest in overall media spending terms. In 2002, according to the US DMA's Economic Model, US$4.0 billion is forecast in expenditures for interactive marketing. The DMA expects that number to grow by 18.9 percent annually to reach US$8.4 billion in 2006. Interactive sales, forecast at US$36.0 billion in 2002, are expected to grow by 20.9 percent to reach US $81.1 billion in 2006.

> The e in e-business enables management to more quickly validate customer requirements across dozens—if not hundreds—of customer segments and move quickly to optimize customer satisfaction in those segments having the greatest growth potential.
>
> The Internet brings an unparalleled level of accountability to the prime directive of the enterprise: *finding and keeping customers.*[32]

Surprisingly, Fast Moving Consumer Goods (FMCG) companies are lagging behind other sectors in their use of electronic media for marketing. As reported in *DM News*,[33] *Neilsen/Net Ratings* says, "consumer packaged goods companies are disproportionately underrepresented for online advertising is mainly [because] of tradition—traditional companies gravitating towards traditional means of marketing their traditional products."

Email: Direct Mail Without Having to Pay the Postman or the Printer

The leading edge for electronic marketing is email. Throughout the world, email is becoming a medium of choice, fast, cheap and increasingly reliable. We use it to talk to our business colleagues, our families and friends, in fact anyone who is hooked up to the system and has an email address.

"Email" said a presenter at one of the numerous marketing industry conferences "is direct mail without having to pay the postage or the printer." If somewhat oversimplified, it's a fair definition. One might add that it also allows the user to do extensive testing with virtually real time results, personalize messages down to the individual and elicit responses with or without payments.[34] It also allows for links to web sites that permit full and attractive selling messages and even interaction. Not bad for a medium that is perceived to be "free," prompting the quip that while there may be no such thing as a free lunch, you can at least have some free bytes.

Whether free or paid for, these bites can and do cause indigestion. "One of the constant themes drawn from the experiences of thousands of people who have test-driven web sites in Vividence evaluations is that users are turned off by marketing efforts that are designed to benefit the company and not the customer."[35]

Of course email is not "free." There is the cost of the lists, usually more expensive to rent or acquire than direct mail lists. And there are transmission costs, etc. However, even being generous in estimating the costs, an email campaign costs no more than 30% of the per thousand cost of direct mail and it can bring in a higher percentage return—or at least it could until SPAM soured the market.

A 2002 survey done by the Association for Interactive Marketing, a subsidiary of the US DMA, put the "average cost per email in 2002 at US$.05" or US$50.00 per thousand, obviously excluding the list cost. Including one hundred percent rented lists, the per-thousand cost of an email campaign should be no more than US$250.00. Even with an undeliverable rate of 10%, this would only add US$25.00 per-thousand for a total of US$275.

Response rates to email vary widely as indicated in Exhibit 9-3. If we accept that the Average Acquisition Cost Per Online Customer in 2002 was estimated to be US$30.00 each[36], the "average" response rate is plus or minus (30/275 = .109) or .11%. Experience teaches that this rate can be substantially higher. Much depends on the level of precision of the targeting and the offer that is being made.

There is no question that Internet users who give the marketer "permission" to send them email marketing communications will revolutionize direct and data driven marketing and will have the lowest CPO. The failure to get "permission" from customers and prospects to send them emails could result in a very negative reaction from the recipients. Direct marketing experts agree that "the real cost of email marketing is in turning off your customers and prospects so they do not remain as customers for you or anyone."

Obviously, permission-based emails produce substantially higher response percentages than those sent to people who have not given the marketer specific permission to contact them. "SPAM" said one electronic marketing guru "is to permission emails what rape is to consensual sex." But even permission-based relationships change. Respondents to a survey by Quris Inc. an email marketing services provider " . . . open and read about 65 percent of the permission email they receive, but when asked to re-evaluate the permission-based email relationships they maintain, they would renew just 47 percent of those relationships." The report went on to say that 68 percent of the respondents asked why permission email subscribers would like to unsubscribe cited "too frequent email" as the main cause followed by "losing interest" in product or service (51 percent), emails were "generally boring" (35 percent) and "offered no significant value" (34 percent).

One of the least intrusive and most effective forms of offer that appear to give the best opportunity for success is the use of email to stimulate "click-throughs" to a web site. Before examining this, however, it is worth looking at the economics of a direct sale from an email initiative.

Exhibit 9-16 is similar to the direct mail template. The "cost input" of the traditional mailing package elements has been replaced with an input box for "Email Distribution Cost" and input boxes for "Other" costs.

What we see is that the total cost of the "email" in this case is 200.91 per thousand and slightly on the high side of the normal acceptable range.[37] To calculate the total cost of a sale we first need to eliminate the number of duplicate names and inputting the "Estimated % of Duplication Eliminated from Lists" accomplishes this.

In this example, the breakeven for a profitable campaign with orders direct from the email is 0.46 percent.

Exhibit 9-16 Email Cost Calculator

Allowable Cost Per Order: 60.00

Lists:

	Available Quantity	Net Qty After Dedup	Test Qty	Rollout Qty	List Cost Per '000	Negotiated Per Order Payment	Estimated Response Rate	Test Cost	Rollout Cost	Cost Per Order	Difference from ACPO
Describe List A	10,000	8,000	1,000	7,000	120.00	3.00	0.50%	190	1,330	51.84	8.36
Describe List B	15,000	12,000	2,000	10,000	135.00	5.00	0.30%	410	2,050	91.06	(31.06)
Describe List C	30,000	24,000	2,000	22,000	160.00		0.30%	430	4,730	94.39	(34.39)
Describe List D											
Describe List E											
Describe List F											
Describe List G											
Describe List H											
Describe List I											
Describe List J											
Describe List K											
Describe List L											
Describe List M											
Describe List N											
Describe List O											
Describe List P											
Describe List Q											
Describe List R											
Describe List S											
Describe List T											
TOTALS	55,000	44,000	5,000	39,000				1,030	8,110		
					Average 145.91		Average 0.34%			Average 82.03	

Sensitivities (+ or -) To Target Response Percentage

	Target	
Degree of Sensitivity	20.00%	0.47%
% Response	0.20%	0.34%
Cost Per Response	135.36	82.03	59.17

E-mail Distribution Cost:

	Per '000
Distribution	55.00
Other 1	
Other 2	
Other 3	
Sub Total	55.00
List Cost	145.91

TOTAL E-Mailing Package: 200.91

Creative Cost of Mailing Package: 3,000.00

Estimated % of Duplication Eliminated from Lists: 20.00%

E-Mail Breakeven Response %: 0.48%

E-Mailing Costs: 9,140

TOTAL Campaign Cost: 12,140

SENSITIVITIES OF E-MAIL PLANNING

If the object of the email is to send people to a web site (rather than make a sale in the first step), we have to move to the next step and discount the number of respondents, again adding in any unique web site costs directly attributable to the email promotion. (The Internet Template, Exhibit 9-18, can be used together with the Email Template, Exhibit 9-17.)

Finally we need to further discount this by the number who go to the web site but do not end up purchasing. Only then do we get a final cost per order. It is a "funnel" process very similar to that described in Chapter 5.

The Economics of Marketing on the World Wide Web

Internet "hosts" (sometimes called ISPs for Internet Service Providers) are sites that accept advertising in the form of banners, pop-ups, buttons and a large range of other forms. So too do specific Internet sites that are not hosts. Many hosts and individual sites will sell you "banner," "target," "newsletter," and "opt-in" positions at negotiated rates just like commercials or advertisements in other media. Sometimes they will charge by number of impressions, by the month or by the "click." But many will also be willing to make commercial deals to run your messages and charge you a percentage of your sales or some combination of these different modes. This and the ever-changing nature of Internet sales makes the economics of using the Internet complicated and each "buy" of Internet advertising an individual case.

In the heady days of the Internet bubble, Internet advertising was a sellers' market and sites with high traffic could pretty much charge what they liked. When the bubble burst and almost every Internet provider was stretched for revenue, the power switched to the marketer, who could aggressively negotiate Internet prices and even make deals based only upon results.

This seesaw has now somewhat stabilized, and some formal pricing structures are becoming more common. But there is still great volatility in the market and this is likely to continue for some time to come. Negotiation is still the best way to get maximum Internet value and the presentation of a credible case for what you can afford, the ACPO if you will, is an effective means of building that negotiation. As Yahoo's Jerry Shereshewsky puts it:

There are a million different variations on "rates" for internet advertising.

At the most basic there are sites with little or no real demand for their inventory. They will do "cost per" deals (like the early days of TV). Cost per deals also range all over the lot. Some are literally cost per order. Many are still 'cost per click' and, of course, the cost people are willing to pay is directly related to the value received.

Most larger publishers and those with real demand for inventory shy away from "cost per" deals because all the control/power is with the marketer and none with the publisher. A poor offer, product or creative eats inventory and never returns revenue.

Next on the list, and becoming increasingly more common, especially in areas like search results, is an auction. Sometimes the variable is cost/per, but more and more often it is CPM; like regular media. But the auction format, done entirely online by folks like Overture allows the market to determine the value of a particular location and moment in time.

At the top of the heap is traditional cost per thousand advertising. The costs can be quite low for "run of network" (probably in the $2–3 CPM range, making it incredibly cost effective compared to television or print) or quite high as specific demographic, geographic, behavioral and/or contextual targeting is brought into play. Prices for certain kinds of placements, using all these variables, can range (in US) upwards of $50/cpm or even more.

A selection of "Recreation & Sports" and the various ways they price for their sites are shown in Exhibit 9-17. This example was taken from AdStop.com a portal aggregating Internet advertising information.

The main ways of paying for Internet advertising:

▶ "Per Impression":

The most commonly used method is to pay for "impressions," the number of times your message appears on the host site, usually quoted on a cost per thousand ("CPM")

Exhibit 9-17 Email List and Advertising Comparisons

Advertising Categories ▾

Compare Category: **Recreation & Sports**

Site Navigation ▾ | Compare Options ▾

WebTrends Live: track your ad and results, verify your traffic.

[Compare] [Print]   [Search!]   [Power Search!]

Your Compare results are displayed below. Click the Compare checkboxes then the "Compare" Button to compare specific Web Sites

Compare	Click for details	Uniques	Pages	Verified	Banner	Button	Target	Newsletters	Opt In	Trades	Discount	Agents
☐	@ Travel Notes - Travel Di...	-	-	N	$.35/cpm	$.27/cpm	$.50/cpm	$.33/cpm	-	N	Y	N
☐	1800 USA Hotel	-	300k	Y	$.26/cpm	-	-	-	-	N	N	Y
☐	a virtual Dominica	19k	50k	Y	$.50/mo	-	-	-	-	N	Y	Y
☐	Accommodation Search Engine	-	-	N	$.30/cpm	-	$.50/cpm	-	-	N	Y	N
☐	Admiralty Yacht Sales	6k	30k	N	$.10/cpm	-	-	-	-	N	Y	Y
☐	Adventure Angling	-	42k	N	$.10/cpm	$.10/mo	$.10/cpm	-	-	N	Y	Y
☐	Adventure Directory	37k	44k	N	$.40/cpm	$.600/mo	$.40/cpm	-	-	N	Y	Y
☐	Adventure Sports Enthusiast...	-	-	N	-	-	-	-	-	N	N	Y
☐	Adventure Sports Online	-	100k	Y	$.30/cpm	-	$.30/cpm	-	-	N	N	Y
☐	Adventure Sports Online	-	-	Y	$.30/cpm	$.30/cpm	-	-	-	Y	N	Y
☐	AdventureBid.com	15k	150k	N	$2.460/mo	-	$2.460/mo	-	-	N	Y	N
☐	All About Spain	250k	2.0m	N	$.30/cpm	-	$.35/cpm	-	-	N	Y	N
☐	All StarStats Online	-	1.5m	Y	$.35/cpm	-	-	-	-	N	N	N
☐	All Things Automotive Direc...	50k	190k	N	$.40/cpm	-	$.60/cpm	-	-	N	N	N
☐	allhotels	-	-	Y	$.75/cpm	$.70/cpm	$.90/cpm	$.65/cpm	$.90/cpm	N	N	N

Exhibit 9-18 Template: Internet Cost Calculator

Template INTERNET

Allowable Cost Per Order: 120.00

Sites / Channel	Product / Format	Number of Periods	Fixed Cost Per Period	Qty of Impressions / Click Per Period	Cost of Impressions / Click Per '000	Response Rate of Purchase	Price Paid Per Purchase to Host Site	Actual Qty	Total Cost	Cost Per Order	Difference from ACPO
AOL - Home Page	Full Banner 468x60	3	100.00	1,000,000	30.00	0.02%		600	90,300	150.50	(30.50)
AOL - Shopping	Pop-up 320x205	2		1,000,000	20.00	0.02%		400	40,000	100.00	20.00
AOL - Chat	Button 120/60	3		1,000	100.00	0.20%		6	300	50.00	70.00
Site 4	100	3	100.00	1,000,000	10.00	0.02%	10.00	600	36,300	60.50	59.50
Site 5	100	3		1,000,000	20.00	0.02%	20.00	600	12,000	20.00	100.00
TOTALS				4,001,000		Average 0.06%		2,206	178,900	Average 81.10	36.90

Sensitivities (+ or -) To Target Response Percentage

Degree of Sensitivity	20.00%	20.00%		Target	
% Response	0.03%	0.04%	0.06%	0.07%	0.08%
Cost Per Response	150.27	112.70	90.16	75.14	64.40

Creative Cost: 20,000

TOTAL Internet Cost: 198,900

CPO with Creative Cost: 90.16

Breakeven Response %: 0.04%

SENSITIVITIES OF INTERNET PLANNING

basis. A percentage of the viewers of the message will "click through" to your site and a percentage of these will purchase. But if the rate is "CPM" the cost of appearing on the site will not relate to click-throughs or sales.

▶ "Per Click":

"Click-throughs" is another payment method, which can be measured electronically. The viewer clicks on your banner or pop-up and is taken automatically to your site or web page for that promotion. You pay the site per click-through, whether or not a sale is consummated.

These "clicks" are measured by the host with existing technology and should be subject to audit by you if you do not agree on the number. Many hosts charge a negotiated amount for each click-through. Some charge a small amount for banners and pop-ups plus a negotiated amount for each click-through. In that case, it is necessary to calculate the combination of the two.[38]

▶ "Per Purchase":

Some site owners charge a percentage of sales resulting from the appearance of your message on their sites. More and more hosts demand a percentage of sales revenues and some combine this with charges for appearance.

It is critical to establish cost benchmarks and that the marketer carefully analyze the comparative costs and values and only then chooses those that are most appropriate to his needs.

The Internet Template provides a tool to help in developing plans for Internet marketing and follows the same format as the other media templates. Because of the fast-changing nature of the medium, it will be necessary for the Internet marketer to make changes in the template to suit his particular needs in the light of changing circumstances.

Media Planning and Testing

Since targeting the right prospects for any marketing initiative is the highest priority, the planning of the media campaign must be developed around establishing the right target—a medium or media that economically reaches as many of the target prospects as possible—delivering orders at less than the allowable and then finding more of them through rigorous testing.

It is always something of a balancing act. To get the equilibrium right we need to make judgments on a number of critical factors. These questions inform the decisions:

▶ Quantity versus Quality:

Does the medium have sufficient "reach" to give you the quantity you want or are you satisfied with tight targeting that provides smaller numbers but better percentage returns?

▶ Cost Per Thousand (CPM) versus Cost Per Order (CPO):

Is the comparative CPM more important than the precision of the targeting that might cost more but deliver a lower CPO?

And are there other media that might give you more for less?

▶ Mix versus Concentration:

For the same expenditure, do you wish to hit the same person many times or different people a few times?

Building a simple "Media Testing Table" (Exhibit 9-19) will focus the work. It is rather like a reverse tennis tournament seeding. Start with the "known" (the best players) and use these as your benchmarks. For these you should have:

▶ Historic CPOs.

▶ Reach (available circulation).

▶ CPM (cost of reaching the audience on a per thousand basis).

▶ Expansion potential (Are there more like them?).

▶ Testing availability (Can you test?).

Exhibit 9-19 Media Testing Steps

DEVELOPMENT OF MEDIA TESTING

STEP 1	STEP 2	STEP 3
KNOWN MEDIA CONTROL	KNOWN MEDIA CONTROL	KNOWN MEDIA CONTROL
	OTHER CATEGORY MEDIA	OTHER CATEGORY MEDIA
		NEW CATEGORY MEDIA
		NEW CATEGORY MEDIA
	OTHER CATEGORY MEDIA	OTHER CATEGORY MEDIA
KNOWN MEDIA CONTROL	KNOWN MEDIA CONTROL	KNOWN MEDIA CONTROL

To these should be added other media from the same category as the known controls. (If you have been using newspaper inserts in weekend publications, you would do well to see if you could add some more). Then add media from other categories, magazine inserts, for example. And so on.

Choosing the Right Media:
An Exercise in Making Comparisons

What we want is to purchase the media that will produce the lowest cost per order and the number of orders we desire. Since there are so many options, the last step in developing a final media plan is to compare the available options. Aggregating all the media data simplifies comparisons. What we see in Exhibit 9-20 is a direct comparison of the most important media elements.

We can determine the comparative reach of each medium and the estimated number of responses from each. We can compare estimated costs per response and whether these are less than or in excess of the allowable. And we can see the campaign cost if we rollout each. Then we can decide what to test and how to obtain the best results.

Exhibit 9-20 Per Thousand Promotion Evaluation

	ACPO	24.00
(Member, Subscriber, etc...)		

Media:	Cost of Media Per '000	Expected % Response	Number of Responses	Cost Per Response	Profit or (Loss) Against Allowable *	No. Responses Per '000: Necessary to Breakeven	% Response Necessary to Breakeven
Direct Mail	1,000.00	3.50%	35.00	28.57	(4.57)	41.67	4.17%
Press Advertisements	200.00	0.50%	5.00	40.00	(16.00)	8.33	0.83%
Press Inserts	250.00	1.00%	10.00	25.00	(1.00)	10.42	1.04%
Package Inserts	50.00	20.00%	200.00	0.25	23.75	2.08	0.21%
E-mail	20.00	5.00%	50.00	0.40	23.60	0.83	0.08%
Input Other 1			-	-	-	-	
Input Other 2			-	-	-	-	
Input Other 3			-	-	-	-	
Input Other 4			-	-	-	-	

* NB: The 'Profit or (Loss) Against Allowable' and the subsequent breakeven calculations do not factor in the percentage of profit or contribution taken into the costs.
Adding this back will change the breakeven numbers.

What you want to accomplish is to define those media that give you:

▶ New ways of reaching an expanded target market.

▶ CPMs comparable to known media or the reasonable expectation that even if they have a higher CPM, they will produce an acceptable CPO.

When you have all this data together, you must:

▶ Look at the total money "budget" you have available.

▶ Look at the total number of sales, "starts" or other results you desire.

▶ Build an expandable media plan that meets these objectives and develop a testing plan to validate your assumptions.

Negotiate with the media for the best possible deals.

Media are the highways that take you to market. Choosing the roads that will get you where you want to go fastest or cheapest is the challenge. As indicated in this chapter, managing the economics of media purchasing is a formidable task—one that often gets short shrift from marketers despite their understanding that without access to the right audience at the best price, the rest of the marketing effort is useless. Understanding the economics of the various media and targeting your prospects in the most efficient manner is paramount and assures accountability.

Notes

1 Over the past decade there has been a rising tide of consumer dissatisfaction with the barrage of advertising messages, especially those delivered through the more intrusive media such as telephone selling and SPAM—the name of the World War II canned meat product now used generically to describe the growing tide of unsolicited emails that appear on our computer screens. In the US and some other countries, laws are being enacted in response to the public outcry against these intrusions of privacy. There is a "No Call" list in

the US where consumers can put their names and commercial calls to their numbers is now illegal. In addition to anti-SPAM legislation, there are also an increasing number of software products coming onto the market to filter or eliminate SPAM.

[2] *MaxiMarketing:* Page 25.

[3] This is what Saatchi & Saatchi founder and brilliant marketer Charles Saatchi called "the single minded proposition, dramatically expressed".

[4] This was wonderfully articulated a few years ago in the UK when two companies were competing for the license to measure TV audiences. One of the companies ran an ad in national newspapers showing a couple on a couch making love. In the background was a television set showing a commercial. The headline said something like: "Our competitor says they are watching your commercial." The couple obviously had more compelling things to do, even if the TV was "on."

[5] *DM News*, April 2003.

[6] Recent legislation in the U.S. and a number of other countries forbidding unsolicited outbound calls and establishing a "no call" list will undoubtedly spread and change the face of outbound calls. The number of people in the U.S. asking to be on the no call list reached 30 millions in just a few months.

[7] There are exceptions in which there are a number of what are sometimes referred to as "curriculum" mailings. These consist of a sequence of communications sent before asking for an order. To determine their efficiency, it is necessary to consider them as a single cost element. A curriculum series of three mailings, each of which costs 800.00 per thousand, would require you to think in terms of a media cost of 3 times 800.00 or a total of 2,400.00.

[8] Sharing the ACPO model results with the ad sales department of the medium has often helped establish a reasonable performance payment basis. Sometimes a combination of a fixed amount for the advertising plus a performance payment is the best course of action.

[9] *MaxiMarketing:* Pages 54 & 55.

[10] "Recent" experience with a medium is important. Media change in the content they present and the context in which they present it. Mailing and email and telephone lists age quickly and lose pulling power if not constantly renewed.

[11] For template users who wish to use more than 20 lists, the section can be extended to any length but it is essential that the formulas for the totals be changed accordingly.

[12] It should be remembered that *the de-duplication procedure will reduce the number of names on some files more than others and that for the purposes of accuracy, new total list quantities should be input after the de-duplication process has been completed.* However, for initial planning purposes, a total percentage should suffice.

[13] If correctly calculated, the ACPO should include the mandated percentage of profit as a cost and thus, the "breakeven" would produce the desired profit.

[14] It is important to note that *the output for all the sensitivities references the total campaign costs including creative in this and the following media Templates* while the average cost per response references only the media costs and excludes the creative and other fixed costs.

[15] In recent years, leading printers throughout the world have made increased use of "Selective Binding" techniques that permit specific inserts—even whole advertising sections—to appear in selected copies of the publication and not in others. The use of these techniques can provide increased targeting based on subscription and other data but usually at a substantially increased cost per thousand.

[16] In this and the Press Media template, the amount of any negotiated per order payment is added to all the media used. Thus, if you have some media where there is no payment, it is suggested that you use separate runs of the template for those media with and without a per order payment.

[17] In changing any of the Templates, users are reminded to carefully follow the directions found in the Template notes on the CD-Rom.

[18] According to Jeff Holland, President of Vertical Media Group, quoted in the September 11th issue of *DM News*, a US trade publication, " . . . insert media represent 7 billion units and has revenue of US $1 billion annually". Add to that the insert business outside the US and the importance of the medium more than doubles.

[19] Where testing of more than a single insert in the same publication is going to be undertaken, it is advisable to input on the template each test separately with the appropriate quantities.

[20] After successfully testing a small percentage of a publication's

circulation with inserts many marketers will rollout to the total circulation making no effort to eliminate the part of the circulation already used. In that case, the total circulation number input under "Available Quantity" should be the total circulation *plus* the test amount.

[21] There is the further problem that many large manufacturers now package their products and the inserts that accompany them at a central point in one country and then the packages are distributed in that and other countries—to make this even more complicated, sometimes, merchandise originally shipped to one country is then moved to another. Language and price and currency considerations must therefore be taken into consideration.

[22] How similar they are to small inserts is attested by the fact that many years ago, the Columbia Music Club in the U.S. had undertaken a take-one campaign that failed miserably. Few people took them and large quantities remained. Noticing that the size of the left over take-ones was almost identical to that of the leading TV listings magazine, *TV Guide*, Columbia's direct marketing agency convinced the magazine to test carrying inserts bound into the center of the magazine using the left over stock. Virtually overnight, this became one of the most successful and sought after response advertising positions in the country.

[23] Roman, Murray. *Telephone Marketing.* New York: McGraw Hill, Inc. 1976. Page 12.

[24] Exhibit 9-12 is a section of the Telemarketing template. The full template, Exhibit 9-13, allows the user to do all the calculations concerned with telemarketing.

[25] Gross Rating Points (GRPs) are the measure of advertising *reach* times average *frequency*, the advertising weight delivered within a given time period. It could also be said to be "the total number of exposures to a schedule of announcements, expressed as a percentage of all possible listeners".

[26] For valuable insights on all aspects of TV direct response, see: Witek, John. *Response Television*, Chicago, Illinois: Crain Books. 1981.

[27] After the acquisition of a leading direct marketing advertising agency by one of the top five general agencies, the media director of the main agency offered to take over the media buying functions of

the newly acquired DM subsidiary. Purchasing more than fifty times as much media, the general agency believed it could buy better than the direct marketing agency. When an actual comparison was made between what the DM agency and the main agency could buy the identical time for, the DM agency was purchasing at rates more than 20% below the general agency.

[28] Wunderman, Lester. *Being Direct*. New York: Random House, 1966. Pages 122—125.

[29] As with other media, response will follow a predictable pattern based upon experience. In TV and radio, response to the first commercials may be low and will rise over a series of broadcasts and then decline as the "cream" has been converted to orders. Understanding this pattern for any given product is critical for planning. Where local TV and radio markets exist, it is good to test representative markets for one to two weeks with a few commercials each day and carefully track the results until they begin to fall. This should provide a benchmark for all other markets.

[30] The actual response rate is rounded up in the illustration to 2%.

[31] "Leads" are requests for further information—the responder "raising his hand" so to speak and signifying interest without a commitment to purchase. When using any medium to generate leads it is necessary to factor into the economics the cost of conversion from lead to sale.

[32] Page 4, Executive Summary, *"Business Case for Brand Resource Management"* 2001 GISTICS Incorporated.

[33] *DMNews*, September 16, 2003.

[34] One important note of caution here is that the smaller the quantity, the less reliable the statistical reliability of the rollout. Thus, before rolling out an email campaign, it is critical that you have a high level of confidence that the test sample is representative of the total. Re-testing a few times before rollout is highly recommended and possible because of the short time it takes to receive responses.

[35] Vividence White Paper: *Stop Losing Customers On The Web*; March 2002.

[36] Association of Interactive Marketing survey on "Commercial Value of Email", Page 18.

[37] Under the lead paragraph saying, "An investment of less than $3,000 in an email campaign is expected to generate $100,000 in

new revenues for a media monitoring and web clipping service" *DM News* (September 23rd 2003) reported " . . . 99,000 emails were delivered with just over 20,000 undeliverable. Nearly 50,000 recipients opened the emails and 684 clicked through. This generated 317 trial orders, and 16% of the trial orders converted to a paid order rate."

[38] Recent research indicates "Consumers often visit an advertiser's web site in the days following an ad impression rather than immediately . . . Though click-through rates long have been the standard direct response measurement for online ads . . . advertisers should consider view-through data, which gauge customer activity following an impression, to get a better idea of performance." *DM News*, October 28, 2003.

►►► **10**

Strategic Planning
for Accountability

In one sense, the whole of this book has been about economic planning for accountable marketing throughout the marketing continuum. Whether the task is developing an ACPO model, choosing the most appropriate selling sequence for products and services, building the marketing database for maximum utility and profitability or deciding what resources should be deployed for CRM initiatives, careful planning is essential. In fact, many of the problems marketers encounter in trying to develop metrics for their marketing are the result of poor or haphazard planning and after-the-fact rationalizations.

With their increased focus on accountability, managements are also demanding a higher level of economic and strategic planning before giving investment approval to new projects. The problem with planning is that it is both time-consuming and not very sexy. It often consists of a few steps forward and then a few backward. Just when the objective seems in sight, some problem arises that could put the entire project in danger, maybe even cause its abandonment. We are never happy when our best-laid plans end up in the trash bin, even if that is the best place for some of them.

An overview of a 9-step planning and testing process is illustrated in Exhibit 10-1.

Exhibit 10-1 Nine-Step Planning and Testing Process

❶	❷	❸
DEVELOP MARKETING OBJECTIVES	DETAILED PRODUCT, OFFERS & TARGETS	BRIEFING FOR DEPARTMENTS AND AGENCIES

❹	❺	❻
BEGIN IMPLEMENTATION	BEGIN TEST PROMOTIONS	FINAL TEST EVALUATION FOR ROLLOUT

❼	❽	❾
ROLLOUT IMPLIMENTATION	ROLLOUT	CRM PROGRAM

Marketing Objectives and the Product: Where Planning Begins

It is amazing how often even savvy marketers fall so much in love with their marketing ideas that they ignore the first three steps illustrated in Exhibit 10-1—forget to carefully define their marketing objectives and the essential characteristics and consumer benefits of the product they are trying to sell. However important the brand or slogan or incentive, these are secondary to agreement on achievable and accountable marketing objectives—the first step of a multistep process. Exhibit 10-2 illustrates the first three of these steps in greater detail.

Developing the Marketing Objectives

The overall marketing objectives will be driven by a number of factors and in most companies, will demand a considerable amount of internal negotiation:

Exhibit 10-2 Detail: First Steps in Planning and Testing

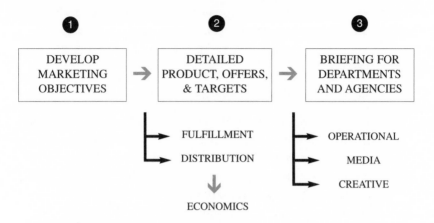

▶ Definition of the product:

Some products are easier to define than others. If it is a "simple" single sale as described in Chapter 5, the product definition should be relatively straightforward. If it is a complex product or a product combined with a service, the definition must prioritize the different elements of what we are selling. Whatever the product or service, it must be realistically assessed in its own right and against competitive products. The question that must always be asked is: How can the product be presented in its best light? How can it be positioned to demand consumer attention and interest?

Computer manufacturers and other electronics product producers pack their products with so many features that they often lose sight of the consumer's understandable desire to easily use the machine—"plug and play" to use the industry jargon: "plug and *pray*" to use the frequent consumer reaction. They appear to believe that the consumer will be attracted to all the goodies packed in the box, even if he doesn't want or understand many of them. Bucking this trend, Dell Computers built its leadership market position by allowing the consumer to configure his individual machine and then manufactured, delivered and supported it "to order."

▶ Definition of the target market:

Who are the prime prospects for the product? Why should they be interested in purchasing it? How can they be economically reached? Are there enough of them to justify the marketing effort?

▶ Agreement on sales objectives:

Do the marketing and sales departments agree on the total product definitions and sales objectives? Getting this agreement is not always easy, especially in companies that have a number of different products. Salespeople frequently have an inherent distrust of marketing: they believe that if they go out and sell, sell, sell, they could do without the marketing folk. Bridging this divide is a major challenge and unless there is genuine agreement on sales objectives, it is unlikely that they will be met.

▶ Agreement on the selling price(s):

Pricing is one of the most difficult aspects of any marketing effort. "Premium," "Penetration," "Economy," "Psychological," "Promotional" are just a few of the many pricing strategies that get significant attention in business schools and fill the pages of management books. Having identified the right target market, pricing can make the difference between success and failure at reaching it profitably.

> Of all the tools companies can use to spur consumers to act, pricing is often the most effective—but also the most blunt. Recent advances in information technology, however, have greatly sharpened this tool, allowing for ever finer consumer segmentation. . . . these advances signal an end to the era of broadly averaged, one-size-fits-many pricing. . . .
>
> The increasing prevalence of more subtle ways of collecting data and transmitting offers makes receiving individualized prices effortless and ultraconvenient for consumers.[1]

Making and agreeing on pricing within any company is difficult enough on simple products: on complex ones it can be one of the most contentious battlefields. Issues of distribution channel competition and differentiation all come into play. Price testing, discreetly undertaken, is recommended wherever possible.

▶ Analysis of the Allowable Cost Per Order:

Building ACPO models for different marketing scenarios assures that if the general assumptions are correct, the marketing program will deliver the expected profit both as a percentage of sales and as a return on the promotional investment. This is, after all, why we are doing the marketing in the first place.

If the numbers don't work or the needed response levels fall outside accepted norms, this is the time to make changes or if the changes cannot be made satisfactorily, to abandon the project. Planning what to do has an important corollary: that's planning *what not to do*.

▶ Agreement on the best and most appropriate channel (s) of distribution:

What is (are) the best channel (s) to take the product to market?

By this point in the planning process, an assessment of the different available sales channels and their pluses and minuses should be reasonably clear. Yet there are many hurdles and conflicting issues that need to be resolved.

A UK insurance company developed a complete economic and marketing plan for using direct marketing to expand the market, dominated as it was by "agents." However, despite the fact that the direct approach looked inviting, in the last analysis the company decided that the risk of alienating their agents was too great even if the *projected* profits from the new distribution channel initiative looked substantial.

IBM originally sold only through value-added resellers (VARs) until competition forced Big Blue to "go direct" while continuing to sell through established channels.

Similarly, companies traditionally operating successfully in the retail marketplace must carefully weigh the potential fallout of opening up alternative channels that can be seen to compete with the existing channel, however unrealistic the fear of fallout may be. [2]

There are many ways of overcoming distribution channel conflicts but it is a delicate area and one that should get considerable management attention as part of the planning process.

Focusing on the Detailed Planning Issues

Once there is general agreement on the objectives, the pricing, the ACPO, and the distribution channels, it's time to tighten the focus and plan the details, Step 2 in the planning process in Exhibit 10-2. What must we do?

▶ Detailed Product Definition:

Configuring the detailed product definition is a matter of taking the general product definition and fleshing it out so that we can describe exactly what we are selling—"making it so clear and simple even my mother-in-law could understand it," said one marketing executive.

Assume that the "product" is a home security system made up of a number of basic components and scaled to different size dwellings. Assume further that in addition to the "hardware" and installation, we are offering a 24-hour monitoring service. We are presented with a number of options:

- Should we offer a "starter kit," the minimum basic hardware at the lowest price point with each additional component as an add-on and the monitoring service as an upsell only after the initial sale has been made?

- Should the "product" be a "subscription" to the monitoring service with the subscription price including the basic hardware?

- Is there another configuration that will have more appeal to the potential purchasers?

These options are just three of many. Each is a different product and each may appeal to different target markets. We need to examine the reasons prospects might purchase and if possible, the emotional touch-points that surround the product. What we must decide is which configuration offers the greatest potential for success or whether to construct more than one product offer targeted at different market segments.

▶ Detailed Offer Definition:

When we have decided on exactly what the product or service is going to be, we have to decide how to make the offer of this to the potential consumer as attractive as possible and how to differentiate it from other similar or even identical products that will be competing for the consumer's attention and money.

Following the old Mafia dictum—"make them an offer they can't refuse"—sounds a better idea than it is. Of course, we can bribe some consumers to purchase any product if the incentive bribe is large enough, but this is seldom economically viable in the short term, almost never in the long term. The "offer," especially if it is incentivized through a discount or premium, may become too expensive and either eat deeply into the profit or make the product too expensive.

If the product is going to be offered exclusively at the retail level, the range of possibilities for offers will depend upon retailers' acceptance and co-operation. This is often a limiting factor and usually comes down to a question of price and sales promotion. If other distribution channels are going to be used, more offer flexibility is possible.

It is often wise to build a table of possible offers, comparing their elements and their costs and even to present these to focus panels[3] to gauge their reactions. A better way, where possible, is to test these offers using a discreet medium such as direct mail and see which offer produces the best result.[4]

Obviously, if different offers are going to appeal to different segments of the prospective market, great care must be employed to make sure that the presentation of the offers is differentiated to align with the different market segments and the tests are designed accordingly.

This is the moment to concentrate on the planning for the fulfillment of the offers. If it is a simple matter of taking orders from wholesalers and retailers and shipping the goods from a warehouse, this should provide few difficulties. But if, as in the case of the home security system, the offer involves a "home security audit," and then installation and monitoring, the fulfillment systems become extremely complicated and need very serious attention to both be able to deliver on the promise and provide the attendant service.

► Detailed Target Definition:

Having decided on the product and offer configurations, we need to carefully plan how large our target market is and how we are going to hit that target audience as efficiently as possible. Overall market research followed by media research (including mailing list research) is critical. So too is the willingness of the marketer not to try and reach too far to get that extra "N" percent of market when the cost of this is likely to far exceed its incremental value.

A large retail bank recently killed an exciting promotion because it couldn't serve all its geographically dispersed customers, instead of being content with the more than 85 percent who lived in areas that could be served. The newsmagazine that hand-delivers its subscriber copies before 3:00 PM on Sunday has to be content with making the home delivery promise to only 75% of its subscribers: The others live too far from the affordable distribution system and must therefore receive delivery by the postal system and not by the Sunday deadline.

Briefing Internal Departments and Outside Agencies

Most of the time we spend in meetings is to try and convince our colleagues of the value of our ideas or be convinced by them of the value of theirs.[5] The very nature of corporate organizational structures means that any major initiative needs a high level of cooperation and coordination among different departments, departments that often have competing priorities. This cooperation does not always come easily and sometimes needs imaginative entrepreneurship to get around the corporate barriers.[6]

Assuming that the needed cooperation can be obtained, operational issues must be resolved so that the product moves as seamlessly as possible from design to manufacturing to market and any after-sale support is in place and effective. Outside service companies (ad agencies, research companies, creative consultancies, etc.) must now be brought into the planning process and both properly briefed and invited to contribute their experience and ideas.

Building the Business Plan

Every major initiative should have a planning document that brings together the data and assumptions on which the initiative is based, the financial analysis and projections. Most importantly, the document should include a timed plan of all the tasks and milestones to make the project a success. Exhibit 10-3 shows a Gantt[7] chart developed for a complex membership-marketing initiative using Microsoft® Project, a powerful planning tool that lets the user input tasks and project milestones, their relationships to one another, needed resources, and other data. The program calculates the times needed for tasks and the start and end dates as well as defining what tasks could, if delayed, impact the entire project. Whether using this methodology or some other, the key is to define the tasks and who will undertake them, the dates they must be completed and the resources that will be applied and to monitor task delivery dates to make sure that one delay does not hold up the whole project.

Exhibit 10-3 Sample Gantt Chart

	Task Name	Duration	Start	Finish	Predeces	Resource Name
1	MEMBERSHIP MARKETING	141.5 days	Wed 4/2/03	Thu 10/16/03		
2	Prepare Plan & Priorities To Accomplish Objectives	141.5 days	Wed 4/2/03	Thu 10/16/03		
3	Describe Activities Needed for Each Phase	2 days	Wed 4/2/03	Wed 4/3/03		SMM,AX
4	Define Internal Resources & Partners	1 day	Wed 4/2/03	Wed 4/2/03		SMM,AX
5	Prepare Budget	4 days	Fri 4/4/03	Wed 4/9/03	3,4	Mkt
6	Prepare Management Presentation	2 days	Thu 4/10/03	Fri 4/11/03	3,4,5	SMM,AX
7	Management Approval of Plan	3 days	Mon 4/14/03	Wed 4/16/03	3,4,5,8	AS
8	Examine Membership Cats by Longevity & Sector	5 days	Fri 4/4/03	Thu 4/10/03	3	Research
9	Determine Financial Info. For Companies (?)	5 days	Fri 4/11/03	Thu 4/17/03	8	Amex
10	Analyse Results	0.5 days	Fri 4/18/03	Fri 4/18/03	9,8	SMM,Mkt
11	Prepare 'New Product' Descriptions	2.5 days	Fri 4/4/03	Tue 4/8/03	3	SMM,Mgmt
12	Prepare Focus Group Questionaires & Bullets	2 days	Fri 4/18/03	Tue 4/22/03	11,10,9,8	Mkt,Outsouce
13	Examine & Select Focus Group Companies	2 days	Fri 4/18/03	Tue 4/22/03	10	AX
14	Conduct Focus Groups & Analyse Results	30 days	Tue 4/22/03	Tue 6/3/03	13,7	Outsource
15	Determining Members' Wants & Needs	5 days	Tue 6/3/03	Tue 6/10/03	14	SMM
16	Balance 'Vision' with Current Categories	1 day	Tue 6/10/03	Wed 6/11/03	6;15	SMM,HG
17	Review Pricing (No. Employees & Revenue, New Cats	1 day	Tue 6/3/03	Tue 6/4/03	6;14	SMM,HG
18	Review Categories, Consolidate	1 day	Wed 6/4/03	Thu 6/5/03	6;17	SMM
19	Review Services & Products	5 days	Tue 6/3/03	Tue 6/10/03	14	HG,SMM
20	Prepare Communication & Rentention Programs	2 days	Tue 6/3/03	Thu 6/5/03	14	Mkt,AX
21	Launch Communication & Retention Prog	2 days	Tue 6/10/03	Thu 6/12/03	20,19	Mkt
22	Review Marketing Materials to Support Acq & Rentent	5 days	Tue 6/10/03	Tue 6/17/03	19	Mkt,HG
23	Review New Member Acquisition Process	5 days	Tue 6/10/03	Tue 6/17/03	18,19	HG,TV
24	Review 'Trainee' Sales Program: Remuneration, Goals	10 days	Tue 8/17/03	Tue 7/1/03	23	HG,JN
25	Map All Marketing Database Actions	5 days	Fri 4/4/03	Thu 4/10/03	3	Mkt,PJR,AX
26	Develop Marketing DB Specification	10 days	Thu 6/12/03	Thu 6/26/03	3,23SS+2	Mkt,PJR
27	Determine Best Prospect Database System	10 days	Thu 6/26/03	Thu 7/10/03	26	Mkt,SMM
28	Appoint Database Vendor	3 days	Thu 7/10/03	Tue 7/15/03	27	Mkt

Exhibit 10-4 Detail: Steps 4–6 in Planning and Testing

④ ⑤ ⑥

| BEGIN IMPLEMENTATION | BEGIN TEST PROMOTIONS | FINAL TEST EVALUATION FOR ROLLOUT |

■ **Product**
• Assure existence of product inventory
• Arrange delivery & installation system
• Arrange "Support," if applicable
■ **Offers**
• Check all aspects of offers and premiums including legal & economic
■ **Promotion**
• Review and OK promotional materials and media
■ **Fulfillment**
• Arrange all fulfillment including call center handling and data capture

■ **Launch Test Promotions**
■ **Monitor**
• Promotional delivery
• Product fulfillment and delivery
• Installation & support
• Payment systems
■ **Correct Errors & Improve System Weaknesses**
■ **Read and Analyze Test Results**
• Begin to make adjustments to rollout plan based on results
■ **Ready Cross/Upsell Implementation**

■ **Complete Test Evaluation**
■ **Confirm or Adjust Rollout Plans & Timings**
■ **Revise Business Plan on Basis of New Data**

Project Implementation

Once the plan is in place, it is time to move from planning to implementation—from theory to practice—and the testing work can start on all the tasks described in Exhibit 10-4. The objective at this stage is to validate the program. In retail marketing, *test retailers or test markets* will probably be used before rolling out. In direct marketing, testing in a *limited range* of media should provide sufficient results to assess whether or not a rollout is desirable. In either case, marginal results should act as a warning and if possible, should lead to further planning and more testing.

The final three steps in the planning and implementation process build on the earlier ones and on the test results. Assuming that the planning has been carefully done and that the results of the tests meet expectation, we are ready to rollout a full-scale marketing program.

Exhibit 10-5 Customer Contact Sequence

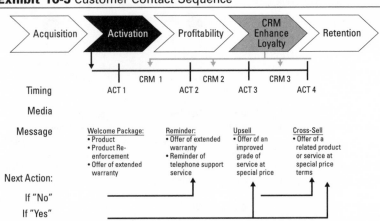

Planning Customer Contact and CRM Strategy

Since most major direct marketing efforts will involve a continuing sale of products and upsell and cross-sell activities, these and the CRM activities need to be planned as part of the total effort. In the life of the customer, when should the first CRM effort begin? When is the optimum time for offering product enhancements as upsell features? How many efforts should be expended, for example, towards a customer who has received a credit card but has not "activated" by using it before these efforts are abandoned?

These are all legitimate questions for the marketer and while the answers will frequently be opportunistic—the result of opportunities discovered after the launch—many can be anticipated and as much work as possible done to put them in place before the launch.

Some marketers use a diagrammatic system similar to that shown as an example in Exhibit 10-5. By plotting each action, defining it by timing, media, and message, a regular rhythm is established, and this can be varied to suit changing situations. Some customers like to be contacted with new offers on a regular basis. Some don't wish to be contacted at all. "Permission"—based communications—communications that the customer has indicated he is eager to receive—are usually more effective than "cold" promotions, especially emails. If the customer is asked how often he would like to be contacted and given some options about the kind of offers he would like to receive, the results are likely to be enhanced.

In Exhibit 10-5, we see that the first time the customer is contacted (ACT 1) after the acquisition phase is when he receives the product. The positive benefits of the purchase are reinforced and an offer of an extended warranty (paid or free) is made.

If the customer *does not respond* to the extended warranty offer in the "welcome pack," he receives a follow-up telephone solicitation the extended warranty and a reminder of the telephone support service. If he doesn't take advantage of that, he is not contacted again until ACT 4.

If *he accepts the offer*, the telephone follow-up of the extended warranty is skipped and the next offer is an "upsell," an offer of product enhancements and then ACT 4.

Likewise, the CRM activities are carefully planned either to utilize specific selling communications or to stand alone. But great care is taken in making certain that they support and do not conflict with the regular promotional sequence.

A major credit card company that had a tie-up with a national chain of cinemas sent all its good customers a free pass to special cinema previews as a CRM project in between promotional mailings. A "control group" did not receive the invitations. Not surprisingly, the group that received the CRM initiative had greater loyalty (less churn) and a greater increase in their card usage than the control group.

How much of the planning contributes to accountability and is measurable?

Much depends on what baseline data the marketer has. If, like the credit card company, the data is extensive, then each marketing action should be specifically measurable. If not, then while metrics are being created, less accurate measures such as increases in sales and fewer customer defections will have to suffice.

Selling the Plan to Management

Selling new marketing initiatives to management, especially those that involve expanded distribution channels, is an essential part of the process. Without management approval and investment, the project will be stillborn. How many times have we seen a well-intentioned project that might have been a major success fail to get approval because it was not presented to management in a way that gave them confidence that the planning had been meticulously done?

Many companies have formal investment request procedures, but these will be impossible to fulfill if the initial planning is weak. The first job is to develop a consensus that the recommended project is something the company wants to and should do and that it will produce the required return on investment. With an increasing focus on accountability, managements want to feel comfortable that the new initiative has a high chance of success, has been thoughtfully and carefully planned, that there are sound measurement metrics in place, and that there are no landmines buried away somewhere and waiting to explode.

The best way to approach this is always with your assumptions and projections based on facts presented in a logical order. A solid business plan, built with the details discussed earlier, and using proven methodologies such as allowable cost per order modeling, critical path charting, and promotional sequence and fulfillment planning provides the basis for getting management approval. Even if management wants your plan boiled down to a single page recommendation (à la P&G and various other large FMCG companies), the existence of a detailed plan as its foundation makes the summary preparation a relatively easy task.

Management will usually want to know:

▶ How much return the project is estimated to generate from how much investment and in what time period.[8]

▶ The degree of risk if things go wrong and how you plan to test to minimize this risk.

▶ The metrics by which the project will be measured.

▶ How the project will contribute to the total product and marketing strategy.

▶ How it will affect other parts of the company and whether or not you have their sign-on.

▶ Your degree of commitment to the project's success: how much you believe in it.

While each company's project approval process is different, presenting comprehensive answers to these questions backed by the detailed work to build confidence that the problems have been addressed is the best way to succeed.

Good planning is both a science and an art. Without it, accountable marketing would be less accountable than it can be and disasters would be more likely than successes. Murphy's famous law says that everything that can go wrong will go wrong. The best thing we can do to mitigate the inevitable things that will always go wrong is to anticipate them in as much detail as possible, first try and prevent them from happening, and then if they do, have a carefully developed plan to deal with them.

Notes

[1] Orin Herskowitz, Michael Haugen, and Roy Lowrance, "The Death of Averaged Pricing." The Boston Consulting Group, Inc. 2001.

[2] A classic case of channel competition and potential retaliation by retailers took place when the first major American book club, Book of the Month Club, was launched. Retailers were so incensed with the publishers for allowing their books to be included in the book club offering that they emptied their shelves of all copies of these books and returned them to the publishers along with a catalog of angry threats about "never buying another book from you." Six months later, many of these same booksellers featured "The Book of the Month Club" selection in their store windows when they discovered that the heavy advertising done by the club actually helped them sell more of these titles than before.

[3] Focus panels are carefully selected groups of prospects or customers to whom the concepts are presented by a research specialist and whose reactions are carefully noted and analyzed. The problem with focus group research is that while it is very powerful in identifying what not to do, it is less effective in determining whether a person will purchase a given product or service.

⁴ See Chapter 9 on Testing.

⁵ The president of The American Heritage Publishing Company—at its time in the 1960s, a very successful American magazine and book publishing enterprise—had a rule that no meeting could be longer than one hour and that no interruptions of any kind would be tolerated. He was convinced—rightly I believe—that we spend all too much time in meetings *making believe* that we are working when in fact they are *an excuse for not working*.

⁶ In his 1966 book *"The HP Way"* Hewlett-Packard co-founder David Packard describes how the "skunk works" was created as a way to let engineers [and by extension others] work outside the strictures of corporate hierarchies with management "looking the other way" so they could develop projects that would have been killed by committees and hierarchies.

⁷ Gantt charts are one of the possible (and the preferred initial chart) planning views. Another is the PERT chart. The Gantt Chart view displays basic task information in columns and a bar graph and allows easy changes and a variety of reports.

⁸ The issue of accounting for marketing investments for direct marketing projects where the cost of acquiring a customer is made up-front and anticipated revenue is spread over a reasonably long period going forward is discussed in detail in Chapter 1.

Postscript: THE FUTURE IS
ACCOUNTABLE MARKETING

" **C** lever clients," said Martin Sorrell CEO of WPP Group in an interview reported in the International Herald Tribune[1], will turn increasingly to the Internet, direct marketing and other "quantifiable" types of marketing. What Lester Wunderman forecast in his politically incorrect "Accountable Advertising" speech more than twenty years ago has now become mainline wisdom.

Accountable marketing is the future; not just for direct marketing but for the entire marketing continuum.

It's hardly surprising. Companies and their shareholders are demanding accountability in all facets of their businesses, and marketing, one of the largest areas of expenditure, is not exempt as it has been in the past. With new tools and disciplines readily available, companies throughout the world are focusing on getting more bang for their marketing bucks and demanding metrics that help them measure the effectiveness of their firepower.

We can see it happening everywhere. Hairdressers are keeping databases of their clients and calculating just how much promotional money to spend to remind clients of the need for a visit and inviting them to try out new services. Having carefully analyzed their margins on car servicing and the importance of staying close to the customers who have purchased cars from them in the past, automobile dealerships are promoting regular servicing at preferential prices. Fine, they argue, for the manufacturers to spend lavishly to advertise new models that can be purchased at *any* dealership: They can measure the value of their former customers, and, understandably, they wish to make certain that next purchase is at *their* dealership.

Companies like Procter & Gamble are more and more insisting that their advertising agencies and consultants share in the risk and the rewards of their efforts. Service companies, they argue, will provide better services if their compensation is directly related to clients' success. To judge success, metrics must be in place and the finer the measurements, the more the comfort on both sides of the table.

Customer satisfaction is high on the agenda of companies in all industries. If their customers are satisfied, they have a much better chance of remaining loyal than if they are not: The whole edifice of customer relationship management is built on the foundations of customer satisfaction. This satisfaction must be measured against a clearly defined baseline.

The inherent fear voiced by marketing "creatives" that accountability means the ascendancy of the bean counters to the detriment of inspired creativity is largely overblown and self-serving, the result of too many years of pampering by the marketing community. Making marketing accountable doesn't mean making it dull. Rather, it raises the level of the creative challenge to use that inspiration to produce results that satisfy because they are measurable—because they certify that the creativity was well directed and the greater their creativity, the better the result.

Accountability begins with a mindset. That mindset demands that every marketing action is carefully planned and made to conform to a model that contains not only strategic but economic criteria. It means that the marketer must migrate his focus from case rate to customer rate, from the value of a square meter of retail space to the value of a customer, from the value of a single transaction to the customer's lifetime value, from thinking about how to get new customers to keeping the ones he has. And he needs to know how much he can afford to spend to acquire each new customer and whether it is better to invest in keeping the best customers he has or getting new ones that match their profile.

Any of us who has ever experienced a complete instrument landing in zero visibility develops a tremendous respect for the pilots who trust their own lives and those of their passengers to the instruments. Happily, as marketers, we never have to fly blind but the analogy is a fair one.

More and more marketers will use the instruments of accountable marketing to navigate their marketing actions. They will find that many of their traditional assumptions need re-evaluation. For example, the whole question of how much segmentation in market definition is profitable will condition how they spend their marketing monies and former assumptions about "growth" are being replaced by new assumptions about profitability. Just as many companies that have survived the difficult years that followed the bursting of the Internet bubble now focus on their "core competencies" today's savvy marketers are increasingly concentrating on their core customers, the relatively small percentage which produces the largest share of the profits.

By differentiating and allocating portions of their marketing spend towards customers whose purchases represent different percentage of their revenues, they are able to overcome the dangers of marketing to the average customer and thereby to concentrate their marketing effort where it will produce the maximum return on the investment. Ask any firefighter, and he will tell you to concentrate the water on the base of the fire, not waste it by spraying drops on the whole building.

Stan Rapp has written, "Only time will tell whether the seemingly incompatible worlds of brand awareness and direct response advertising have at last found common ground in the most unlikely of client budgets—the expenditure for mass brand-building advertising."[2] Like many others in the industry, he sees true accountability for every part of the continuum, if not here already, not so far over the horizon. But how far out in time sits that horizon is extremely hard to tell. Richard Madden, planning director of the international agency TBWA/GGT Direct in the UK takes the view, ". . . when . . . you're dealing with clients with multiple distribution channels, brand valuation, return on shareholder equity and so forth, we're really stuck in the dark ages."[3] Perhaps, but many observers see a bright light and the accountability glass as more than half full rather than only half empty.

In its January 31st, 2003, 10K filing with the US Securities and Exchange Commission, Dell Computer Corporation wrote:

Dell provides a single point of accountability for its customers. Dell recognizes that as technology needs become more complex, it becomes more challenging for customers to efficiently address their computing needs. Dell therefore strives to be the single point of accountability for customers with complex technological challenges. Dell offers an array of services designed to provide customers the ability to maximize system performance, efficiency and return on investment.

If this industry leader and marketing and manufacturing pioneer is concentrating on a *"single point of accountability,"* it's hard to imagine that the future is very far away.

Dell's fantastic success has been in fine-tuning its business and marketing processes and making them highly accountable. No one would argue that this has in any way reduced the company's creativity. In fact, Dell's creatively disciplined approach to every aspect of its business is frequently credited as an underlying factor of its success.

Accountable marketing is neither a fashion nor a fad that will enjoy a brief moment in the sun and then be replaced by something a little newer and sexier. It is destined to become a core competency for all marketing actions from the start to the end of the continuum, and its disciplines are certain to make all marketing more effective and more profitable.

Notes

[1] 5 February 5, 2004.

[2] "Something New Under the Advertising Sun,", *The DMA Insider*, Fall 2002. pg. 10.

[3] "Strong Measures" *Marketing Direct*, November 2002, pg. 21.

▶▶▶ Index